# D IS FOR DYSFUNCTIONAL— AND DOO WOP

# D IS FOR DYSFUNCTIONAL— AND DOO WOP

## SONGS OF A HOOSIER SCHIZO

*How a poor girl from the Midwest was
programmed for silence but finally found her
voice and eventually learned to sing solo*

*Enjoy!*

MARY ELLEN STEPANICH, PHD

*Mary Ellen Stepanich*

abbott press®

A DIVISION OF WRITER'S DIGEST

Abbott Press books may be ordered through booksellers or by contacting:

Abbott Press
1663 Liberty Drive
Bloomington, IN 47403
www.abbottpress.com
Phone: 1-866-697-5310

ISBN: 978-1-4582-0988-7 (sc)
ISBN: 978-1-4582-0987-0 (hc)
ISBN: 978-1-4582-0986-3 (e)

Library of Congress Control Number: 2013910023

Printed in the United States of America.

Abbott Press rev. date: 05/31/2013

For Great Niece Sarah (who has received excellent programming, but she is not allowed to read this until she is twenty-one or at least old enough to know better!)

# CONTENTS

———————•◆❋◆•———————

# Acknowledgments

There have been many people who have encouraged me in whatever I've attempted over the years, but the most encouraging ones—my husband, father, and mother—are no longer living. The living folks who have provided the motivation for me to bring my thoughts to paper are the members of The Scribblers and The Lady Scribblers, writers' groups in Ventana Lakes, Peoria, Arizona, who listened to my personal ramblings, provided feedback, laughed at my funny stories, and even shed a tear or two at the sad parts. Thank you, Scribblers.

Special gratitude goes to Maralys Wills, a renowned writer of memoir and a genre-hopper extraordinaire, for her encouragement and advice. Thanks also to writer friends Melba Beasley, Nancy Bailey, and especially Sheila Lester, who critiqued the final product and were kind enough not to throw up.

Finally, thanks to the people at Abbott Press who helped the final product to see the light of day.

# DISCLAIMER

---

All of the events described in this memoir are true to the best of my recollection. Given the number of brain cells I have destroyed, either by illness or lifestyle, some events and stories may be slightly exaggerated. Consider it poetic license. Of course, many of the names have been changed to protect the innocent—and the guilty.

# Note to Reader

---❖---

We are what we are because we have
been where we have been.
—Sigmund Freud

All families are dysfunctional in some way. Maybe it's Uncle Elmo the dipsomaniac, or Grandpa Bernie the child molester, or perhaps it's a favorite aunt who just divorced her sixth husband because she doesn't realize she keeps falling in love with the same type of "dip-shit." Where does dysfunctional behavior come from? What is the source? Is it an errant gene in the DNA or learned behavior; i.e., nature or nurture? There are many theories—pick one. Perhaps Richard Rodgers and Oscar Hammerstein II had it right in one of the more serious songs, "You've Got To Be Carefully Taught," from their musical, *South Pacific*. (© 1949 Williamson Music Inc., New York, NY)

This is not a how-to book—it's more of a how-not-to book. It's the story of one family's dysfunctions, as seen through the eyes of the elder daughter: that would be me. I started life as an innocent, happy child, but my exuberance was soon stifled as a result of disastrous value programming. That programming included being molested at age four, then having my mouth taped shut on the first day of school by an autocratic battle-ax of a teacher who wanted to stop my flow of eager questions. The final blow came as a result of my third divorce from a cheating, abusive husband. My ever-critical mother commented, upon hearing about the breakup, "You can't get along with anybody, can you?" Of course, what I really needed to hear was, "I'm so glad you're okay."

Some results of the dysfunctions in my family are inconsequential; others are extremely costly in terms of missed opportunities and lost love. But all of them have, at their core, an element of humor, at least in the retelling.

Most of the problems I encountered throughout my life were the result of value programming—the tacit and implicit lessons taught by parents, teachers, peers, relatives, and even the geographical and cultural environment surrounding a growing youngster. Dr. Morris Massey, in his popular 1972 video presentation, "What You Are Is Where You Were When," teaches that the programming of a person's values, good or bad, is the unforeseen but inevitable influence by forces that are not necessarily under any parent's direct control.

These learned values, however, are immutable and remain with the individual throughout his or her life, wreaking havoc and dysfunction with the carelessness of a pinball careening and clanking around the arcade machine. In a few rare instances, the poorly programmed person (usually as the result of some trauma or tragedy) can finally recognize the closely held values that are no longer functioning for optimal outcomes—and choose to ignore them.

When asked, "What do you desire most in life?" most people would recite the litany spelled out in *The Secret,* a how-to book by Rhonda Byrnes. (©2006 TS Production Limited Liability Co., Atria Books, New York, NY.) She gives advice on how to acquire wealth, love, health, or knowledge—and maybe even a Lamborghini sports car. If anyone had asked that question of me during the first forty-two years of my life, the answer would have been, "I want someone to listen to me!"

I was like so many of the children born and raised in this country in the 1940s who grew up to be insecure adults, or "schizos," which is a term coined by Dr. Massey to identify the unique personalities of my generation. With one foot in the Great Depression and pre-war poverty, and the other foot in the New Deal and post-war affluence, we schizos grew up being influenced, or value programmed, by the people, places, and phenomena of the decade and not necessarily in a way designed to create confident, assertive adults.

My fellow schizos and I were bombarded from birth with conflicting messages, such as "Be careful, it could happen again, you know," and "Go for it, you can live a better life." No wonder a generation of Americans grew up confused and insecure in their own skins.

After forty-two years, I was brought face to face with the early childhood programming that made me the person I had become: relationship-shy, thrice divorced, disappointed in career, with childhood dreams demolished. Ironically, it was during a Strategic Management class in my organizational behavior doctoral program of studies at Purdue University that this revelation hit me "upside the head," as my father would have said. As a result, I found my own voice that had been suppressed for years and learned to verbalize my wants and desires while silencing the inner critic—the one that sounded remarkably like my mother.

I was a member of a normal (whatever that is) God-fearing, church-going, midwestern, small-town family of the mid-twentieth century: mother, father, daughter, son, four grandparents, fourteen aunts and uncles, twenty-one first cousins, and countless great-aunts and uncles and second cousins, all of whom knew best how I should live my life.

As you will see, I managed to ignore them—eventually.

Mary Ellen (Blevins Trowbridge
Brannen Batterton) Stepanich, PhD
Peoria, Arizona
December, 2012

# PROLOGUE

·•❋•·

# LOOKS LIKE WE MADE IT

Success is a journey, not a destination.
—Ben Sweetland

"Mom! Guess what? I can't believe it. You'll never guess what just happened!"

I suppose the excited edge to my message was dulled somewhat by the thousand-mile trip over the telephone lines from Arizona to Indiana. My mother's reply sounded rather matter of fact. "Well, what happened?"

"Kenny Oldham just called me. Remember Kenny? One of my classmates, Heddy, married his younger brother . . ."

Mom cut me off with her usual family tree gossip whenever anybody from my rural Fort Branch hometown was mentioned, whether I knew him or not (or even cared.) "Oh, yes! Wasn't it awful? Roy died way too young. I don't know why Heddy got married again. You know, there was a lot of talk going around town about her second husband—what was his name? You know the story, don't you? He took some of that new male hormone medicine—is it Niagara? And he got caught trying to seduce this young girl. I think she was the babysitter. Anyway, he was sent to prison as a sex offender! I just felt so sorry for Heddy. You know, she was so ashamed of what that man did, she took back Roy's last name after the divorce . . ."

It was my turn to cut off the flow of gossip. "Mom! Listen, will you? Kenny asked me to be the guest speaker at the next Fort Branch High School alumni banquet! Me! The class nerd! Can you believe it—after all these years? I'm just—flabbergasted!" Here I was, sixty-four years old, with a bachelor's degree, an MBA, and a doctorate, and I was as excited as I was the first day of grade school. Unfortunately, when I get excited, everything I ever learned in my twenty-plus years of schooling leaves me, and I resort to the language of my youth, growing up in the backwaters of Gibson County, Indiana.

"Well, that's fine." As usual, my mother didn't waste needless time on useless praise or congratulations. With her laser-like skill, she got right to the heart of the problem. "What are you going to talk about?"

I was too thrilled to let Mom's lack of enthusiasm get to me this time. "Kenny said they wanted me to talk about academic excellence. The alumni association is pushing a program to get contributions for college scholarships, and they wanted someone who had—and I quote—'a history of achievement in academe.' I just can't get over it! They want *me!*"

Actually, when Kenny called and asked me to be the guest speaker, I couldn't help but ask him why I was chosen.

"We wanted somebody with a PhD, preferably a woman." He confided in me that the male speaker from the previous reunion, who also had a doctorate, was a trifle boring. I guess my reputation had preceded me.

The second week in June arrived before I was totally prepared for it. While I was booking the airline ticket for my trip home, as the reservation clerk completed the paperwork I suddenly thought to ask, "Does the airline offer a senior citizen discount?"

"Yes, we do," she responded.

"How old do you have to be to get the discount?"

"Sixty or over."

"Great! Then I qualify—I'm sixty-four."

She confirmed the flight schedule and fare and then asked, "May I reserve a rental car for you when you arrive in Evansville?"

"No, thanks, my parents are picking me up at the airport."

There was a moment of silence, and then I heard a choked laugh. "You are sixty-four years old and you still have living parents who drive and can pick you up?"

"I'm luckier than most, I guess."

Like so many who retire to a new and different location, my parents had moved to Cherokee Village in 1978 when Daddy retired at age sixty-two. But they soon felt the tug of family and home and wanted to return to the place of their births as well as the birthplace of their children. In 1982, they concluded that retirement in Arkansas hadn't worked for them, mainly because most of their new friends were dying of old age. They returned to Lafayette, Indiana, where both their children were professors at Purdue, then moved back to our hometown of Fort Branch in the early 1990s. What pleased them even more than coming home was the fact they could now afford to buy the Romerhausen place, a ranch-style home built of Bedford limestone, just around the corner from uptown. Mr. Romerhausen had been a successful life insurance agent. I believe I still have a policy he sold my mother for twenty-five cents a week. Mom would say with pride, "I always dreamed of living in a stone home."

I should explain that uptown Fort Branch was two blocks of family-owned shops with western-style false fronts that looked like they might have been transported from 1880 frontier days. Many of the storefronts were made of hammered tin, which was probably worth more than the entire stock of merchandise in the stores.

When my younger brother arrived at our parent's house to attend the reunion (Bill was also a graduate of Fort Branch High School), my mother told my professor sibling that I had been asked to speak at the reunion. He said, "Oh? Why?" (Brothers! Why couldn't I have been an only child?)

Perhaps the reunion committee may have expected something a bit more esoteric in my presentation. Nevertheless, I related all my experiences with the Fort Branch public school system in my humorous speech entitled, "Academic Excellence: Who Needs It?" However, I concluded with the tales of my ultimate success in higher education and answered that question, "We all do!"

While I was gathering memories of my early value programming to relate in this memoir, I began to realize it was some sort of miracle that I was now relatively happy and content with my life. From the day of my birth (which I always claimed to remember) to the present peak of success, there have been struggles—struggles to be accepted by peers; to be heard and heeded by parents, teachers and relatives; and to be appreciated for the person I was, deep inside, by a multitude of husbands and lovers. With a little bit of mental mining of memories, I was forced to come face-to-face with the cause of my life-long struggles for normalcy.

I had been programmed, not for success, but for failure.

# PART I

---◦•❀•◦---

# INTRO

(A good girl receives bad programming
and loses her "voice.")

# CHAPTER 1

·•❊•·

# BABY, IT'S COLD OUTSIDE

A baby is God's opinion that life should go on.
—Carl Sandburg, *Remembrance Rock*, 1948

A guttural, animal-like scream split the air in the dimly lit front room of the weather-beaten farmhouse. A kerosene lamp burned on a table next to the bed where the nineteen-year-old girl lay writhing in agony. She weighed barely a hundred pounds soaking wet, which she was now, drenched in the perspiration of pain and terror. In the small bedroom at the rear of the house, three children huddled together on the feather bed, clutching the handmade patchwork quilt to their chins. They were frightened and confused by the sounds coming from the front room. What was happening to their older sister? Why was she screaming? Why was Doc Gwaltney here?

Old Doc Gwaltney and his wife, Barbara, had driven their 1932 Model T Ford sedan to the Dorsam farm in the middle of the night. They had driven through snow so deep it had threatened to strand them on County Road 168 before they could get to the farmhouse and the difficult delivery that awaited them. Barb Gwaltney often served as her husband's midwife. While it was true that most babies in Gibson County arrived after midnight, she would have preferred to stay in bed on this night. It was close to twenty degrees below zero, and in some places the drifted snow was deep enough to bury their old Ford.

Barb's husband, whom everyone affectionately called "Doc," was the only doctor in this part of the county, so he was always on the road somewhere, delivering babies, setting broken bones, and stitching up wounds. Farming was a dangerous occupation. Corn-picking machines tore off little pinkies, horses kicked their handlers' heads, and tractors ran over big toes.

Although he could keep up with this hectic schedule, Doc was beginning to show signs of aging. His gray hair was thinning and his waistline thickening under his vest, where he proudly wore his father's watch with its caduceus fob in his vest pocket. Most of the townsfolk said his dad had served in the Army Medical Corps. And now, with war rumblings in Europe, both Doc and his wife had concerns for the future safety of their son, Tab, who had aspirations of becoming an aviator in the Army Air Corps. But they pushed these thoughts aside and concentrated on the difficult delivery that promised to keep them both awake for the next several hours or more.

The teenager on the bed was my mother, Edna Marie Smith Blevins, and she was about to give birth to me, her first child, under the primitive conditions of a rural Indiana farmhouse with no electricity, on the coldest day of the year—January 8, 1940. My father, William Blevins (or "Bud" as his family called him) was the typical expectant father, sitting alone in the lean-to, add-on kitchen, feeling helpless and strangely unnecessary. I don't know if he paced, as most new fathers do, but I know he was worried. He himself had almost died at birth. He had been cast aside behind the stove as a stillborn until he finally got the strength to find his voice and complain to let people know he was alive! He knew the dangers of childbirth, especially with only a country doctor in attendance. What if something went haywire?

The three youngsters in the back bedroom were the Dorsam children, my mother's younger half-siblings: Ella, aged twelve; Elma, who was ten; and their baby brother Earl, who was only seven. This was their first experience with childbirth, although they had seen many animals being born on their farm. But momma cats and cows were generally quieter about it. My Aunt Elma, the only participant still living, recently commented on the event: "There was a lot of noise, and we didn't understand what was going on."

As Emma Dorsam wiped the perspiration from her daughter's pale, thin face, Edna looked up in terror at the doctor she trusted to take care of her and her soon-to-be-born child. "Doc! Is something wrong? Why doesn't the baby come—*Ooooww!*"

"Now, take it easy, girl. Let's see if we can't help things along a mite." Doc turned to Emma. "Could you bring me a dishpan of clean, hot water?" After he scrubbed his hands, he directed the next request to his wife. "Barb, get the ether canister and gauze out of my medical bag."

Doc deftly handled the canister as he dripped a small amount of ether onto the gauze pad that Barb placed over Edna's nose and mouth, and soon the pregnant girl stopped moaning and moving erratically. Doc and his wife worked diligently to save the fetus that seemed to be in some difficulty and wouldn't move through the birth canal, as it should. Perhaps I had a premonition of the trials and tribulations that lay ahead in life and simply said, "Oh, the heck with it! I think I'll just stay where I am."

In fact, the umbilical cord was wrapped around my throat, which impeded the delivery. It seemed that even before birth, things were conspiring to shut my mouth! But that time, I outwitted those forces and finally emerged, screaming and crying. I'm not sure anyone noticed, but it was obvious I was going to sing soprano.

I don't remember this next part, of course, but both my parents told the same story. As soon as the baby slipped into his capable, welcoming hands, Doc Gwaltney offered the baby to his wife, who quickly wiped the afterbirth from the infant and cleaned her up while Doc ministered to the new mother. "Edna, you have a beautiful, healthy baby girl."

"Really? She's okay? Let me see her!"

The baby, wrapped in a clean, warm flannel cloth, continued to complain about being manhandled and thrust naked into a freezing room. Edna, however, was just thankful it was over and the baby was whole and seemingly undamaged. By this time, Bud, the new father, was standing by his wife's side, gazing with pride at his first child, a six-pound, bald-headed screamer. The new mom handed the baby to her young husband and, as if by magic, the baby stopped crying. He placed the infant carefully in the palm of his hand, looked into her eyes, pointed his index finger at her as if to make an important point, and spoke the words that would follow her for the rest of her life: "You, my little girl, are going to get an education."

Did I hear him? Was that what implanted in me the insatiable desire to learn, learn, and then learn some more? Who knows what a newborn infant really hears? The actions of the parents throughout the child's upbringing and the opportunities they make available to their offspring probably form its inner core of dreams and ambitions.

Despite the difficult delivery, Doc Gwaltney charged my folks his usual fee for birthing a baby—twenty dollars. Mom had saved the money to pay the doctor. Daddy worked hard for that money, laboring as a hired hand for Herb Johnson, a local farmer. All throughout the previous fall, he shucked corn by hand and was paid four cents per bushel. Daddy was a slender, lightweight, tow-headed twenty-three-year-old, but he was strong and could easily shuck a hundred bushels of corn a day. So, my birth cost five hundred bushels of corn, which was a big chunk of Daddy's hard-earned money. I'm just glad I wasn't born on credit. That's a terrible way to start life!

Like any new father, Daddy wanted to tell his parents about the birth of their newest granddaughter. Although Grandma Dorsam had a telephone, it was a battery-powered wall model that had to be cranked to place a call. The transmission could reach only a few miles, just enough to call the neighbors and connect to the central operator in the nearby small town of Fort Branch. Besides, Grandma and Grandpa Blevins didn't have a telephone. Poor farmers didn't have the time or money to waste on such frivolity. I'm sure it's hard for today's young people to imagine a world without cell phones, text messages, or tweets.

It was cold the night I was born (seventeen degrees below zero) and my parents were so poor they couldn't afford antifreeze for their 1929 Chevy. In the winter Daddy had to drain the water from the radiator when they reached their destination so it wouldn't freeze and ruin the engine. That worked fine as long as the temperature didn't fall below zero. However, on this night, as soon as he opened the radiator drain, the water froze, causing the engine block to burst.

Not to be deterred, Daddy grabbed a bicycle and pedaled three miles through knee-high snow to give his parents the good news.

When he got to the Meyer place where my paternal grandparents were renting, they were gone. They'd left a note on the door saying they were moving to Oakland City, another small town in Gibson County. All Daddy could do was leave a note to his parents announcing my birth and then ride his bicycle through the bitter cold to get back to the Dorsam farm.

My parents had considered naming me for my two grandmothers, Emma Katherine Dorsam and Bertha Ellen Blevins. But they finally settled on Mary, the name of one of their good friends, and Ellen, Grandma Blevins's middle name. I shudder to think how close I came to being named Emma Bertha Blevins! Mary Ellen is bad enough. I can still hear my cousins' taunting cries, "Mary Ellen, watermelon!"

Mom and Dad stayed at the Dorsam farm for about three weeks. Grandma Dorsam bought three dozen diapers for me. She said that was the number of diapers needed to raise a baby until it was toilet trained. For years, my mother delighted in telling me how she scrubbed my diapers on a washboard and boiled them in lye soap. That probably encouraged me to become toilet-trained as soon as possible. Who wants to sit around all day on diapers that were soaked in lye soap?

Mom once gave me her recipe for lye soap, just in case I would ever need it: "One can of lye (about a fifteen-ounce can), one can of old bacon grease or lard (about one-half gallon), and water (enough to liquefy). Cook these ingredients in an iron kettle hung over a wood fire out in the yard until it gets thick. Place the mixture in an old flat dishpan. When the mixture gets cold, cut it into large squares. Place the squares on a board to dry. To use for laundry, shave the soap bars into flakes."

I never found it necessary to make lye soap. Thank goodness somebody invented Tide.

When Mom and Dad were married in July 1938, Mom was barely eighteen years old. She weighed only ninety-eight pounds and stood five feet eight inches tall. As I remarked at my parents' fiftieth wedding anniversary party, "My mother was so thin when she got married that when she put on a dress with vertical stripes, in her size it had only one stripe. She was determined none of her relatives could say she *had* to get married, so for the first year she made Daddy sleep in the barn."

Somehow, I managed to arrive a year and a half later, although my mother was still a clueless teenager. Nevertheless, she raised her child to the best of her ability. From 1940 to 1944 I was an only child and I reveled in the attention. After all, when you are the center of your little universe and the apple of your Daddy's eye, life can only be good. The next chapters will recount some of the absolute joy I experienced during those years—exploring fields and barns, discovering the warmth of kittens and baby chicks, and always singing, singing, singing!

However, there were times in those formative years when the circumstances, people, and environmental factors that influenced and helped to form my value system (my beliefs about right and wrong) would cause me to doubt myself and what everyone in my family, especially my mother, said was right.

# CHAPTER 2

—◦❈◦—

# YES, SIR, THAT'S MY BABY

Give me a child for the first seven years, and you
may do what you like with him afterwards.
—Jesuit maxim

M uch of a child's value programming occurs during the first
six or seven years. Yet how many adults remember those
early years or what values they might have been taught?
Most people will confess they have very few memories from before they
began school, even though those times may have been the happiest of
their young lives. And those who profess to remember anything from
ages one through six, as I do, probably acquired those memories from
parents who delighted in telling stories about them around the kitchen
table at Thanksgiving or at the family reunion picnics at the local state
park. My mother always reinforced those stories with scrapbooks and
photo albums.

I'm told I cried a lot as a baby. How was my mother to know I was
simply exercising my vocal chords for a future career as a singer? All
through the night, the creaky old rocking chair would rock in tempo
to the lullaby my mother sang to me in an attempt to quiet my infant
style of singing:

"Hush, little baby, don't say a word. Mama's gonna buy you a
mockingbird. If that mockingbird don't sing, Mama's gonna buy you

a diamond ring. If that diamond ring turns brass, Mama's gonna buy you a looking glass."

An analysis of the words to this little ditty reveals a very depressing future: mockingbirds that mock and don't sing, and diamond rings that turn to brass. Was she being prophetic about my future? Nevertheless, Mom would try to dissuade me from my lamentations by showing me the pictures in her photo album. "Look, Mary Ellen, who is that?"

It's a picture of a tiny, bald-headed baby of indeterminate gender taking a bath, sitting in a dishpan outdoors on a field of clover grass, holding onto the sides for dear life and staring at something in the bottom of the pan. Her expression seems to say, "What *is* that between my legs and what am I supposed to do with *that*?" As I recall, I didn't get a decent explanation until it was too late.

In the background of the picture is a weathered two-story barn with some boards missing on one side and a hayloft opening near the top. Nearby stands a hickory tree behind a barbed-wire fence with fence posts made of tree branches that had been cleaned of bark and jammed into the ground. The clear sky above the barn shows birds whirling about. In southern Indiana in the 1940s those birds were called, *spatzies*, a German word meaning "little sparrows." The spatzies in the picture seem to be searching for dinner—maybe a few insects to take back to the nests to feed their hungry broods.

Although we were poor, I don't recall ever being hungry. We had a tiny, rent-free house supplied by the farmer Daddy worked for, a Jersey cow called Ruth—named for the lady who sold it to us on credit, some laying hens from Grandma Dorsam for eggs, and a huge garden of vegetables cultivated by my father and canned for the winter by my mother. Once in a while, our table was graced with servings of that wonderful concoction—bologna—which cost an exorbitant ten cents a pound, but my mother got it free from the grocer by trading the cream from the cow's milk. With a meal of eggs-over-easy, fried baloney, and fresh milk, who could ask for anything more?

Some snapshots in the album seem to have a hint of sadness about them. There's my grandmother Blevins in her feed-sack print dress with her hair gone gray before its time. She's holding the arm of Daddy's younger brother, Charles, wearing his CCC (Civilian Conservation

Corps) uniform, standing next to his teenage sister, Berta, who wears a hanky in the breast pocket of her scandalously short dress (at least for 1940), hemmed a daring inch above the knee.

They are headed for Henryville, Indiana, to take Uncle Charles back to the CCC camp where he was stationed. The Civilian Conservation Corps, the brainchild of President Franklin Roosevelt, was a public work relief program that operated from 1933 to 1942. It was part of FDR's New Deal to provide unskilled manual labor jobs related to the conservation and development of natural resources in rural lands. The CCC employed young, unmarried men from poor families who had difficulty finding jobs during the Great Depression. Uncle Charles was paid thirty dollars a month, and was required to send twenty-five dollars home to his mother and sisters. He remained in the CCC until he enlisted in the army at the beginning of World War II.

In the center of this family photo is my father, Bud Blevins, the only one smiling into the camera. He's dressed in a white shirt, dark grey suit, and tie, holding the cutest infant in all of southern Indiana (me!). Although it is a beautiful summer day, the baby is attired in a long cotton dress, ribbed stockings, and hand-knit wool booties and sweater, topped off with a hand-crocheted bonnet. The camera doesn't reveal the sweat pouring down the poor baby's back. It seems that the greatest fear of every mother or grandmother in 1940 was that her child might get too comfortable.

The fact that the infant's mother is not shown in the photograph leads me to believe my mom was the photographer, probably using the old Brownie box camera that I remember seeing as a youngster. The pictures are affixed in the album with small corner paper pockets, glued to the pages to hold the photos securely without damaging them. All the photos in the album are black and white, either grainy or foggy in texture, and show family and friends wearing startled expressions as though they were caught doing something shameful.

One of my least favorite photos reveals my father, shirtless in bib overalls, kneeling in the dirt of the barnyard and pulling a tiny tusk from the mouth of a baby piglet. It's a great picture of Daddy, but I hated what he was doing. I can still hear the terrified squeals of the little pig as it was subjected to this seemingly inhumane treatment. Perhaps this picture is the source of my life-long fear of dentists. The farmer-owner, Herb Johnson, ordered Daddy to pull the tusks from the baby pigs to keep them from hurting themselves and killing each other when they, and the tusks, were fully grown. How ironic—the adult pigs then would be butchered to provide bacon, pork tenderloins, and ham hocks, so what was the point?

Another picture in the album shows Jimmy Moore, Daddy's best friend from his boyhood days in Patoka. Jimmy is wearing a silly grin while Mary Lou, his young wife, is giving him a bear hug. They also were poor farmers and had a baby boy about my age. Mom would point to the picture and tell me about these two friends:

"Jimmy used to say, 'Come over and we'll go in debt to buy a quarter's worth of pork chops and have dinner.' We'd put you babies to bed on a blanket on the floor, and then play cards until two or three o'clock in the morning. We didn't need money to enjoy life in those days."

Sad to say, Mary Lou, for whom I was named, died of tuberculosis before I was five years old.

Examining the photograph album became almost an annual event. When I had nothing else to read (or pretend to read), I would pull the photo album from its place of honor under the coffee table and ask my mother to tell me the story behind the picture.

"Who's 'at, Mommy?" My tiny finger pointed to a photograph of a toddler holding what looked like a goldfish.

"That's you, and that's the sunfish you caught when Daddy took you fishing."

Although Daddy loved me intensely, he never admitted that he really, really wanted a boy. I suppose that's the dream of every young father who wants a boy to follow in his footsteps—to teach the lad to hunt, fish, and repair broken down jalopies. But Daddy never made me feel that I was a second-class citizen. When I was a toddler, he took me with him everywhere. I remember being in a rowboat in the middle of a lake when some men came by in another boat and yelled to Daddy, "What's the matter, buddy, don't you have any *boys?*" Now that hurt!

I loved to pretend to play Mom's huge guitar, which she bought from the Sears and Roebuck catalogue, probably on credit. There I am in the next picture, about three or four years old, with the guitar hanging around my neck by a strap, singing at the top of my lungs. My daddy accompanies me, strumming his mandolin and beaming at me with fatherly pride.

Now, there's a special picture—a mother and her child. It's obviously Easter time, because there are daffodils in a small flowerbed in the background. The mother is wearing a navy blue suit and a jaunty hat crowned with white flowers, tipped attractively over her right temple. At her side is a charming toddler wearing a sailor dress, hand stitched by her mother, topped by a navy blue cape and sailor hat. Mom was an accomplished seamstress and she made many such adorable outfits for me when I was little. This picture of my mother and me dressed in our spiffy Easter outfits has a special place in my own photo album.

I must admit, I enjoyed being the center of attention in those early years, the only child of a poor but happy young couple. Most of us probably absorbed those memories without conscious thought, and they became the foundation of our grown-up loves, hates, and value systems.

Lincoln Steffens once declared, "The best picture has not yet been painted," (excerpt from "This World Depression of Ours is Chock-full of Good News," *Hearst's International Combined with Cosmopolitan*, October 1932, p. 26.)

However, given the future complications of a life that started out so innocently and sweetly, I might want to turn that around to say, "The *worst* picture has not yet been painted."

# CHAPTER 3

⁕

# PUT YOUR ARMS AROUND ME, HONEY

I'm youth, I'm joy! I'm a little bird
that has broken out of the egg!
—Sir James M. Barrie, *Peter Pan*, 1928

The headlights of the old Model A Ford dimly cut through the starlit night as it chugged along the two-lane road leading to Charlestown, a small city on the southeastern side of Indiana, across the river from Louisville, Kentucky. The driver was twenty-four-year-old Bud Blevins, my father.

In the fall of 1940, Daddy's older sister, Lucille, and her husband, Dan Truckey, had gone to Charlestown, Indiana, looking for work. They came home to Gibson County at Thanksgiving saying, "Anybody can get a job over there!" So, my father gave up laboring as a hired hand for one of the local corn and pig farmers, where he was paid a dollar a day—and that was only when the farmer had work for him to do. Daddy drove to Charlestown in an old Ford with no spare tire and exactly ten dollars in his pocket, hoping to find a job and a better life for his wife and baby daughter.

When he reached Charlestown, Daddy stayed with Dan, Lucille, and their three children in a fifteen-foot house trailer while he searched for a job. There was no spare bed for him, so Lucille put a board over the sink in the kitchenette at the front of the trailer, and that became Daddy's temporary sleeping quarters.

He applied for a job at the DuPont defense plant, where they made gunpowder for military guns and bombs. Daddy was very thin at five feet ten inches and weighed only 137 pounds, so he didn't meet the company's minimum weight requirement of 150 pounds. For three weeks he worked as a day laborer for the state highway department, laying sod on the right-of-way and eating all the bananas and milkshakes he could afford.

When he applied again at DuPont, he wore high-top leather shoes, heavy thermal underwear, a bulky wool shirt, pants, and jacket, and he filled his pockets with dirt to add a few more ounces. He stepped on the scales and the needle whirled around and around, then stopped at 145 pounds. Although still underweight, his persistence was rewarded and he was hired on January 3, 1941. According to my Uncle Dan's stories, "DuPont was so desperate for workers they'd hire anybody still breathing."

After Daddy received his first paycheck, he returned to rescue his wife and baby girl from Gibson County, where Mom and I were stranded in the country in the middle of winter with no transportation and dwindling firewood supplies. Although Mom hated to leave her nearby mother and younger siblings, she was thrilled with Daddy's improved income. Their cow, Ruth, was fostered with Grandma Dorsam, their few sticks of furniture were stored in a granary on Great-Aunt Bertha's farm, and the little family embarked on an exciting new journey, filled with hope and promise.

Because DuPont was engaged in war work, all the employees at the defense plant were locked on the job. That meant Daddy wouldn't be drafted into the US Army. However, as he came to find out, being in the army might have been less dangerous. His job at the plant consisted of monitoring several cookers, stirring the cotton wadding into the nitroglycerin mixture, which then cooked to create the substance that became gunpowder. The mixture was so volatile it would sometimes blow up, hurling the parts of the steel mixing machine like shrapnel throughout the factory. If a worker saw the nitro soup change color, he'd yell, "She's gonna blow!" He would then hit the panic button that opened all doors and windows and initiated a warning siren. The siren meant an explosion was imminent, and the workers would rush from the building to escape the blast, holding their breaths to avoid the deadly fumes.

Ironically, thirty years later my Aunt Lucille's eldest son, my cousin Sonny, was working at the identical job in that same DuPont gunpowder plant when his machine blew up, and a piece of the exploded steel fragment sliced off the top of his head like a melon, disclosing his brain resting in the ruins like a pinkish grey pudding. A very talented surgeon put my cousin's head and brain back together, and after a few years of therapy, he learned to walk and talk again and eventually even trounced me playing chess.

Our first year in Charlestown was still no frills for my family. Housing was hard to find because of the influx of workers at the defense plant, so for the first several months we lived in a tent. Although the structure was made of canvas, it had a wooden floor and wood panels halfway up the sidewalls. After a few months of Daddy's steady income, we could afford to move to a tiny house trailer. My mother always told me I walked later than most babies because the trailer was so small I could get around the place holding on to the walls and furniture. I'm sure what I was thinking was, "Why work hard if you don't have to?"

From hearing my mother's stories—not from *my* memories—I know they enjoyed living in the trailer court. They had many friends, and there was plenty of room for me to run and play in the dirt, which my mother claimed I loved to do. Unfortunately, my folks had to move when the Health Department shut down the trailer court and made everyone leave. It's a miracle I suffered no poor health consequences as a result of my close contact with that particular patch of dirt. However, doctors have recently identified certain anomalies in my lungs they say are the result of spores that are present in the earth of the Ohio River Valley. (Hmm—maybe the Health Department knew something we didn't.)

Shortly after the Japanese bombed Pearl Harbor, my folks found a three-room house to rent out in the country not far from Charlestown.

The house was owned by Mr. Buttoroff (everyone call him "Butt-off") and was so poorly made you could sit at the kitchen table and see daylight between the walls and the ceiling. Daddy went back to Gibson County to retrieve our furniture from Great-Aunt Bertha's granary and the family cow, Ruth, from Grandma Dorsam.

About this time, some events were etched into my memory files.

There was a chicken house on the property, so in the spring of 1942, my mother ordered fifty baby chicks from a mail order catalog. I remember the softness of those chicks and how I loved to hold them in my hand and caress them against my cheeks. But just as the chicks were beginning to get their feathers, a tornado struck, blew away the hen house, and buried the little chickens in the muddy potato patch. Mom managed to find twenty-five or thirty mud-soaked chicks that hadn't blown away, and she put them in the oven to warm. When they dried out, they started coughing up mud and dust, but they survived. I watched over those chickens as though they were my own children. And when they began to lay eggs, I would bring the fruit of their labor into the house and announce, "The hen sitteded down!" This grammatical *faux pas* has been the source of much family jest throughout my life.

After a year in the country, we gave the cow and chickens to Mr. Butt-off and moved into town, to a tiny, white-painted, four-room bungalow clustered with five other look-alikes around a circular *cul de sac*. Mom and her neighborhood friend, Lucille Liter (whose husband, Bub, also worked at DuPont), used their sewing talents to make stuffed animals to sell for a few extra dollars to supplement the wartime ration book.

My mother, Edna, was a stay-at-home mom in those days. She felt her job was to take care of her husband, her daughter, and her home. To keep me from being constantly underfoot, Mom encouraged me to look at catalogs or magazines and pretend to read. She would say, "Read me a story." So I would tell the story that I thought was being told in the Sears, Roebuck and Co. catalog. That was the only reading material my folks could afford—it was free! I even turned the pages as I pretended to read. My mother started the reading habit that has resulted in my current home being filled with floor-to-ceiling, wall-to-wall, book-filled shelves.

As a young woman, Mom played the guitar and harmonized with her girlfriends and cousins as they sang their favorite songs of the 1940s. I quickly learned those popular songs and would sing along with my mother. When I was about three years old, my parents and I were eating at a local cafe, and three men in navy uniforms came into the diner. I squealed, "Mom, I wanna sing my song to the sailors!" She stood me on top of the table and I serenaded the boys in navy blue, complete with appropriate movements, "Put your arms around me honey, hold me tight, huddle up and cuddle up with all your might." I must confess, I still have the desire to do that today whenever I see a man in a navy uniform, but I usually manage to resist the urge—most of the time.

Charlestown is situated smack dab in the middle of Tornado Alley, and one summer morning in 1943 a cyclone—as we Hoosiers called it—struck the town. Daddy was working the night shift at that time, sleeping during the day. I remember looking out the front window and seeing a dark sky filled with whirling clouds of debris. I thought it was pretty. As I recall, I said, "*Ooooooh!*"

Mom happened to be walking past the window, saw the sight, and shouted to Daddy, "Bud, it's a tornado!"

Daddy came running out of the bedroom. He was completely naked (he slept in the nude) and I remember thinking, "Where did Daddy get that banana?" Of course, I was too young to know anything about a man's anatomy—*that* would come later—much later. He saw the tornado heading straight for our house, grabbed his pants, and hustled Mom and me into the garage. We had no basement, so Mom and Daddy lay on top of me on the garage floor as the tornado passed harmlessly over our house like the angel of death at Passover.

However, the twister cut a terrifying swath through the rest of Charlestown. The funnel struck a small gasoline service station not far from our house, and it exploded in a fiery inferno as though it had received a direct hit from a B-52 bomber. The tornado did not stop until it reached the Ohio River, where it parted the water like Moses at the Red Sea and then dwindled into nothing more than a strong wind.

Aunt Lucille and her family had recently moved to the Projects—hastily built housing units with affordable rents for the working class.

As soon as the tornado passed, we piled into our car to go check on my aunt's family, about a half-mile away. As we neared their block, we saw a sofa sitting on the upper branches of a maple tree. Mom pointed and yelled, "That's Lucille's new couch!" When we got to their house, we saw not much more than broken sticks and stones. Ironically, a metal kitchen table with a red Formica top was standing in the middle of the debris, untouched, with a covered bowl of beans sitting on top.

The folks salvaged what they could find. My aunt's family, if memory serves me correctly, had taken refuge in a tiny cellar. They all squeezed into the rumble seat of our 1934 Plymouth to come live with us temporarily. I was put in charge of carrying the bowl of beans, which I balanced carefully on my three-year-old lap. I really don't remember if we ate those beans, but considering there were now eight hungry mouths to feed, we probably did.

I have many memories of my early years living in Charlestown, although I was just a small child. Perhaps that's because everything seemed so strange and new to me, sometimes traumatic, or it may be because my mother and father told me the stories so often.

Some memories were pleasant, such as going with my parents to visit Fountain Ferry Park in Henryville. However, some memories were not so pleasant. I remember one of Daddy's coworker buddies catching and handing me a grasshopper to hold—I suppose he thought it would fascinate me. However, when I realized it was alive, I screamed and threw it at him. To this day, I am terrified of bugs! A neighborhood boy, who was a year older and a head taller than I, grabbed my tricycle away from me, rode it down the driveway, and broke the pedal. I cried for my loss and then became so angry I threw the broken pedal at him. I also loathe all bullies.

One day, I was standing in the front seat of Daddy's 1931 Ford sedan, the type with the long gearshift lever mounted in the floor. I was turning the steering wheel and pretending to drive when the car suddenly popped out of gear and started rolling backward out of the driveway. I yelled, "*Wheeee!*" as the car rolled down and came to a stop with a quiet bump at the circular evergreen-filled island in front of the house. By the way, I still love to drive, although I rarely yell "*Wheeee!*" anymore.

Automobiles always have had a special fascination for me. I was four years old and following my parents through a Montgomery Ward store—which Daddy always called "Monkey Wards"—when I spied the most adorable kiddie car. It was a maroon Ford convertible replica powered by four-year-old-sized pedals, with a white windshield and grill and a steering wheel that guided the car left and right. I had to have that car. I begged my parents, I pleaded, I cried. I refused to leave the store without it. I'm embarrassed to say I think I threw a tantrum. The only-child syndrome was at work, and we left the store with that kiddie car. It cost fifteen dollars, about a week's take-home pay for my father, so I know what my parents sacrificed to satisfy their only child. I played with that car until I couldn't squeeze my little body into it anymore.

Today, when I remember those early years, it's as though I'm looking through my mother's photograph album again. I see a little brown-haired girl with a bow in her hair—more bow than hair. Her mother and father are seated on a piano bench and she is standing between them with a possessive hand on her father's shoulder, always smiling as she looks at the camera, as if she is proud of herself and her special place in life—the first and only child of a poor but happy family.

If only the joy depicted in those photographs could continue.

# CHAPTER 4

---·❀·---

# ON THE BANKS OF
# THE WABASH

My hometown was so small, the "You are
entering . . ." and "You are leaving . . ."
signs were nailed to the same post.
—Herb Shriner, Indiana comedian

Growing up in southern Indiana during the 1940s and 1950s was like living in perpetual reruns of *The Real McCoys* and *Father Knows Best*. (Of course, in my house, it was Mother who always knew best.) Our family was hardscrabble dirt poor, but I was oblivious to that fact. After all, I didn't know any other way of life; the rest of my relatives and most of the people in my small hometown were in the same boat.

All I knew was that Daddy could do anything: fix a broken doll, cure a wart by rubbing it and saying, "Hocus pocus, dominocus," or grow tomatoes the size of cantaloupes. He could catch a fish—sometimes two at a time—on a rusty old hook, shoot a bird between the eyes at one hundred yards with a .22 rifle, kill a tree squirrel with a single shot of his twenty-gauge, skin and filet his prey in two minutes flat, and cook it to perfection in a feast fit for a royal table.

Of course, those great meals were punctuated by the sound of each of us spitting out the shot pellets onto our chipped and cracked Woolworth plates.

Mom was the strict disciplinarian of the family; she would not tolerate back talk, sassing, pouting, or questioning of her authority. "Because I said so!" and "I'll give you something to cry about!" were her watchwords of parental authority and civil obedience. She was a second-generation German-American who believed that showing affection to a child would lead to his or her ruination. Perhaps she didn't realize she was creating a multi-married, push-me-pull-me, social misfit who would struggle to become an accepted member of society. Or, perhaps she was harboring within her fragile psyche a family secret that drove her to behaviors that made perfect sense to her but that to me, seemed to come from the devil himself.

In 1944 my mom was pregnant with her second child, and she wanted to be with her mother and Doc Gwaltney when her baby was born. She begged Daddy to move us back to Gibson County. At that time, the war was progressing well for America, and DuPont opened a window of opportunity for workers to be released from their contracts. Daddy accepted the release, and we moved back to the place of my birth.

In his video, *What You Are Is Where You Were When,* Dr. Morris Massey points out the importance of place in forming a child's value system. I'm convinced that many people of my schizo generation were raised in similar environments—small towns and farms in the heart of this country, known as the Midwest. Occupying a spot in the center of the nation's heartland is my home state.

Indiana is known as the Hoosier State. There are several versions of the origin of the nickname. Some say that the first settlers to the area, when they heard someone at the cabin door, would call out, "Who's yar?" More recently at a basketball game, Indiana University's famous coach, Bobby Knight, became so enraged at a call by referees that he tossed a metal folding chair onto the court. Thereafter, folks would say the state's nickname derives from the question, "Whose chair?"

The name of my hometown came from pre-Civil War days when an army fort was built on a branch of Pigeon Creek, which emptied into the Wabash River that formed the southwest border of the state. The "Fort on the Branch" ultimately became Fort Branch, Indiana. The sleepy little town has not grown much in the two hundred-plus years of its existence. My brother, Bill, says, "That's because every time a baby is born, somebody leaves town!"

Fort Branch was (and still is) largely a blue-collar farm town, situated by the side of a major north/south nation-bisecting route—US Highway 41—and relatively unknown to Hoosiers and the rest of the country. At the time I was born, the town was so small there were only three streets leading westward from the highway into town. The road on the north side—County Road 168—skirted the edge of town and headed beyond Fort Branch to Owensville, another one-horse town with no claim to fame other than being the home of one of my high school heartthrobs.

The street that led into the center of town—Locust Street—went past my grandma Dorsam's white-painted, clapboard-sided, craftsman-style bungalow where she and her family had moved after Grandpa sold the farm. Four or five wide concrete steps led to a wrap-around front porch that held a large swing. I can still picture my grandmother standing on the porch, wearing a flour-dusted feed-sack apron, urging me, "Hurry up, Mary Ellen, before the aunts eat the cookies."

When I was six years old, my grandma Dorsam's dormant cancer returned with a vengeance and she died in 1946. I was puzzled by the sight of my dear grandmother lying quietly in that big box in front of the fireplace in the bungalow's front room. Death is not always clearly understood by the very young. (Viewing of the deceased was usually held at home in those days.)

My two aunts, Ella and Elma (Mom's younger sisters), were only ten or twelve years older than I when they had to take on the role of homemakers, caring for their father and younger brother. They also were responsible for giving me opportunities as a teenager I never would have experienced otherwise, such as attending opening night at the

Mesker's Amphitheater in Evansville, watching live stage productions of the operettas *Chocolate Soldier* and *Brigadoon*, and going to concerts such as "Johnny Cash in Person!"

There was a sign on the highway at the head of Locust Street advertising Emge Foods, a meat processing and packaging plant, Fort Branch's major employer at that time. The sign's primary purpose was to indicate to the local farmers where to turn off the highway so as to reach the two-block-long uptown area. There, they might pick up a couple bags of feed at the Farm Bureau Co-op or cash the monthly subsidy check at the Farmers and Merchants National Bank.

In addition to the Farm Bureau and the bank, uptown boasted the Ben Franklin five and ten cent store, Doc Stormont's drug store, and the Star movie theatre. Bud Gentry, who would marry my Aunt Elma a few years later, was the only employee at the theater. He was the ticket seller, the popcorn popper, the concession stand operator, and the projectionist. As my father would say, "He was busier than a one-armed paper hanger!" Bud wouldn't let any of us kids in for free, of course, but the movies on Saturday cost only a dime. My baby brother, Bill, and I brought our own popcorn from home, a sure sign that we were among the town's poor folks.

On the south side of town, coming off the highway, there was a gravel road—Coal Mine Road—that had a steep hill that my brother and I called Tickle-Belly Hill. We would urge our father, "Faster, Daddy, faster!" and he would take the hill at the highest speed our old Ford could manage. As the car crested the top, we became airborne for a moment, which would give us a tickling sensation in our stomachs, just like that of a roller coaster—not that we had ever experienced a real roller coaster, of course.

When we continued on the road, we passed the ruins of an old coal mine. The only reminder of the once thriving mine was a smoke stack that still poked its proud nose into the sky. Then, we bounced over the railroad tracks and on to the site of the Emge slaughterhouse and meatpacking plant. I always thought that part of town smelled like cow dung and pork bellies.

Like most small towns, Fort Branch sported almost as many taverns as churches, of which there were five—Catholic, Baptist, Methodist,

Presbyterian, and Nazarene. There was one library, funded by the Carnegie Foundation; one elementary school, Marlette, named for a former school superintendent; and one high school, named simply Fort Branch High School. When I was a young girl, there was only one grocery store, Kuester's (pronounced keester), located in the enclosed front porch of the family home. They were descended from some of the original German settlers of the town. The church graveyards were full of Kuesters, Kruses, Messerschmidts, Romerhausens, and Titzers.

The town had two fraternal lodges—the I.O.O.F. (Independent Order of Odd Fellows), and the Free and Accepted Masons. The Odd Fellows met in a large room on the second floor over the bank, and the Masons had their own meeting hall housed in a red brick Victorian mansion a block away. These two fraternal orders symbolized the dichotomy of the town. The working class men such as my father belonged to the I.O.O.F., and the wealthier merchants and bankers belonged to the Masons. That changed several years later after the end of World War II when Fort Branch began to acquire a middle class. My daddy eventually became a Mason, and was Worshipful Master of the Lodge in the 1960s—quite a step up from his backwater beginnings.

There was a train depot and a parking lot across from the block of frontier-style storefronts in uptown Fort Branch. During summer nights when I was very young, movies were projected on the sidewall of the depot, and the children and townspeople would gather on wooden benches for the free show provided by the local merchants. My memory is full of the laughter, suspense, and romance of those movies. I especially loved the cartoons—I suppose that was the first time I heard Porky Pig's "Th-th-th-that's all folks!" from the screen. The adventure serials were exciting, but unfortunately we didn't always get to see them in sequence. The word *cliffhanger* takes on new meaning when you never learn how the hero got out of his predicament.

This parking lot was also the usual gathering place when the town had holiday festivities. I recall one parade of children on Halloween, when we would march around in our homemade costumes, usually fashioned from old sheets or items from the ragbag. There were no ready-made costumes and no Party City stores in those days. Pompous and prosperous town merchants would award prizes for the most original costumes. One year, I was surprised when one of the judges, Scats Wright, the owner of the local Ford dealership, tapped me on the shoulder and pinned a ribbon on my chest. I had won a prize for being "most patriotic." I didn't understand that, because I was dressed as a fairy princess! Apparently, the near-sighted judge thought my homemade magic wand was Lady Liberty's torch.

Every Christmas, the Masons distributed free bags of candy, nuts, and oranges to the children of the town. We would line up at the depot parking lot and then march in a long line down the block to the Masonic Hall. There were years when that bag of goodies was nearly the only thing my baby brother and I received for Christmas.

Eventually, Daddy's working life was steadier, although arduous. In all those years of haves and have-nots (mostly have-nots), I never heard my father complain. He was cheerful in the face of adversity and kind to everyone he met. He shouldered more than his share of life's burdens and chores. I remember when he was working the day shift at Emge's, coming home for lunch every day because we lived only one block from the plant. Mom was at work at the drug store, and somebody had to feed my brother and me. One day while he was fixing our lunch, he looked out the kitchen window and saw one of his friends on the sidewalk, heading back to the Emge plant, and he went out to chat with him for a moment. As they talked, Daddy suddenly stopped. "I gotta run into the house—I've got a pie in the oven."

The other guy guffawed and taunted, "Yeah, I'll bet."

Daddy said, "You wait right here." He ran into the house, returned a few moments later carrying a perfectly browned, lattice-crossed cherry pie, and held it up proudly for inspection.

His friend shook his head. "Damn. You'd make somebody a good wife."

Daddy made his family a good husband, father, caretaker, tutor, playmate, spiritual leader, role model, and breadwinner; and he surrounded us all with a special love we will carry to the end of our days.

My cousin, Sharon, who lived in my hometown of Fort Branch until she died recently, sent me an e-mail to which she attached a story she'd received (origin unknown):

> A man who was writing a book about churches visited several while traveling across the country. In every church, he saw a golden telephone with a sign, "Talk directly to God—cost, $10,000." However, when he stopped at a church in Wabash, Indiana, he saw the same golden telephone, but this time the sign read, "Talk directly to God—cost, thirty-five cents." When he asked the minister about the bargain price, the pastor smiled and replied, "Son, you're in Indiana now—God's country. It's a local call."

So why do so many Hoosiers go barefoot? Because when you're in Indiana, you're on holy ground!

# CHAPTER 5

·❋·

# HIS SISTERS AND HIS COUSINS AND HIS AUNTS

You can pick your friends, but you can't
pick your relatives. (And you can't pick
your seat in a crowded theater.)
—Anonymous

When our little family moved back to Fort Branch, Mom and Dad rented a big, yellow, mouse-infested barn of a house that we labeled—no surprise—the Yellow House. It was located one block from my maternal grandparents' home on Locust Street, a street that seemed to me at the time to be as wide as a river. Today, it looks too narrow for two cars to pass each other. Did the street get smaller, or did the cars get bigger? Actually, when you're only two feet tall, the world can seem huge.

I was loved and coddled almost daily by my teenage aunts, Ella and Elma, and graciously tolerated by my pre-teen uncle, Earl. One day, Uncle Earl took me for a ride on his bicycle. With the typical wisdom of an eleven-year-old, he perched me on the back fender. Within minutes my foot became entangled in the spokes of the back wheel. My ankle didn't break—four-year-old bones usually bend, they don't break. But to this day, sixty-plus years later, I still bear the scar on my ankle.

One day at the end of her workday at Emge's, my Grandma Dorsam stopped at our house to see if I wanted to go home with her for the evening. My mother was not at home—she had taken my infant brother, Bill, to my Grandma's and was giving my aunt Ella a home permanent. My father was working in our garage, so my grandmother told me to run and ask him for permission. I went to the garage and asked Daddy if I could go home with Grandma.

Without looking up from working on the car, he said, "No, it's too close to suppertime."

I ran back to my grandma and smiled innocently, "Daddy said okay." As we drove away, I ducked down behind the front seat, in case Daddy was looking. Needless to say, punishment later was sure and swift. I learned then that lying is not the best way to get what you want. Too bad some of my future husbands never learned that lesson.

In 1945, the summer of my brother Bill's first birthday, my folks invited Daddy's younger sister, Berta, and her new husband, Orris, to accompany our family on an outing to the White River for some boating and fishing. Daddy tied the boat oars and some bamboo fishing poles to the door handles on the driver's side of our car, a 1937 Ford four-door sedan. As I recall, the style of that car had the front door and the back door handles together, side-by-side. The front door opened and swung forward, and the back door opened and swung toward the back. Not long thereafter, car companies ceased manufacturing this incredibly unsafe design.

All six of us got into the car from the passenger side. I stood up on the back seat between my aunt and new uncle, so I could see all the scenery whizzing by at forty miles per hour. That was the favorite place for this five-year-old to ride in the car. Mom sat in the front seat, holding baby Bill on her lap. Of course, we didn't have seat belts or child safety seats in those days.

Before we left town, we stopped at Atterbury's Marathon station for gasoline. Daddy climbed over Mom to get out on the passenger side because he wanted to talk to the station owner. Everyone else remained in the car.

An old Model T Ford pulled up to the gas pump behind us. The driver, a local farmer still in his bib-overalls from his morning work, helped himself to the pump's gas hose, because the station attendant was busy filling our gas tank from the front pump. After the farmer finished fueling his Model T, he tossed a half-dollar to the attendant and jumped into his car, started the engine, and pulled away from the tank.

As he drove the car away, the bumper accidentally hooked on the gas hose, which then sprayed gasoline all over our car. The attendant rushed to shut off the pump, getting himself sprayed with gas in the process. The act of switching off the pump created a spark that ignited the gasoline in the pump, which ignited the gas that had sprayed on our car and on the service attendant. Flames were suddenly shooting out of both gas pumps.

Mom grabbed my brother by his arm and jumped out the passenger side door, running between two burning gas pumps—and a burning gas station attendant! My aunt and uncle were right behind her, having completely forgotten about me. I was standing in the backseat, taking it all in, but beginning to become a little concerned. It was getting hot! I couldn't decide whether to yell "Wheee!" or "Help me!"

Mom screamed at Daddy, "Bud! Save Mary Ellen! She's trapped in the backseat!"

By then, flames had completely enveloped the passenger side of the car. Daddy grabbed the boat oars and fishing poles that had been lashed to the driver's side door and broke them with his bare hands. Then he jerked the door open, and pulled me out of the backseat. We ran across the street to the public library lawn and watched our car melt into a pile of burned metal. Mom later wrote in her memoir, "It still gives me cold chills to think how close we came to losing our precious daughter." The attendant recovered, by the way.

I've often heard stories of the astonishing amount of strength provided by the adrenaline rush that comes to parents when their children's lives are in danger. My father was always a beacon of strength to me, and I will never forget him or the day he saved my life.

(Upon reading the first draft of this book, my brother said, "Now I understand why you always freak out when you see a fire.")

There were times when my star was definitely *not* on the ascendant. I had terrible teeth. My mother claimed that was because they had no money while she was carrying me, and she couldn't afford proper pre-natal nutrition and medication. Even my baby teeth were rotten, so Mom took me to a dentist when I was five years old. The dentist was not prepared to deal with children. He placed a board across the arms of the dentist's chair for me to sit upon so he wouldn't have to bend over to examine my mouth. The man was gruff and grumpy, and the shiny picks and pliers and other dental instruments on the tray were terrifying to me. They reminded me of the time Daddy pulled the tusks from the baby pigs. So I started to cry. The dentist—whose name I apparently have blocked from my memory—told my mother, "This child is impossible! I cannot work on her teeth." He then sent us home.

My mother was humiliated. She was always more concerned with what other people thought than how her children felt. She made Daddy beat me with his razor strop when he got home from work because I had misbehaved at the dentist. The razor strop, a thick leather belt-like strap used to sharpen straight razors for shaving, was the usual mode of punishment at our house. I suppose that was because tree switches were not that close at hand. Actually, I think they used it because the razor strap was more painful. Some parents say, when they are punishing their children, "This hurts me more than it does you." That is *not* the case with a razor strap!

We now lived closer to the home of my paternal grandparents, Grandma and Grandpa Blevins. I was allowed to spend time with them on their small farm in rural Gibson County just outside Oakland City, another backwater community near the coalmines in southern Indiana where Grandpa worked. They had a small house with a sagging front porch whose floorboards were bent and broken and a well outside the kitchen in the backyard with a hand pump for drawing fresh water. They had no indoor plumbing, just the inevitable stand-alone outhouse, complete with a half-moon cutout on the door.

I've seen that design on outhouses all my life, but only recently discovered that the custom of so adorning an outdoor toilet goes back to colonial days. Few people could read at that time, so the crescent moon on outhouse doors was used as the symbol for women, while a star cutout indicated an outhouse for men. It is thought that men let their "necessary rooms" fall into such bad shape that it was the women's outhouses that survived the test of time. Thus, the half-moon symbol became synonymous with outdoor toilets. My subsequent experience with men and their bathrooms certainly lends credence to this notion.

I loved being with Grandma and Grandpa Blevins, even though I hated using the outhouse. Grandma was short and plump, and when she sat down, I would try to sit on her lap, but it was like clinging to the top of a steep-pitched roof. I had to hang on to her neck to keep from sliding off. Grandpa drank a lot of beer—and often offered it to me—but I didn't like the taste. I loved his stove-perked strong coffee, however, especially when he sweetened it with three or four teaspoons of sugar and a half-cup of milk. I drank coffee that way until I was thirty years old. (That was about the time I started counting calories. The scrawny kid had begun to transform into the zaftig grown-up.)

Grandpa also mesmerized me when he would play an old fiddle while he clogged and tap-danced. I would laugh and clap with delight. Little did I know, but he was half-drunk at the time. Sometimes he would pop popcorn for us in a wire basket held over the flames in the open, fieldstone fireplace. Grandpa was a loveable character, but he was not the best of role models. Years later, Daddy told me about a time they came to pick me up after a week's stay with my grandparents. I was in the garden, beating the ground around a small corn plant and mumbling, "Som' bitch, som' bitch." As the old saying goes, little pitchers have big ears.

Although I loved my grandparents, I didn't have as much fun when my older cousins, Aunt Lucille's five children, would come to visit at the same time. Their favorite game was Teasing Mary Ellen. They liked to play dodgeball—and I was the one who had to dodge! They've never let me forget the time they hit me in the butt with the ball and I spun around angrily: "What are you trying to do? Knock my *brains* out?!"

But one of those cousins, Tommy Dan, was not like the others. He was a little goofy, but he was very sweet to me. Aunt Lucille always said he wasn't quite right because she had hemorrhaged badly while carrying him during pregnancy. One summer day, we were all playing in the woods near my cousins' house in the country outside Mackey, Indiana, where there was a tree with a large branch, about six feet off the ground, that looked just like a horse with a saddle. The other cousins, his sisters and brothers, would climb the tree and have imaginary horse races. Tommy Dan urged me to climb the tree, even though I was smaller than everyone else. He said, "Don't worry. I'll help you."

He boosted me up into the tree, I rode the imaginary horse for a while, and then I asked Tommy Dan to help me get down. He said, "Stick out your legs; keep them stiff and I'll lift you down and set you on the ground." I can't believe I trusted him. I stuck out my legs; he grabbed my ankles and I stood up and took a nosedive into a bramble bush. The other cousins, of course, laughed themselves silly at stupid Mary Ellen.

There is one brief incident in my early formative years that I have tried both to suppress and to face squarely in an attempt to avoid any long-term psychological consequences. I suppose something similar has happened to many young girls.

An older male relative came very near to sexually abusing me. I was four or five years of age and had been left in his care while my parents were gone for the evening. He liked to hold me in his lap and kiss me, which I didn't mind, although I thought he was creepy. He then told me he would give me a nickel if he could look inside my panties. I really wanted that nickel, so I agreed. However, after he pulled aside the waistband of my panties, looked, and then attempted to touch me, an alarm must have gone off in my head, because I said, "No!" I grabbed the nickel, pulled up my overalls, and locked myself in the bedroom where I stayed until my parents came. I never told a soul and have harbored that secret to this day.

By now, at five and a half, I was very eager to start school, possibly because I wanted to escape a world where adults thought they had a right to use me, abuse me, and laugh at me, and other children made fun of my naïve innocence. I thought, "There must be place for a kid like me—scrawny, skinny, and smart."

Obviously, I had yet to learn the meaning of the word *gullible*.

# CHAPTER 6

⬦❋⬦

# SCHOOL DAYS, SCHOOL DAYS

Education has for its object the
formation of character.
—Herbert Spencer, 1851

Public school teaching methods have evolved over the years from what they were when I was a child—some better, some worse. In my early schooling, teachers subscribed to the adage, "Spare the rod and you'll spoil the child." The rod was usually a paddle hanging by the teacher's desk for all to see what awaited them if they failed to behave. And the paddle always looked well used. Most children learned this lesson well: "A child should be seen and not heard."

Later, mostly during the 1960s, America went through a period of Dr. Benjamin Spock's influence that gave rise to the "Me" generation, categorized as "challengers" by the organizational behaviorist, Dr. Morris Massey. Using Spock's approach, parents began to feed their children self-indulgence instead of instilling self-control. As a result, children became more outspoken, defiant, and demanding of gratification. In fact, they came to view self-gratification as a right. I have some girlfriends from that generation—shopping is their favorite form of therapy.

Today, litigious fears hamper a teacher's attempts to teach or even maintain any semblance of discipline, culminating in young people who are either aggressively belligerent or deliberately anti-social. One of my friends, recently retired from public school teaching, tells horror stories of elementary students who would openly defy and even curse her in class. When the parents were called in for parent-teacher conferences and advised of their children's behavior, they would shrug and say, "So?" As the saying goes, "The nut doesn't fall far from the tree."

There is no doubt that my first teachers and their autocratic approaches had some life-long effects on my personality and character. It was yet another example of value programming gone horribly wrong.

My small town had no kindergarten or pre-K schools, so I started first grade at age six and three-quarters. My January birthday, according to the local school board, prohibited me from starting the previous year. I was so jealous that my neighborhood friends had already started school, so I compensated for that by making them play "corporation" with me. We would have company meetings; I would write out the minutes, and then officially seal them with the notary public seal belonging to our spinster neighbor, Hope Hyne. As a matter of fact, I've attended many corporate conferences in my lifetime that had no more substance than those childhood neighborhood meetings.

Hope had suffered a bad fall as a child that left her with a severely malformed spine, resulting in a hump back. She lived alone with her elderly father in a small cottage across from our house. Mr. Hyne had been a night watchman at Emge's until he retired. He loved to sit on his front porch swing and tell tall tales to all the children on the block. Hope was a good neighbor, albeit a bit of a "nosy parker" at times. She watched the goings-on at our house like a hawk, reporting whatever my brother and I did, which caused me a lot of anguish later in my teenage years.

Because my parents always encouraged my learning, by the time I was six years old I could read quite well. I was a regular in the children's section of the local Carnegie Public Library and possessed my own library card. I also could print short sentences, spell many words, and do simple math. For example, when I was four years old and had to have a tonsillectomy, the doctor who gave me the anesthesia placed the ether mask on my face and told me to count to twenty—if I knew how to do that. I bragged, "I can count to one hundred!" Of course, I don't remember saying anything after "two."

My mother may have made some mistakes in value programming her only daughter, but the incident that stifled my emotional voice—and led to my life-long yearning to be listened to and heard—occurred on the most important day of my young life: the first day of school.

I was so excited to be attending school—finally! However, I hated the fact that Mom forced me to wear those repulsive, thick cotton stockings, the kind held up by a garter belt. What humiliation for a six-year-old! I believe I was the only kid in school who had to wear those throwbacks to the 1920s. Fortunately, Mom soon allowed me to forego the stockings, probably because I kept tearing them and they soon became darned to death.

My first grade teacher was Miss Smith, who was a member of our church and a friend of my parents. I have changed her name, not to avoid any embarrassment or lawsuit, but because I have blocked her name from my memory. My father always told me about *his* first grade teacher who was Miss Smith. Daddy had a lisp as a youngster, so he called her "Mit Mit." For that reason, I have chosen to name my first grade teacher Miss Smith, in honor of my father.

Despite my ensemble embarrassment, I was eager to please the teacher by demonstrating the extent of my knowledge. Consequently, when she would ask a question of the class, I would call out the answer whether or not she asked me directly.

About mid-way through that first day of school, Miss Smith grew impatient with my exuberance. She came up to me and stood right beside my desk. I looked up at her in happy expectation, knowing she was going to tell me what a good student I was. I just *knew* she was so proud of me. To my horror, she leaned over and placed a big piece of Scotch tape on my mouth!

"Now, maybe you'll be quiet."

I was mortified. The students around me tittered and laughed at my shame. I have never experienced, in public, anything so traumatic and belittling. The rest of the day was blanked completely from my mind, and more than fifty years passed before I could tell my own mother about the incident.

When I got home, Mom greeted me at the front door and quizzed me eagerly about my first day at school. Non-responsive, I mumbled, "It was okay," and escaped to the room I was still sharing with my baby brother, Bill. I didn't want her to know that the teacher punished me for doing what I *thought* was right.

That was the end of my youthful spontaneity and the beginning of my quest to find my lost voice. Teachers, relatives, neighbors—and four husbands—would continue to squash any of my attempts to be listened to or heard.

But I hadn't quite learned my lesson yet. A few weeks later, we had a spelling bee in class, and I couldn't stop myself. One of my little classmates was stumped when asked to spell the word *it*, so I spoke out, a bit exasperated, "*I*-tee! *I*-tee!"

Miss Smith called my mother later that day, "I think Mary Ellen needs something to challenge her. First grade isn't doing it. I suggest piano lessons." Mom didn't bother to tell me about the conversation, however, until fifty years later. She just let me go on thinking the teacher hated me.

Thus, despite the fact that we had very little money, my parents somehow scraped together fifty cents a week, and I started piano lessons when I was six years old. I was not that happy about it—I'd rather have had tap dance lessons, like the pretty girls in my class. But tap dance lessons cost more.

My folks had borrowed three thousand dollars from my maternal grandparents in 1945 to buy a little four-room house near the Emge plant. There was an old sink in the kitchen, with a hand pump for cold water only. The house had no hot water, no bathroom, and no electric receptacles. The only electricity source was a light bulb hanging from the ceiling on a three-foot-long cord in the center of each of the four rooms. There was a cellar with an outside door that had to be lifted in order to go down the steps to a small, coal-burning furnace and fruit cellar. The property included a detached tumbledown garage with a two-hole outhouse toilet in one corner and a coal shed in another.

One of the Emge daughters, Christine Elpers, together with her husband and two children, lived in a large brick residence back of our house, behind the huge wall of arborvitae bushes that separated the rich from the poor. Their daughter, Eileen, had a mean, ugly English bulldog that would bark and chase after my brother and me whenever we had to go to the outhouse in the garage. The dog frightened us so much that we would "hold it" until our little bladders were ready to burst before we would venture out to face the wrath of the dog. I think that my brother, Billy Earl, may have utilized his special male apparatus to go in the bushes near the back door, rather than face the angry bulldog.

There was a related event that really embarrassed me at the time but I now realize was perfectly understandable, given the circumstances. I was visiting my Grandma Dorsam one weekend—I loved to play with the miniature porcelain doll and baby elephant she kept in the hinged window seat in the dining room. While I was playing, I had an urgent need to pee. My Aunt Ella was putting on makeup in the bathroom (they had an indoor one), but she called out, "Come on, it's okay."

I rushed into the bathroom, hoisted myself up onto the commode, and let go. The pee went all over the lid and the floor. In my haste, I didn't notice that the lid was closed—after all, our outhouse had an *uncovered* hole. My Aunt laughed at me so hard she had to leave the room. I was, once again, humiliated beyond redemption for doing what seemed perfectly natural to me. I knew I wasn't stupid, but why did I continue to do stupid things? What was missing from my early programming that left me inept in social situations?

Over the next few years, Daddy added another bedroom and an indoor bathroom (thank goodness!) onto our house, built a new two-car garage with an attic, rewired the house, dug a basement, installed a coal furnace with automatic stoker, laid hardwood floors and carpeting, and even relocated the front porch from one side of the house to another. Because we lived on a corner, this changed our address from tiny Foster Street, only one block long, to the larger Victor Street. We now had an address that bore the same street name as the wealthy Emge families: Conrad "Coony" and Christine Emge Elpers, their son Bob Elpers and family, and Fred and Barbara Emge Bender and their children.

I was so proud of what my father had accomplished. However, that pride actually got me into a "world of hurt." As it says in the Bible, "Pride goeth before a fall." It was the time of year for the tax assessor to gather data about property improvements, and he happened to come to the house when I was the only one at home. Once again, I wanted to demonstrate what I knew, and when the nice man asked me if I could answer some questions about the house, I assured him that I could. I proceeded to tell him all about the additions that Daddy had made to the house—the indoor bathrooms, the extra bedroom, and the basement.

When my mother came home from working at the Ben Franklin dime store, I bragged to her about how well I had done in giving the nice man all this information. She was so angry I thought she was going to kill me. (Which she did, almost—the razor strop, again!) I didn't know that it meant we would have to pay more taxes; I just thought I was giving the correct information. So, this time, I was punished for telling the truth. No wonder I grew up to be so confused about making the right choices. Incidents like this one, and my school experiences, laid the foundation for my emerging "schizo" personality.

Meanwhile, at the end of first grade, and over my mother's objections, I was double promoted into the third grade. I suppose my mother was concerned about my ability to socialize with the older students. I think what *really* happened was the second-grade teacher threatened to resign if she had to take *me* in her class!

Unfortunately, what I remember from those early school years is not all fun and games. Because I had skipped a grade, my classmates were older than I, which can have a significant effect when one is seven years old. There was a Christmas program at Marlette Grade School with a Santa Claus appearance. My classmates were scoffing and saying it was not a real Santa Claus. Another little classmate smirked in my ear, "They're all fake. There ain't no real Santa Claus. Our folks just made 'im up to make us do what they say."

"You take that back! There is *so* a real Santa Claus! I heard him talking to my mom in our living room last Christmas!" Needless to say, I was the source of much ridicule among my classmates for many years because I still believed in Santa Claus. I suppose it was my Daddy's voice I heard, but it certainly had sounded like Santa Claus would have sounded if he had come to town.

Going from first grade to third grade had other ramifications, academic as well as social. We had printed all of our work in the first grade, but students were expected to write in cursive in the third grade. In those days, cursive writing was taught in the second grade of school. Therefore, I had to teach myself to write by looking at the foot-high cursive letters marching around the room above the blackboard, and drawing them on my papers. This explains why the only bad grades I ever received in school were for poor handwriting. Of course, I excuse my illegible handwriting today by saying, "All doctors have poor handwriting!"

I managed to keep quiet and behave myself in class until the fifth grade. The teacher, Mrs. Lambkin, was teaching arithmetic and put several students to work at the blackboard writing out the problems and solutions for the day's lessons. When they were done, she dismissed them, saying, "That's fine." I raised my hand immediately and contradicted her, "No, that third problem is wrong!"

The teacher glared at me. "If you think you can teach this class better than I can, you come up here!" I was frozen with fear, and I didn't know what to do. When I started to get up from my desk, she lost it. I'm not sure that I remember correctly, but I think she may have thrown the arithmetic book at me.

As a matter of fact, a few years ago I saw an elderly Mrs. Lambkin at my friend's beauty parlor, and she told Wanda, "Mary Ellen was the smartest child I ever taught."

Ultimately, I think what I finally learned from that and other school and home episodes was to keep my mouth shut. Unfortunately, people and events sometimes conspired to break my vow of silence. In high school study hall one afternoon, my neighbor, Ruthie, poked me in the back and whispered, "What questions are we supposed to answer for Algebra?"

I turned to her with my finger on my lips and a frown on my face. She poked me again, "Come on!"

"Chapter 5, odd-numbered questions," I whispered, gangster style, out of the side of my mouth—and looked up into the face of Mr.

Barrett, the study hall teacher, who handed *me* a detention slip. I had to stay after school like a delinquent! As they say in corporate America, "No good deed goes unpunished."

It does seem to me, in retrospect, that most of my early memories are of punishment—by other kids for my naïveté, by cousins who were bigger and meaner, by parents who thought I was being disobedient when I was only frightened or trying to do what I thought was right, and by older adults and teachers who simply thought of me as—irritating.

Recently, after my parents passed away, I discovered a yellowed, crumbling, and stained piece of paper in a box of letters and documents my mother had saved. It was a poem I'd written when I was about eight or nine years old, entitled, "I Wish." In that poem, I voiced my frustrations with life and a possible hope for my future. (Apparently, I hadn't learned yet about using the subjunctive mood.)

I Wish

I wish I was a little bird,
and lived up in a tree.
I wouldn't say a single word.
I'd just sing with glee.

I wish I was a butterfly,
flying from flower to flower.
I'd fly away, away up high,
and land on a faraway tower.

I wish I was a little kitten
with shiny, yellow fur,
Not like the one who lost her mitten,
for I'd just play and purr.

I wish I was a little pup
with master kind and keen.
He'd teach me to roll over and sit up,
and I would never be mean.

But since I'm just a little girl,
and will grow up someday,
I'll try to help this sad old world
become a better place, some way.

# CHAPTER 7

---·•✦•·---

# WORKIN' FOR A LIVING

The world is moved along, not only by the mighty
shoves of its heroes, but also by the aggregate
of the tiny pushes of each honest worker.
—Helen Keller

Throughout most of the twentieth century, the major employer in Fort Branch was Emge Foods, a meat-processing and packing plant founded by Oscar Emge, a local German butcher. Old Grandpa Emge, as he was called affectionately by all the town folk, could be seen—and heard—driving around town in his enormous black Chrysler, always in second gear. Fort Branch was small, and the old man didn't drive fast enough to need the third gear, anyway. But his car made a distinctive groaning noise that announced his presence wherever he went.

At one time or another, almost all of my family members had worked at the Emge plant, at the Emge farm, or for the Emge family. My maternal grandmother Dorsam worked there, packaging meat. My mother's sister, my Aunt Elma, worked in the business office operating a comptometer, which is a now-extinct abacus clone business machine that required the operator to have fingers of steel and the dexterity of a monkey. I know, because I learned to operate one in my business machines class at Fort Branch High School. Young people today are lucky that Bill Gates and Steven Jobs invented computer software.

My mother cleaned old Grandma Emge's house, a Victorian cavern filled with velvet tuffets and black-walnut-finished chiffoniers. Mom inherited several of those furniture items when the old lady died, including a bed with a headboard of ornate carvings and inlaid woods of different colors and textures. My first husband kept that bed after our divorce, and its whereabouts is now a mystery.

I was a babysitter for the Emge's grandchildren and great grandchildren. When I was a teenager, I took care of great-grandchild, Nancy Elpers, so often she began to call me "Mommy." I was only twelve when Barb Bender, one of the Emge daughters, first asked me to babysit for her children. I had often taken care of my brother and several young cousins, but never for pay. The first day I sat for Mrs. Bender, as I was ready to leave, she asked me what I charged. I said the first thing that came to mind, something I had read in a Nancy Drew book, "Fifty cents an hour." She didn't hesitate and gave me two dollars for the four hours I'd been there.

When I got home and showed Mom my newfound wealth, she was not happy. "That's too much! Take it back." And I did, reluctantly. In hindsight, I believe my mother was suffering from servant mentality. She believed we were not in the same class with the Emge family and we *deserved* to be treated as servants.

When I returned the money, I told Mrs. Bender that my mother said it was too much. She then paid me thirty-five cents an hour, and that was my hourly wage for the remainder of my high school years working for the Emge family, both babysitting and cleaning their houses. The lesson to be learned here is clear: The low wages you settle for as a starting salary will continue to be lower than any of your contemporaries for the rest of your employment with that organization, no matter what jobs you perform, nor how well.

In summers, my teenage brother worked on the Emge farm caring for the livestock and harvesting corn and wheat. One of the Emge horses kicked my brother in the face and gave him his distinctive slanted-to-one-side nose. Fortunately, he was wearing a heavy pith helmet at the time, which cushioned the blow somewhat.

My father worked at the Emge plant for thirty-four years, from 1944 until he retired in 1978. His first job at Emge's was on the hog kill, a barbaric process in which the pigs were hung by their back legs from a conveyor belt while they were still alive, and then their throats were slit by the hog kill workers as the pigs passed overhead. The blood from the slaughtered swine sprayed on the workers, and many of them, including my father, were infected with brucellosis, a debilitating disease more commonly called undulant fever because of the way the accompanying fever would rise and fall inexplicably.

My father survived by taking an experimental, expensive antibiotic—chloramphenicol. My veterinarian brother now says the dosage given to Daddy was too high, so it must have been a cure-or-kill treatment. Although Daddy recovered with no aftereffects, many other workers were not so fortunate. Obviously, this was before OSHA—the Occupational Safety and Health Act of 1970: the one good thing the Nixon administration did for the country's working class.

Daddy received no income during his illness—there was no workers' compensation law at that time. In order to bring in enough money for our family's subsistence and pay for the expensive medication, Mom took in washing and ironing in addition to cleaning and wallpapering other people's houses. Once, after Mom had washed, ironed, and neatly folded a client's laundry into his clothesbasket, our cat leaped into the basket, expecting to find a warm, cozy place to snooze. Instead, he received a whack on the behind, and we all had to smack the dust and cat hair out of the clean clothes before the client arrived to retrieve his laundry. I thought this was funny, and I started to relate the incident to Mom's client when he came to pick up his clean clothes. My mother managed to choke off the story with her famous one-more-word-and-you-die look.

After Daddy recovered from the undulant fever infection, he worked in the night shipping department, where he was constantly cold because of the refrigeration and always exhausted because he had to sleep during the day. With two boisterous children being hissed at by Mom to "Be quiet!" this was no easy task.

In order to get in out of the cold, Daddy took some automobile mechanics classes. After a couple years working as a grease monkey apprentice, he was promoted to a mechanic's position maintaining the company's automobiles and delivery trucks. Daddy was a natural at that—he had a long history of buying and fixing up old cars to sell at a profit.

My father had graduated from Patoka High School, but my mother had not had any formal education beyond the tenth grade. As a young girl, she had a chronic lung infection that caused her to miss too much school, so she quit at age sixteen. She must have been very proud of Daddy's education because I recently found a scrapbook she had made in which she carefully preserved every one of his automotive mechanics class certificates.

The down side of this promotion meant that Daddy often would be called by his boss in the middle of the night to drive to Kentucky, Illinois, or Ohio, to fix a meat delivery truck that had broken down. He loved to tell the story about rigging up a hoist, lifting out a truck's engine block, and making repairs in a Paducah, Kentucky, shopping center parking lot—in the middle of the night!

Probably as a result of my lower middle class background, and the fact that my family knew only labor, never luxury, I grew up being more Democratic in my political thinking, rather than Republican. Recently, one of my fellow writers in my critique group, an obvious right-wing thinker, was angry with what he perceived as a leftist, liberal subtext in one of my stories. He wrote to me in an e-mail, "I fought and bled for my country. What have you ever done for your country?!"

What I wanted to say was this: "I got up and went to work every day, and I paid my taxes without complaint or avoidance. Those taxes were used to pay for your uniform, your gun, and the GI Bill for your education—which obviously you did not use."

But I didn't say it. (Where was my "voice" when I needed it?)

When the Emge plant closed in May 1999, it had been in operation for nearly a century and had been the life-blood of the town and its citizens. There were no buyers for the plant, so it remained empty for the next decade. On June 18, 2010, a fire started at the abandoned plant in some hay that was stored in one of the buildings. Flames quickly spread throughout all the buildings. The fire was fought for five days by firefighters from three counties. Who knows? Perhaps the decades of splattered pork and beef fat had permeated the walls and simply fed the fire.

After several days of burning, the buildings were totally destroyed. I was visiting family in town during those five days, and it was tragic to watch an ancestor being figuratively burned at the stake. The death of the Emge Meatpacking Company was a sad day for the town and for all of us for whom it had meant a livelihood and a connection to people and places of the past.

Shakespeare said, through Marcus Antonius's speech at the burial of Julius Caesar: "The evil that men do lives after them. The good is oft interred with their bones." I'm inclined to disagree. When I visit Fort Branch and reconnect with old friends and relatives, I tend to remember the good times and the people who were kind to me.

However, when I think a little harder, I also remember the evil.

# CHAPTER 8

---

# MEMORIES ARE
# MADE OF THIS

Teachers who educate children deserve
more honor than parents who merely give
them birth; for bare life is furnished by the
one, but the other ensures a good life.
—Aristotle

Education became a better experience for me when the Fort Branch school system hired Miss Rice to teach music, both in elementary and high school. Although a pinched-face, no-nonsense, spinster lady, she evoked in me a passion that has burned stronger and hotter than any love affair. Because of Miss Rice's guidance, music became an all-important part of my life.

I continued to take piano lessons throughout my school days. While other children were trying to escape piano practice in order to go outside and play baseball, I would gladly practice my piano—I was able to escape doing the dishes! My mother would stand in the kitchen doorway, drying the pots and pans, a dreamy smile on her face, as I played Beethoven's "Fur Elise" on the ancient upright piano we had inherited from my grandparents.

At age eleven, I was asked to sing on the local radio station with Wanda, one of my church girlfriends. The citizens of Gibson County were regaled every Sunday afternoon by our pre-adolescent voices singing familiar hymns, such as "Beyond the Sunset," in two-part harmony. Before long, I was singing and playing for churches, Girl Scout functions, ladies social groups, and public school events—even serving as the high school accompanist.

However, something happened in the summer after my twelfth birthday that threatened to end my budding singing career. While preparing to go to town with my folks for our weekly grocery shopping, I glanced in the mirror and saw a strange sight. Even though I knew I was smiling, my face displayed a smile only on the right side. I was frightened, but decided to say nothing to my parents.

However, you can't hide anything from your mother for long. Mom soon noticed that something was wrong. She quizzed me, "Where have you been?"

"Just swimming at the Mount Carmel city pool."

"How long has your face been like this?"

I hesitated before telling her the truth. "Well, since yesterday."

Mom called the town's only physician, Dr. Geick (pronounced Gyke), who took us into his office that same day. After examining me, he pronounced, "It's not polio." Mom heaved a sigh of relief—that was a common disease in those days, especially for those who'd been swimming in community pools.

"I think she has something called "paralysis of the seventh nerve." There is no known cure at this time, but we'll start her on some antibiotics, and I want you to see a specialist in Evansville." The affliction has more recently been named Bell's palsy and is caused by a virus, therefore impervious to antibiotics. But we didn't know that at the time.

The specialist prescribed twice-weekly treatments of electric shock, administered by an instrument that resembled a flat light bulb on the end of a thick wand. This Frankenstein-inspired tool was rubbed over the afflicted side of my face, sending a shock to the nerves—and to my very soul—in the hope that this would stimulate the paralyzed nerve back to life. It was painful but effective, although I was left with an absolute phobia about electricity.

My mother would sit by my bedside while I slept because my left eye would not close, even when I was asleep. Mom kept closing my eyelid in an effort to keep my eyeball from drying out, which she'd been told might lead to blindness. Her efforts paid off because, even though my left eye is weak, I still can see. I have often wondered why they didn't simply tape my eye shut at night. Nobody hesitated to tape my mouth shut in first grade, did they?

The miracle of my recovery will be accepted and understood by those who believe in the power of heavenly intervention. My mother prayed and prayed, and within a few short weeks I gained full control of my facial muscles with no discernible aftereffects other than the need to wear glasses to correct my weak eyes. I have known, throughout the years since, several people who have had the same disease, and they've been left with a completely—or at least partially—paralyzed side of the face. Mothers are, indeed, God's instruments on earth.

As if that illness weren't traumatic enough for a twelve-year-old to overcome, nature sent me another blow that same summer. I was playing a rather rough and tumble game with my friends, and ended up straddling my neighbor, Joan, in my moment of triumph. She looked up from her position on the ground and announced, "You've been sitting in something, and you got dirt on your panties."

I wasn't sure what was what, so I just threw the panties in the dirty clothes. When Mom was doing the laundry later, she saw them and knew immediately it was time to have "the talk." She approached me with the soiled panties and said, "I see that you're old enough now, and I have to tell you about something all women do."

"You mean, have a baby?"

She then went on to explain menstruation, and that this phenomenon would occur every month. I was furious. "Every month! And this doesn't happen to my brother? That's not fair!"

Of course, as I have subsequently discovered, that's just one of many things that are "not fair" in the battle of the sexes.

There were times when Mom took her role as God's instrument a little too seriously. I was a young teenager with a new dress I couldn't wait to wear, and the only place I had to wear it was church. The dress had a full, gathered skirt, and a peasant style bodice with puffy, gathered sleeves and an elasticized neckline that could be slipped down over the shoulders. I would do that whenever I was feeling like a sexy, enticing thirteen-year-old.

I had walked to church that day, wearing my new dress but with the neckline raised to a chaste, virginal level. Mom and Dad were already there, having taken my brother early to Sunday school. When I showed up in the choir room—Mom and I both sang in the choir—she looked at my dress and said, "Go home and change clothes. That dress is not fit for church."

No amount of arguing would change her mind; I had no choice but to go home and change. I thought, "Well, heck! The choir robe would have covered it up, anyway." I wanted to grow up and be pretty, and Mom wanted me to stay young and ugly. Why else did she give me all those frizzy Toni home permanents?

When I was fourteen, Mrs. Brown, the faculty sponsor of the Sunshine Society, a social group for high school girls, came to me with a request that had another long-lasting effect on me. "I want you to get four girls together and learn the song, '*M-o-t-h-e-r,*' to sing for the Sunshine Society's annual mother-daughter banquet." She had found a songbook entitled, *Beauty Shop Memories* that had an arrangement of the song in four-part harmony, voiced for young women.

That was the beginning of the Sunshine Quartet. My friend Wanda and two other girls in my class, Jeanie and Sheri, learned the song, "*M-o-t-h-e-r*", in barbershop harmony to sing for the banquet. Jeanie even wrote a special verse, "*D-a-u-g-h-t-e-r,*" for the occasion.

The Chordettes were popular at that time—they were a Sweet Adelines barbershop quartet that had won Arthur Godfrey's talent contest in 1948. They were featured regularly on the Arthur Godfrey radio show for several years. I bought every copy I could find of the Chordettes' barbershop songs in sheet music. Using their arrangements as a model or template, I taught myself to arrange music in four-part harmony for my quartet. I'll admit my first attempts at arranging did not result in kosher barbershop, but it had four-part chords.

The Sunshine Quartet became the singing stars of the school, especially when we performed my special arrangement of "Memories Are Made of This," the popular song by Dean Martin. Dressed in red and white striped vests (made by my mother), straw hats, and canes (made by my father), we appeared throughout southern Indiana, even winning a local talent contest. I often wondered if the Dapper Dans of Disneyland saw us and copied our outfits!

One weekend, the quartet was hired to sing for a women's sorority in a nearby town, but I had accidentally left the accompanist's music in my locker at school. Mom drove us to the high school and served as lookout while the girls and I broke into the building through an open window in the gymnasium. I think that's when I learned that old show business adage, "The show must go on!" That's also when I realized just how far a stage mother would go to ensure her daughter's musical success—even aiding and abetting breaking and entering!

After high school graduation, the members of the Sunshine Quartet went their separate ways, married, and had children (well—I had husbands, not children). We didn't see each other for twenty-five years. At the twenty-fifth reunion of the class of '57, all four of us were present, and the class asked us to sing. We had to dust off a few cobwebs in the brains, but we managed to recall one of our songs. I can still hear Jeanie singing in her low alto voice, "Sweet, sweet, memories you gave-a me."

Our class then voted to have a reunion every five years so we could see each other more often, and the Sunshine Quartet entertained at almost every reunion. I dread the day when we can no longer relive those happy high school days by singing songs of the 1950s—"Mr. Sandman," "Why Do Fools Fall in Love," and "Goodnight Sweetheart"—and reminisce about the basketball games where we cheered on our mighty team, the Fort Branch Twigs. (I know, I know, a *twig* does not necessarily instill terror in the hearts of opponents.)

One of my special high school friends was Dannie, a Roman Catholic who had attended Holy Cross, the local Catholic elementary school, from grades one through eight. The Catholic students joined the rest of us non-Catholics for the four years of high school. I must admit we were startled in ninth grade when the Holy Cross kids would stand up while answering a teacher's questions. Maybe that explains why they got better grades. By the end of the freshman year, however, they were just as disrespectful as the rest of us.

Dannie was a smart kid, and we shared mutual interests in English and literature. One day during the summer between ninth and tenth grades, the two of us rode our bicycles to the local picnic area favored by the high school crowd. It was a cemetery, but it was the only place we could go for solitude away from the watchful eyes of parents. (Hey, we just talked!)

On the way back, Dannie and I stopped our bikes to chat amiably on the neighborhood corner under a streetlight before heading home. Just then my father drove by. Daddy leaned out of the car window and shouted to me, "You get home—now!"

Although Mom and Dad didn't openly express the thought, I knew they didn't want me to become involved with a Roman Catholic. They subscribed to the notion that the Catholic priest dictated that every woman must have at least a dozen children "in the name of the Lord." They had better plans for me.

At this point, I should mention that a few years after I was widowed, I happened to be visiting my parents in Fort Branch at the same time that Dannie was visiting his father, who lived next door to my folks. The two of us sat outside in lawn chairs, talking until well after dark. When I came in, Mom looked at me and said, "I think your father and I might have made a mistake in keeping you two apart." Too late, darn it—Dannie had a lovely wife.

I almost scuttled my parents' great plans for me when I was a senior in high school and fell in love with Joe, a boy from the nearby town of Owensville. He had graduated from high school the previous year and operated his own electronics repair shop out of the front of his father's sheet metal shop. This was in the early days of television, and he was a whiz at fixing TV sets. Of course, television reception in 1956—at least in our part of the state—included just one station from Evansville that broadcast a few hours a day, another with sporadic reception from Bloomington, and very snowy wrestling matches coming from Louisville, Kentucky.

There was one program we did get in the afternoon that I remember watching every day after high school classes—Dick Clark's *American Bandstand*! I taught myself to jitterbug by dancing while leaning against the refrigerator. Unfortunately, I didn't have a lot of opportunity to show off my skill. There weren't many refrigerators on the dance floor.

Anyone who has ever lived in a small town in the 1950s will empathize with me in this story. Joe was often at our house while Mom and Dad were at work. We would watch TV, play games, or just daydream. (Okay, okay, we also necked!) One afternoon when Joe left the house, our nosy neighbor, Hope, was on her front porch across the street. When Mom came home from work at Doc Stormont's drugstore, Hope told her that Joe was zipping his trousers as he went to his car. I had a difficult time convincing my mother that I was still chaste and that Hope—a lifelong spinster—was engaging in wishful thinking.

We dated steadily, breaking up briefly when Joe was enticed by a girl (I called her a slut) from his hometown. Mom was so angry about Joe's behavior that she encouraged me to drive by his other girlfriend's house while he was there. As I slowly drove past, Mom reached over and pressed the lever on the special moo-cow horn on my 1950 Ford. I guess she wanted to let him know that *we* knew what he was up to. Mom was, once again, the stage mother.

Joe and I did make up eventually and made plans to marry, until I was lured away by a force that was stronger than both of us. As a result of my high school academic records, I was selected as valedictorian of my senior class and received a full merit scholarship to Indiana State Teachers College. The ISTC registrar invited me to campus shortly after high school graduation to get acquainted with the school and to register early for classes. I was determined that I was not going to college but was going to marry Joe and settle down in Gibson County, Indiana. However, Mom and Dad convinced me just to take a look at the college before making a final decision. (And who says parents are dumb!?)

So, in late May 1957, Mom drove me to Terre Haute, Indiana, to preregister for classes at Indiana State. Joe decided to go with us. On the way north on Highway 41, we stopped at a farmer's market near a peach orchard. Mom took a picture of Joe leaning against the giant peach statue—known as the Big Peach—in front of the orchard. Daddy always said of the photo, "It's a picture of a worm on the peach."

When we pulled onto the campus at Indiana State, I felt as though I had entered Emerald City, and the registrar was the wizard. Joe later told me that he knew his "goose was cooked" when he observed the gleam in my eyes once I saw the campus. I was enthralled with the perfectly manicured lawn on the quad, the alabaster walls and columns of the library, and the ivy-covered brick of the classroom buildings and women's residence hall. A young man from my hometown, Keith, worked at the college library. He gave me a tour of the place, and I was as impressed as if it were the Library of Congress.

I went back to Fort Branch, gave Joe his ring and walking papers, packed my matching twin sweater sets, and practiced Gregg shorthand in preparation for taking on Indiana State and the Fighting Sycamores. I was really going up in the world—moving from lowly Twigs to giant Sycamores!

# CHAPTER 9

—◦❋◦—

# HE AIN'T HEAVY, HE'S MY BROTHER

Deal with him as a truant, if you will,
But claim him, keep him, call him brother still.
—Oliver Wendell Holmes, 1883

(Note: I wrote this chapter in 2009 and presented it to my brother on the occasion of his sixty-fifth birthday and retirement from Purdue University. Some of the story has appeared elsewhere in this book.)

My brother, William Earl, was born on D-Day—June 6, 1944, the day the Allies invaded Europe—and he's been storming beachheads ever since. He was named for our father, William, and our mother's brother, Uncle Earl. In those days, in the mid-40s, it was customary for young people in midwestern and southern states to be called by both first and middle names. I was always Mary Ellen and I refused to respond to Mary. Similarly, William Earl was called Billy Earl until he was a teenager, when he rebelled and demanded to be called just plain Bill. Nevertheless, I called him Billy Earl until he grew big enough to beat me up, but most of our relatives continue to call him Billy Earl or Billy, to this day.

Now that I think of it, everyone born in southern Indiana had two names, at least in my family. I was Mary Ellen, my brother was Billy Earl, and I had cousins named Tommy Dan, Bonnie Jean, and Alan Wayne. My first husband, born and raised in Martinsville, Indiana, was named William Robert, and you can guess what his family called him—Billy Bob.

I really didn't understand why Mom and Daddy wanted to have another baby. Weren't we perfectly happy, the three of us? I found out why, in April 2006, when my brother Bill gave the eulogy at Daddy's funeral. He remarked that not long before our father's final hospitalization, he had asked Daddy, "Why did you and Mom decide to have a child in the middle of a world war?"

Daddy didn't hesitate as he answered, "Because your mom said, 'It's time to have another baby. Aunt Bertha says we shouldn't raise an only child.'"

They didn't let me in on the rationale, however. All I knew was that an interloper was coming to take my place with my parents. I have a few distinct memories of my brother's arrival. That's when I started to eat dirt from the freshly plowed garden near our house. I don't know why it tasted so good, but it reminded me of dark chocolate fudge—at least in texture. It had an earthy smell, like new potatoes. I was so angered by my brother's birth that I told Mom when she brought the baby home from the hospital, "Take it back! I want a girl."

I remember folding one of his earliest baby photographs into a paper airplane. Perhaps I hoped he would simply fly away. Another time, I accidentally dumped over his baby carriage—at least I think it was accidental. He wasn't hurt—much. Today, I take great joy in teasing my brother about the fact that I was born at home with no frills, attended only by Doc Gwaltney, a country doctor, and that he had the privilege of being born in a hospital in pampered splendor.

When Billy Earl was less than a year old, the family moved from the Yellow House, as we called it, to a small house my parents purchased for three thousand dollars, borrowing the money from Mom's parents. The tiny bungalow was located on the west side of town at 307 W. Foster Street, just one block from Emge's Meatpacking Company where Daddy worked. Our father would remark proudly, "We now live in the stick-and-plumb section of town. *Stick* your head out the window and you're *plumb* out of town!"

Daddy worked very hard to remodel and update that old house. He dug a basement himself, by hand, with only a pick and shovel. Little Billy Earl helped, or as he lisped, "I hepped!" Daddy would dig in the basement, and Billy Earl carried out some of the excavated dirt in his little toy tin pail. Daddy made the basement walls of thick cinder blocks to support the house frame. The finished project boasted a front rumpus room, an enclosed toilet and shower, a furnace room and coal storage bin, a laundry area, and a fruit cellar to contain the hundreds of jars of Mom's home-canned fruits and vegetables that grew in the large garden that Daddy tended with loving care. My brother and I would steal the ripe tomatoes from the garden and eat until we developed a rash!

There had been a large maple tree growing near the corner of the house. The tree was rotten and it constituted a potential hazard to the roof, so Daddy cut down the tree, branch by branch. Then came the backbreaking task of removing the tree roots and the huge stump. Every day, two-year-old Billy Earl would put on his overalls, pick up his toy hatchet, and announce he was going to help Daddy "work on the 'tump." (Apparently, Bill had a problem saying his els and esses.)

Bill adored his father, and wanted to do everything his Daddy did. He fished with him, hunted with him, gardened with him, and even helped Daddy work on the family automobile. There they were, clad in greasy overalls, bodies draped over the front fenders, and heads poked under the hood while they tinkered with something in the engine— spark plugs, oil pan, cam shaft, or valve lifters. These words have always held a special fascination for me, like "Open, Sesame" to Ali Baba.

Everyone in the family agreed that Bill looked exactly like his father did as a young boy. I have a picture of Grandpa Blevins, Daddy, and Bill at age seven; Mom always said they looked like "three peas in a pod." Except for a little difference in body shape (my brother is taller), Bill today looks remarkably like Daddy did then.

My brother and I experienced the usual sibling rivalry. However, I have to admit that Bill really was a sweet child. I remember when I was about seven or eight years old, I dressed up in a costume I had made from crepe paper and pretended I was Cleopatra. Somehow I managed to coerce three-year-old Bill into pulling me through the neighborhood in our Red Flyer wagon while I perched on my little red rocking chair throne in the center of the wagon. I guess I wanted to be a star, even then!

When Bill was four years old, he had measles. My parents had to go out one evening and they left me in charge of my sick little brother. His fever spiked and he began hallucinating, screaming that bugs were crawling all over him. I was only eight then, and I had no idea what to do, so I walked him around the house and encouraged him to pet his little dog, Spotty, a beagle that Daddy had trained as a hunting dog.

"Don't cry, Billy Earl, come and pet Spotty. See? Good doggie!" Of course, Spotty wasn't really in the house, but what did the kid know? He was hallucinating! Thankfully, his fever went down when I finally got him to sleep.

Most of our arguments as children were typically mundane—such as who would wash the dishes and who would dry, who could make his or her chocolate milk last longer than the other could, and who would get to eat the last fried chicken drumstick. My mother knew how to cut a chicken in such a way that there were at least six drumsticks, because she knew we'd fight over them.

Bill was fortunate that he had pretty good hair days, although I did tease him about his "straw hair." But that was not his fault. When he was eleven years old, in 1955, his uncle Earl was in the Air Force and sported a scalp-revealing flattop haircut. I suppose either Bill or Mom decided he would look as good as Uncle Earl in that cut. And it would be cool in summer. But Bill's hair was so fine, the hairs wouldn't stand up straight the way Uncle Earl's did. They just fell to the side like limp linguini or sagging straw. Unfortunately, I can't tease him about his straw hair anymore—now I have it!

When Bill and his neighborhood pal, Millard Newton, were about twelve, they built a wooden clubhouse out of scrap lumber they found here and there. It wasn't much to look at, more like "That Tumbledown Shack in Athlone," but to the boys it was their golden palace of Kublai Kahn. They would eat, meet, and sleep in their little fortress, where no girls were allowed. One night, Daddy went out to the clubhouse to warn the boys, "There's a bad storm brewing,—you'd better get home."

They quickly took off. Millard didn't pause a second before dashing out into the night—without his pants.

Because I had skipped a grade in elementary school, Bill and I were together in the Fort Branch High School building for one year—his seventh grade and my twelfth. By the time I was graduated from high school in May 1957, he was taller than I was—that's when I stopped picking on him. A year later he had achieved his full height of six feet three inches and towered over everyone. By the time I finished college and he was a senior in high school, I was rather proud of the way he looked.

Bill was a great student and very active in high school, especially in extra-curricular activities. Some that I remember were: sports, especially basketball and football; music, playing trumpet in marching band and playing tuba in his own German band; church choir and youth groups; and Boy Scouts, from Cub Scouts to Eagle. As a Boy Scout, Bill did a lot of traveling. Daddy took the boys to Florida in 1957 and to Canada in 1958, the same year Bill became an Eagle Scout at age fourteen. They went to the Missouri Ozarks in 1959, and attended the Scout Ranch at Philmont, New Mexico, the summer of 1960. Bill then went on to the National Scout Jamboree in Colorado Springs, where he met President Dwight D. Eisenhower. He received the Life Award, the Lincoln Trail Award, the God and Country Award, and the Order of the Arrow.

In addition to school and extra-curricular activities, Bill always worked—mowing lawns, slinging burgers at the Dog n' Suds, and wrangling hay and horses at the Emge Meatpacking Company Farm, where one of the Emge horses reared up, slashed a hoof downward at Bill, and broke his nose. His Blevins beak, inherited from his grandfather, still lists to one side.

My brother was a very talented musician, playing several instruments during high school and even designing and constructing a hammered dulcimer. One spring at the high school's annual Lilac Festival, Bill dazzled the audience by playing "Stardust" on his trumpet, emulating Louis Armstrong, even holding the trumpet with a handkerchief, just like Satchmo. His little German oompah band was absolutely charming. Mom taught him to set the tempo for the guys, counting out in German: "*Eins, Zwei, Drei, Veir!*" Bill was so sure he had learned enough German from Mom that he could test out of German at Purdue and meet his foreign language requirement. That ploy didn't work.

His uncertain knowledge of the German language also caused him a few problems as an adult. One year, he was on a vacation in Europe with his wife. They rented a car to visit the famous attractions of Europe on their own timetable. Bill familiarized himself with the rules of the road of each country and was confident in his ability to navigate the various cities and towns successfully.

Their trip included a stop in Koln (Cologne), Germany, to view the cathedral that, though damaged, had miraculously survived the bombing that had completely destroyed the city during World War II. Bill parked the rental car on a street a few blocks from the cathedral and carefully noted the name on the street sign so he could find the car again on the crowded avenue.

When Bill and his wife finished their sightseeing, they sought the car, only to discover it was gone! He checked the street sign, and yes, it had the same name, so he was sure he was in the correct spot. He stopped a policeman and explained that his rental car was missing. He knew it was stolen, because he had carefully noted the name of the street where he parked—Einbahn Strasse. The policeman (probably stifling a guffaw) explained to Bill that he had parked by a sign proclaiming it was—a one-way street. With a bit of searching, they finally found the car.

Recently I found a postcard that Mom and Dad sent to Bill in 1959 while visiting relatives in Ohio. I guess Mom wanted to make sure he was keeping up with his schedule, because the message was: "Dear Bill: If we don't get home by the time you're supposed to take your guitar lesson Saturday, call Rex and tell him you don't have a way to get there. Tell Hope she doesn't have to stay over at our house Saturday. If you can get the mower started, you'd better mow the churchyard 'cause it needs it. We'll be home some time Saturday. Love, the folks." (Whew! Busy boy!)

During his growing years, Bill seemed to have arms and legs that had wills of their own. There is a scene in one of our home movies that shows him trying to straighten a drooping sunflower—by dropkicking it into place. Perhaps he was demonstrating what a great football player he would become. Actually, participating in high school football wasn't all that easy for him. He would play his trumpet while marching in the pregame performance, then suit up in jersey and shoulder pads and head for the playing field.

Bill was an even more outstanding basketball player. Mom always bragged about how cute he looked in his basketball uniform, all six feet plus of him, with his short shorts and tall knee socks. She couldn't stand the droopy drawers that basketball players wear nowadays. He was a star player and won several free-throw awards. He would stand still, look at the basket, take a deep breath, and then—whoosh! The ball would go through the net without touching the sides. I believe he was one of the first practitioners of psycho-cybernetics, although we didn't know to call it that in those days. Daddy simply taught him to visualize the ball going through the net in one fell swoop.

In 1955, our mother located her grandfather, Raymond "R. D." Smith, in Oklahoma. He gave Mom information that helped her find her birth father, Paul Smith, who lived nearby. While she was alive, Mom's mother had forbidden her to search for her birth father. (I wouldn't find out the reason for that until many years later.) Mom also found her real father's brother and sister-in-law, our beloved Uncle Glen and Aunt Alta. They would accompany us on many family camping trips north to the Dakotas and southwest to Utah and Colorado.

Our family excursions, although frequent, were rather primitive. Mom and I slept in the car and Daddy and Bill slept on cots in a tent. However, we managed to see most of the United States's tourist attractions without spending a lot of money. We even visited Washington, DC, camping on a hillside within sight of the US Capitol Building.

One summer during Uncle Glen and Aunt Alta's Indiana visit, they asked to take Bill and me home with them to Oklahoma. Our folks agreed and said they'd come out a week later to bring us back home. I guess we were both spoiled a bit by these new relatives, primarily because they had no children of their own. On the first morning of our visit, Aunt Alta asked Bill what he wanted for breakfast. Bill replied, "Bacon and tomato on toast, and a chocolate milkshake." Not only did Aunt Alta fix this special request for Bill that morning, he got it every day.

Doc Pumphrey, the local veterinarian, and his wife, Inez, were youth leaders at our Presbyterian Church. Bill and Doc enjoyed each other's company, and Bill became interested in the veterinary business, helping Doc on his house calls to local farms. Bill decided to follow in Doc's footsteps and attend the School of Veterinary Medicine at Purdue University. Doc was very proud of him, and I think he hoped that Bill would return to Fort Branch and join him in private practice. But Bill was seduced by academe and followed the path to professorship.

While he was a student at Purdue, Bill was a resident of the State House, a men's cooperative residence rather like a fraternity house, with a house mother to cook and maintain order—more or less. All the residents slept in the attic-like, unheated dormitory area. I remember Bill telling tales of some of their escapades. The one I thought was most gross was a contest among the young men, during which they would hold a lighted match near their rear ends and attempt to create a flame-thrower effect by emitting bodily gases (i.e., farts) into the match fire. (I think the winner of the contest was nicknamed Hairless Joe.)

After graduating from Purdue with his doctor of veterinary medicine degree in 1968, Bill went to Iowa State University to pursue a master's degree in radiology. Dr. Bill was hired to the faculty at Purdue's School of Veterinary Medicine after his graduation from Iowa State. That was quite an accomplishment, because most universities of Purdue's caliber, as normal practice, do not hire their own graduates to tenure-track faculty positions. It's not that they think their graduates aren't good enough. It's just that this policy enables the university to sow its seeds of wisdom on the vast fields of academic knowledge and also to import fresh ideas that have been developed in other institutions. (By the way, I also earned a doctorate degree from Purdue and was hired to the faculty as a tenure-track associate professor. Both Blevins kids made it big!)

I suppose Bill wanted to appear a bit more professorial than his youthful appearance belied, so he grew a mustache, eventually a beard as well, and started smoking a pipe. He shaved the beard when it started sprouting more and more grey hairs, and he dropped the pipe when he thought he'd developed a cancerous spot on his tongue. (Turned out he was fine.) He still sports a mustache, and he has forgiven the grey hairs. He has had to—they're *all* grey!

Bill's academic success at Purdue was legendary. He received rapid promotions and tenure and became the youngest full professor in the history of the department, if not the university. Soon, he was the head of the Radiology Department, later renamed Diagnostic Imaging. It's hard to believe that our family's little tow-headed, straw-haired cutie pie was now Dr. Blevins, doing research that could eventually save human lives and teaching students, young and old, who would go on to teach other veterinarians around the globe or establish lucrative practices. Not long ago, a friend of mine in San Diego told me that her husband, recently retired as a veterinarian and having sold his practice for millions of dollars, had been a student of my brother Bill at Purdue.

In 2007, Mom and I were privileged to attend an award ceremony for the vet school. Bill was to be awarded the Raymond E. Plue Outstanding Teacher Award for his extra efforts to influence and inspire students. Mom and I felt honored to be seated at the table with the benefactor and namesake of the award, Dr. Plue himself, who had been one of Bill's students in past years. Bill's acceptance speech exemplified what an extraordinary professor he has been; he was humble yet brilliant, emotional yet pragmatic, and he brought me to tears as I realized that this paragon was the same boy who had pulled me around our home town neighborhood in a little red wagon.

Dr. William Blevins retired from the professorship at Purdue in 2009, but he remains active in the global veterinary community. He still consults to other veterinarians and clinics, but spends his spare time (what little there is) living his dream—building his house and his farm at Spring Valley Ranch, Warren County, Indiana.

But no matter how many accolades he has received, no matter how many animals' lives he has saved, no matter how many doctors all over the globe seek his advice and expertise—Dr. William E. Blevins will always be little Billy Earl to his big sister.

# CHAPTER 10

MARCH ON, YOU
FIGHTING SYCAMORES

It is, Sir, as I have said, a small college, and yet,
there are those who love it."
—Daniel Webster, 1818

My mother drove me to Indiana State to begin college classes in September 1957. I would be staying in the only women's dormitory on campus, the women's residence hall. The residence hall was under the command of a middle-aged, gray-haired lady who could give meanness lessons to Lucretia Borgia. The college had an unusually large influx of students that fall, and many late registrants were assigned temporarily to bunk beds in the hall's front parlor. Apparently, the college knew from experience that within a few weeks the dropouts would allow the hall to accommodate everyone. And that's exactly what happened.

I was nervous about meeting my roommates. After all, I'd been sleeping in my own room for many years. Now, because of the crowding, we were assigned three to a room, rather than the usual two. The room had a single twin bed and a bunk bed. My mother and I were sitting on the twin bed when my first roommate, Janet, came bursting into the room. She was tall and slender, somewhat gangly, with short wavy black hair and a wide grin that split her face with a red lipstick gash. This bubbly, voluble girl hit the room like an Indiana tornado wearing a hat.

Janet immediately dumped her belongings onto the top bunk and announced that we would switch beds next quarter. At that time, Indiana State was on a quarter system, rather than semesters. My mother's first impression was, "Oh no! She's going to steamroll all over my daughter." As she was leaving campus that day, Mom warned me, "Don't let that girl boss you around."

Wearing my new matching twin sweater set, I put on my best lady-like manners as I greeted this jolly girl from Merrillville, a small town in northern Indiana near Gary. Janet said she was from "the Region," which is a nickname given to those northwestern Indiana towns in close proximity to Chicago. Janet later told me her first impression of me was, "Oh no! She's a southern belle fashion plate!" Little did she know, but I had blown most of my babysitting money on several new matching sets of wool skirts, sweaters, and cardigans; I didn't want to look like a hayseed, even though I still felt like one.

Our third roommate soon arrived—a sweet, shy farm girl named Mary. We three were as different as could be, but we soon became the best of friends. When I visited Janet and her husband last summer, she surprised me by inviting Mary for lunch. It was as though all three of us were eighteen again.

During the first week of classes at Indiana State, all students were required to attend an Introduction to College Etiquette session, the object of which was to socialize the new students to college life and its dos and don'ts. The instructor would introduce different scenarios and require us to role-play the behaviors we thought were appropriate for those occasions. The teacher would then critique our behavior.

I was told that I would be passing some friends seated at a table in a fine restaurant and I should greet my friends. Never having dined at a fine restaurant, I chose to act just as I would have done in Fort Branch at Max's Snack Bar. "Hi! Great to see you guys! What have you been up to lately?" The students at the "fine restaurant" and I chatted for a while, just as though we actually knew each other. I was really pleased with my role-playing.

However, the teacher was very critical of my behavior. "When greeting friends at a restaurant, simply greet them briefly and move on. It is gauche to intrude on them with endless, meaningless chatter." Obviously, she'd never been to Max's Snack Bar! So, once again, the clueless nerd reared her ugly head.

Janet's exuberance and *joie de vivre* often led me astray. We soon made friends with Dottie, another girl from southern Indiana. During our sophomore year, she became pinned to Buz, her steady fraternity boyfriend. Being pinned means the boy gives his girl his fraternity pin to wear, which symbolizes that they are engaged to be engaged. Buz's real name was Ersel, a family *faux pas* he would rather forget. His father was drunk when he was born and told the doctor the baby was to be named Hershel. However, his drunken slur sounded like Ersel, which was the name recorded on the birth certificate. Thus, the boy became "Buz."

After the pinning, we gave Dottie the usual treatment on such occasions. First, we watched as the men of Sigma Phi Epsilon (Buz's fraternity) serenaded Dottie from the dorm courtyard. Then, after she was asleep, we secretly gathered all our friends, sneaked into her room in the middle of the night, carried her to the community bathroom, and threw her in the shower for the traditional "wetting down." We all had a terrific time—until the wicked housemother came charging into the shower room yelling at Janet and me, calling us hoodlums and troublemakers.

We really didn't deserve that. Just because we encouraged the young men who staged a panty raid on the women's residence hall by waving our panties out the window like red flags to the bulls at Pamplona—that doesn't mean we deserved to be called troublemakers!

I'm sad to report that Dottie passed away in 2011 after raising a fine family and working as a teacher and social worker, leaving Buz a widower.

Janet majored in elementary education, and I was a one-hundred-hour business education major, meaning that almost all of my classes would be in the Business Department, with very few electives. Janet and I shared only one class together—Basic Communications—and the first day of class the professor, Dr. Watson, asked each of us to give our name and course of study. When he got to Janet and asked her major, she was ready for him. She responded, "Elementary, Dr. Watson." (Way to go, Janet!)

Mary left us after only one quarter. She requested to room with someone who was quieter and more studious. She cried when she told us, "I love you guys, but I have to leave. Grades come easy to you two, but I have to study." I think her hard work paid off, because Mary became chairman of the Home Economics Department at Mishawaka High School, where she taught for thirty-nine years.

In 1959, another residence hall was built—Burford Hall—and Janet and I moved to classier quarters without bunk beds. Of course, the men on campus had to give the new hall a nickname, and because it housed only young females, it soon became known as "Hereford Hall." Janet's mother had an old picture (circa 1890) hanging in the basement. It showed a cow being milked by a young farm girl. She gave that picture to us for our dormitory room, and we hung it lovingly in "Hereford Hall." Today, the picture hangs in a place of honor in my home—in the bathroom.

We were not allowed to cook in our rooms or to do anything to cause any undue harm to those sparkling new digs. But Janet was not to be deterred by something as mundane as rules. She brought an old popcorn popper from home—the type with the heating element in the bottom and a metal bowl-shaped pan on top. We used it to pop popcorn, of course, but it had another use, to heat canned soup. Janet also had an antique toaster—the kind with the sides that flipped down. So we had buttered toast with our soup whenever the dorm served something not to our liking, such as the meal we all called Mystery Meat. That was a dish consisting of unidentifiable cuts of animal parts glued to a stick with a gelatinous substance the cooks called gravy.

Janet and I roomed together our entire four years at Indiana State. We would alternate staying with each other's families at holidays. My mother and father were like second parents to her, and she loved my little brother, Bill. By now he was not so little, as he had acquired his full height of six feet three inches. Janet's favorite way to greet Bill was to pinch his arm and then snap her fingers on his shoulder, giving him what she called a "snipper-snapper."

Janet made up many words or phrases just to fit the occasion. The phrase *la scatia platabia* meant "point of no return" or "I can't take this anymore." We used that phrase most often toward the end of the semester when we were studying for exams, as in "I have reached my *la scatia platabia*!" The phrase "We *neeed* it" would refer to anything we wanted that society or parents deemed unnecessary. On one occasion when the gang from Indiana State (Dottie, Ruth, Rosie, and Janet) visited my house, Mom gave a party and invited my high school friends (Judy, Rosemary, and Ruthie). Janet thought it would be a great idea to build a spook house. She spied an old vacuum cleaner in the basement and declared, "We *neeed* it!" It was probably that experience in the spook house that caused me to abhor vacuuming today.

Janet also taught me to eat pizza—after all, she was from the Region. We didn't have pizza in Fort Branch at that time. I think that was the official Region-al dish. Unfortunately, I learned my pizza-eating lessons too well, as my well-padded hips will attest.

At one of the school holidays in the late 1950s, Janet came home with me, together with several college friends, including Elsie Masumoto from Hawaii, and Mom invited many of my high school friends to a party at my house in Elsie's honor. Elsie had brought a traditional Hawaiian *muumuu* with her, and she danced the hula for us while I sang, "We're Going to a Hukilau," accompanying myself on a ukulele. She attempted to teach all of us the hula, and Mom filmed home movies of the hilarious results. Janet dancing the hula looked like Ray Bolger, the scarecrow in the Wizard of Oz, on "uppers."

In a speech class later in the year, Janet gave a lesson entitled, "How to Dance the Hula." She hung an orange, an apple, a peanut, and a coffee bean from a string around her waist and demonstrated the hip movements: "First, you bump the orange, then bang the apple, push the peanut, and *griiind* the coffee bean!" As I recall, she received an A+ for that speech.

Elsie's mother was so grateful to my mother for entertaining her daughter at the school holidays that she sent Mom a huge bouquet of anthuriums from Hawaii. I don't think Mom ever got over that, and until the day she died, she thought the anthurium was the most beautiful of flowers. Today, I have a large basket of silk anthuriums in my home, in honor of Elsie and her kindness to my mother.

Visiting Janet's folks in Merrillville, Indiana, was special. Her father worked at the steel mills in Gary, Indiana. With permission from the headquarters in Pittsburgh, he took us on a tour of US Steel. He was a quiet, gentle man who never raised his voice; Janet said she only received one spanking, and that wasn't her fault. Mr. Dean simply let the women of the household—his wife and two daughters, Janet and Vivian—run things as they willed.

Mrs. Dean was a terrific cook. She even fixed slimy okra in such a way that I actually enjoyed it—she French-fried it. Janet's mom was a delightful woman; I think Janet inherited her natural sense of humor from her mother. On Sundays, Mrs. Dean would get partially dressed, put on a robe, fix breakfast, and then complete the process of dressing for church. She would sometimes put on her hat before she put on her dress. I have warm memories of Mrs. Dean rushing around the house in her slip and stockings, with a hat perched on her graying curls.

During the spring of my freshman year, I was asked to join a sorority, Sigma Kappa. Although Janet decided not to join a sorority, it was a good fit for me. They needed my GPA (grade-point average) and I needed the social crutch and creative outlet they provided.

Because of my membership in the sorority, I starred in the campus revue, singing "That Old Black Magic" with hair sprayed silver and wearing a black, sexy, dress tight enough to *seem* sprayed on, as well. While I performed, I could imagine that the stage in the student union auditorium was actually a New York City theater on Forty-Second Street and Broadway. For one moment, I *was* a star.

I also wrote a cheer for the Homecoming weekend pep rally and won the prize, a silver cup, for my sorority. I would include the cheer here, but some things are best forgotten.

The sorority decorated a float for Homecoming and I was chosen to ride on the float. It must have had a circus theme because I have a picture of me clad in satin shorts, fishnet stockings, top hat, and cutaway coat, holding a whip like a circus lion tamer. Either that or I was dressing for a *very* special date!

Although my tuition was paid by scholarship, my family had to pay for my dormitory accommodations, clothes, and books, which they could ill afford. So, my hometown friend, Keith, recommended me for a position at the college library. I started working there as a reserve section assistant (at sixty cents an hour), and was soon promoted to the Cataloging and Book Repair Department, where my pay was increased to a whopping ninety cents an hour! I am ashamed to admit, however, that I read almost as many books as I repaired or catalogued while working there.

Janet's finances weren't much better than mine. She once gave me a treasured LP record, *Victory at Sea*, because she owed me two dollars. (I still have the record.) On the other hand—so she tells me—I once borrowed her only black sweater, which I never returned. I have no idea what happened to that sweater, but when she reminded me recently of that oversight, I sent her one of my mother's black sweaters, which she accepted graciously.

I had a portable record player that I received for graduation to provide music while we studied. One of the LP records that Janet and I loved to play was Wagner's opera, *Tristan und Isolde*, which we would play incessantly while we daydreamed about the fellows in our classes. The main theme builds and builds until it achieves a climax that we both thought sounded very sexual. I guess one good nerd deserves another.

The boy I was daydreaming about was Gary Coates, a Steve Allen look-alike with a devilish, come-hither smile and obvious less-than-honorable intentions. He was a member of the Theta Xi fraternity, Indiana State's BMOC (big men on campus). We dated once—perhaps the result of a dare he received—and he asked me at the end of the date, "What would you do if I kissed you?"

I answered, perhaps a little too eagerly, "Kiss you back!" I think he may have sensed that I was more serious than he was. He never asked me out again. So, girls, the old-fashioned directive, "Play hard to get!" is probably a good rule to follow.

As I wrote earlier, I began my undergraduate studies as a one-hundred-hour business major; my parents believed I would have better employment opportunities with a business degree. But after two years,

I couldn't stand life without music, so I added a minor in music, with voice as my major instrument and piano as the minor instrument. I was able to complete this course of study by taking classes at night—private voice and piano lessons—and by special individual study with the instructor. I don't recommend the latter. Orchestral score study when you are the only student sitting in front of the professor is highly intimidating.

As a music student, I had many performance opportunities. I starred in Thorton Wilder's opera, *Sunday in New York*. Also, one of my fellow music students wrote an original comedy-musical play entitled, *The Prince from Pendlepoop*, based loosely on the operetta, *The Student Prince*. I played an elderly teacher in love with the prince's valet. I received lots of laughs and applause, especially when the young man playing the valet swooped me into his arms and bent me backwards in a lip-lock, inadvertently revealing my frilly undergarments to the audience. He decided to repeat the incident at every performance—anything for a laugh!

Because I minored in music, I was required to give a senior voice recital and sing in three languages. I chose English, French, and Italian. Each section of the recital was a selection of songs in one of the three languages. My vocal coach, Mr. Angell, was also my accompanist.

After I had completed the first group of songs in English, I began to arrange myself in a pre-planned pose, leaning on the piano, getting ready for the next selection of songs to be sung in French. However, I forgot momentarily that we had planned to exit after each section of the recital. Mr. Angell looked at me with panic on his face because he had not brought the music for the second session with him. I woke up after a few seconds, bowed, and hurried off stage. I think the audience thought I was milking the applause—and why not?!

I did date when I was in college, but nothing serious or permanent. I always wanted more than the boys offered, and they probably felt the same way about me! There was one shy, bespectacled sophomore—whose name I have conveniently forgotten—who would get so excited just kissing me goodnight in the dorm's front hallway that he had to carry a large notebook in front of him when he left.

I should say a word about those goodnight scenes. All women were required to be in the dorm, all men outside, and all doors closed and locked by 10:00 p.m. So, at 9:45 every night, dozens of couples lined the front hallway and the lounge, locked in passionate embraces and making out as though the world would end in fifteen minutes. Then, at 9:59, guys with lipstick-smeared faces and sheepish grins made a mass exodus from the dorm. The next night, the scene was repeated. Perhaps that's why we called the lounge, "The Passion Pit."

Wabash College was a men's college located a few miles northeast of Terre Haute in Crawfordsville, a small town just south of West Lafayette, the home of Purdue University. Apparently, there weren't many coeds at Purdue and absolutely none at Wabash College, so whenever that school held a dance, the young men would ship in busloads of girls from Indiana State and nearby St. Mary's, a Catholic college for women.

When Wabash held their Homecoming weekend, I volunteered to be a date *du jour* with one of the young men at Wabash College. The group of us from Indiana State were bused to the campus, introduced to the housemother at one of the fraternity houses, and met the men who would be our dates. The guys turned over the house and the housemother to the girls and spent the weekend with their buddies elsewhere. There was a mixer on Friday night, a football game Saturday afternoon, and a dance Saturday evening, all heavily chaperoned.

After the dance, we adjourned to the basement of one of the fraternity houses for a party. We played a game in which we sat around a table, with a drink in front of us, and participated in a get-acquainted ritual. In unison, everyone patted the table twice, clapped hands twice, snapped fingers twice, and then called out the name of another person at the table. If you missed your turn, or couldn't remember someone's name, you were required to take a swig of your drink, usually beer. Needless to say, the more swigs of beer, the more misses. This continued until everyone was drunk and disorderly. (Where's a housemother when you need her?)

The next day, all the Cinderellas were bused back to Indiana State with nothing more than a homecoming souvenir and a memory—and maybe a headache here and there—to remind them of a fun weekend.

One young man who attended Janet's church, and whose family lived in the Region, romanced me throughout my senior year. Janet thought he was a great guy and encouraged the relationship. My entire family liked him, although my grandpa Blevins teased the painfully thin boy incessantly. His name was Jim Somerville, but my grandfather always called him "Slim Somerville," the name of an old cowboy movie character actor.

Jim surprised me with an engagement ring a few weeks before graduation. Suddenly, I was faced with the same dilemma that had loomed over my future just four years previously. Is this what I want? Is this all there is? I broke the engagement two days before graduation. My parents were disappointed because they really thought a great deal of Jim. Daddy accused me of breaking the engagement because I was afraid to have sex. Mom knew me better than that, I guess, because she said, "Not likely." (I'm not sure what she meant by that. What had she found out—that I hadn't told her?)

On our many trips to Janet's house in northern Indiana, she and I would often ride with Jim Kaiser, another student from the Region. They started dating in the last semester of college, and were captured on film for a candid shot of campus that appeared in *The Sycamore*, our college yearbook. Daddy would joke with Janet about her love life because she had said once, "I don't have a heart—just a pump." Her pump must have been working overtime, because Janet and Jim were married just a couple of years following graduation.

Although Janet and I went our separate ways after college, we've always kept in touch and remained close friends. Whenever I make my annual trek back to Indiana to see family, I always take time to visit Janet and her husband. I was especially moved when I learned that she had named her first child to commemorate our friendship. Her daughter was named Janelle, combining both our names, Janet and Mary Ellen.

She and Jim have raised three wonderful children—a girl and two boys—who are all married now with families of their own. Janet (the girl with just a pump for a heart) and Jim (the mild-mannered industrial arts teacher) now live on a farm near Plymouth, Indiana, as comfortable together as two old poops. And by the way, that's how I know it is Janet on the phone when she calls, because she always says, "How are you, you old poop?"

And so, despite four years of exploration, graduation with honors, several close encounters, and a few nerd-like *faux pas*, true love had managed to elude me and I was facing yet another, "Now what?"

# CHAPTER 11

•❀•

# NEVER ON SUNDAY

They have the time, the time of their
life . . . in Chicago, Chicago.
—Frank Sinatra

I graduated from Indiana State College at the age of twenty-one,
after exactly four years of study—which was usual in those days,
but somewhat unusual today. Now, it seems that every campus
sports third-year freshmen, and perennial students living on the largesse
of loan-strapped parents haunt the ivy-covered halls.

During my senior year, I allowed myself to become engaged to
a young man I didn't really love. I think I was suffering from senior
"marriage-itis"—which was the norm in 1961, when an engagement
ring was a necessary accompaniment to a cap and gown for every
graduating coed. Of course, few girls today are that—misguided. (I
was going to say "stupid" but decided to give some coeds the benefit
of the doubt.)

My fiancé was a junior majoring in education at Indiana State, and
he still had another year to finish his degree, so I would need to take
a job to support us during his senior year. The only jobs available to
young women in Terre Haute, Indiana, at that time were secretarial
jobs paying about fifty dollars per week. When it dawned on me that I
had nothing to look forward to but a life of babies, diapers, and brain-

numbing existence in some backwater town in southern Indiana, I broke my engagement two days before graduation and begged the dean of my school to help me find a job, as far away as possible from Terre Haute.

Dean Muse called his friend, Paul Pair, the owner of the Pair Schools of Business in Chicago, and arranged for an immediate interview for me. I donned my little straw hat and short white gloves—an outfit befitting a well-brought-up young lady of 1961—and asked the depot stationmaster in my small hometown to flag down the passenger train to Chicago. I also suggested to the stationmaster that he change the sign at the edge of town to read: "Population 1,201, soon to be an even 1,200."

As the train approached Chicago, I couldn't help but recall the words of Carl Sandburg, who described Chicago as the "hog butcher to the world." We passed miles and miles of pens containing thousands of animals waiting to be slaughtered. When we reached the Chicago train station, I consulted a city map and decided I could walk the several blocks to the Loop, where I would be meeting Mr. Pair at the Chicago Athletic Club. However, the map did not warn me that I would be walking through the infamous Skid Row en route. Nevertheless, I arrived at my destination safe—and only slightly unsound. It was a heck of a long walk!

Yes, I know, that was terribly naïve of me to think I could walk through Skid Row unharmed. But none of the men lying in the gutter or leaning bleary-eyed against the buildings made any attempt to halt my progress. I guess they could see my clenched-jaw determination.

I must have impressed Mr. Pair sufficiently, because he offered me a position as a teacher of typewriting and secretarial practice at his school, to begin in two weeks. I hurried back to Fort Branch, packed my bags, said good-bye to my hometown, and got aboard the next train to Chicago for the ride of a lifetime. My primary goal at that time was to rid myself of my reputation—that of the oldest living virgin in the state of Indiana!

My first few months in the big city, I lived at the YWCA, an institution that at that time was more prison than apartment. Although the rent at the Y was affordable, the room was small and devoid of any charm, with only a narrow cot, a chair, a small desk, a freestanding sink, and a closet the size of a steamer trunk. I'm sure the cells in Joliet Prison were larger. What's more, my fellow residents were unfriendly and even worse, uncaring. I stored my week's supply of Metrical (a 1960s version of Slim Fast) in the communal refrigerator in the lounge; I was trying to lose the pounds put on by college dormitory food. The next day I would find one or two bottles missing. And this was supposed to be a home for young *Christian* women? So much for the eighth commandment, "Thou shall not steal."

However, the city had so much to offer a naïve girl from the country that I rarely spent any time in my cubicle. After all, there was the Museum of Science and Industry, the Natural History Museum, the Adler Planetarium, the Art Institute, McCormick Place, Edgewater Park, and the famous bars of State Street (that great street) to explore. One of my favorite haunts was the Painted Penny, a bar in the heart of Chicago's night life section known as the Near North Side, where cocktails cost forty-nine cents each, and change included a painted Lincoln one-cent coin.

The school where I was to teach was named for the founders, Paul and Pauline Pair, who closely resembled the same-sounding fruit. They were round-on-the-bottom in shape, but they could be hard and gritty at times. The Pair Schools—one for stenographers and one for bookkeepers—were located in the heart of downtown Chicago. To get to the schools, I rode a city bus from the Y, located on Oak Street, to the intersection downtown at Wabash Avenue and Adams Street.

At first I was a bit frightened to board public transportation in such a huge city. My only previous experience with so-called "public transportation" was in Fort Branch—the horse-drawn Federal Express wagon driven by the local deaf mute. But I needn't have worried. Chicago in 1961 was just a large small town, full of friendly, helpful people. For example, one day while I was waiting to board the bus to go home, I dropped my wallet, and loose change scattered all over the pavement. My fellow passengers scrambled to help me retrieve my coins before we all boarded—an act of kindness that was usual in those days, but almost unheard of today.

I had been living and working in Chicago for three months, teaching typing and office practice at the Pair Schools. During the day, I was a dedicated and determined business teacher, training the hodge-podge of humanity who sought some modicum of skill to help earn a living in the resurgent economy of the early 1960s. "Put your fingers on the keyboard, like this—left hand on A-S-D-F, and right hand on J-K-L semi-colon. That's called the home row. Strike the keys, don't punch them. Let's practice: A-D-A, J-L-J, A-D-A, J-L-J. Good. Now, strike the keys on the row above with each middle finger: D-E-D, K-I-K, D-E-D, K-I-K. Good! Now we can type a word: L-I-K-E, L-I-K-E. No, Mrs. Swartzkof, use the fingers that are resting on the home row keys. No crossovers allowed."

Many of my students were young, fresh out of high school, and knew nothing about business or working for a living. They were eager to learn, however, and couldn't wait to jump into the corporate waters and swim with the sharks. Others were already worn out, either from working in factories on assembly lines or taking care of husbands and children. In some cases, the children were grown and gone, and in a few instances, the husband was just—gone.

The most pathetic students were the widows in their fifties and sixties who were not only bereft of husbands, but also of income. It was almost heartbreaking as I tried to overcome their fears and anxieties to teach them to strike the typewriter keys sharply, rather than punch them carefully. That always resulted in faint letters surrounded by shadows, rather like their own lives that seemed to be faint reminders of former selves, now surrounded by ghosts.

In the evenings, I could shed my teacher persona and reveal my true self—that of a fun-loving young woman, barely of legal drinking age, but eager to enjoy the bright lights and nightlife offerings of Chicago, "that toddlin' town." I knew I was reasonably attractive, of medium height with brown hair done up in the latest style, a French twist. On the other hand, I had to admit that I lacked a few inches in the bosom department, plus I was a victim of that old adage, "Men don't make passes at girls who wear glasses." With a heavy heart, I realized that one of these days I would have to come to grips with the personal problem that consumed my thoughts almost every waking moment and invaded some of my dreams—that is, the problem of my Virginity (with a capital V.)

Where I grew up in southern Indiana, girls who went all the way were considered trash and were not respected by their peers or the town's upstanding citizens. Inevitably, once a girl gave in to a boy, he no longer desired her, other than for what he could get, and then he'd dump her. That's what happened to one of my friends. Well, it hadn't happened to me, by gum. Actually, not much of anything had happened to me, even during four years of college.

Early in September, I saw an advertisement in the newspaper for a cheap apartment farther up the North Side on Winthrop Avenue, close to Edgewater Beach and in walking distance of Lake Michigan. A telephone call to the number listed in the ad reached the building manager, which resulted in an appointment to view the apartment the next Friday evening.

"You better make a decision fast 'cause there's a lotta people innerested," burped the burly superintendent, hooking his thumbs in his sleeveless undershirt. When I simply smiled, the super shrugged, turned, and led me up the uncarpeted wooden stairs to the third-floor walk-up.

Well, this should certainly help the weight loss plan, I thought. Huffing and puffing, I climbed the stairs to the place I was already calling home, sweet home. My rose-colored glasses revealed a cozy nest (okay, so it was tiny) that had everything a young woman would need. There was a bedroom with two twin beds separated by a down-at-heels dresser, plus a small closet; a bathroom with a sink attached to the wall, a wooden-seat toilet, and a tub that was built to fit the Munchkins of Oz; and a living room with a worn couch, an armchair, and a Murphy bed one could pull down for guests—provided all the furniture was moved into the hall.

Finally, there was a miniscule kitchen that was too small even to stir up trouble. It held a sink stained with the evidence of former tenants' meals, a two-burner stove caked with boiled-over—something, and a small refrigerator that had probably held only beer and very little nutritious food. Not a problem, I thought, since the only thing I know how to cook is Kraft Macaroni and Cheese from a box.

"I'll take it!" I wanted to seal the deal before the super could think of a rebuttal. I handed him cash for the first and last month's rent and followed him to his basement office—actually a janitor's closet—to sign the lease and receive the keys.

"I am now a homeowner!" Well, sort of. I danced up the stairs from the basement and out onto Winthrop Avenue. Thinking I would take a look at my new beachfront access, I headed east toward the water for what I assumed would be a short walk. Four city blocks later and after crossing a heavily traveled Lake Shore Drive, I finally reached the grassy park next to Lake Michigan. Oh, well, another page in my weight-loss plan.

Now, I had to find some form of rapid transportation to and from work. The Y had been only a short bus ride from the school, but the apartment was several miles north of the Loop. Near the school was a subway station, where fellow teachers said I could catch the Howard Street rapid transit train that would take me to Bryn Mawr—the stop closest to my new apartment. The next Monday after classes, with a little fear but mostly excitement, I descended the stairs into the bowels of the city to seek the underground train that would take me to my new home.

The concrete steps and the platform, where dozens of people were waiting for the next train, were stained and dirty. I didn't want to think about the source of those blotches. Blood? Urine? Vomit? Yuck! My brain refused to go there, but instead I worried that I wouldn't identify the train bound for Bryn Mawr and might board the wrong one.

With a rumble and a loud *whoosh*, a train roared to a stop right in front of me, the doors opened, and crowds of unseeing and uncaring passengers shoved their way through the waiting masses and up the stairs to their destinations—either work or play. I could hear Daddy whispering in my ear, "Go on, you can do it." So, I took a deep breath and plunged forward, barely making it onboard before the automatic doors slammed shut behind me.

Because I was returning home in the mid-afternoon, I easily found an unoccupied seat, facing forward. I sat close to the aisle, rather than at the window, because there was nothing to see but the walls of the tunnel rushing past. I was almost afraid to look at the other passengers—they might be robbers or rapists. Besides, everyone seemed to be preoccupied with his or her own thoughts.

Suddenly, light filled the car! I hadn't noticed that the train had gradually ascended from the depths beneath the city to rise high above the street and between the dark brick buildings that looked out onto the tracks. The sight was so unexpected that I couldn't hide my country-girl astonishment. I laughed involuntarily and even applauded in delight at the scene, now realizing why my friends had called this now-elevated train "the El."

A tall, dark-haired man was seated across the aisle and a couple rows forward, in a seat facing to the rear. He noticed my reaction and smiled in amusement.

When I saw the fellow's smile, my breath caught in my throat and I smiled sheepishly, a bit embarrassed by my actions. I'd never seen such a handsome man. His full head of hair was black and wavy, his face long and clean-shaven with high cheek bones, his eyelashes curved and black like spiders clinging to a silky web, his lips full and moist, as though he had just kissed me. Or was I merely daydreaming? Was it his smile at my naiveté that made me blush, or my own thoughts imagining how he might solve my—problem?

I knew I must be daydreaming still, because he quickly arose from his seat and came across the aisle, grabbed the upright commuter pole next to me, leaned down and smiled as he said, with a voice that seemed infused with the honey sweetness of grapes grown on a sun-kissed Greek isle, "You haf the most beootiful smile."

There were many possible responses going through my mind at breakneck speed, one that my mother would recommend (a nose-in-the-air cold shoulder), and others that made me blush at their boldness, such as giving him my name, address, and the promise of my first-born child.

Before I could choose, however, the gorgeous creature spoke again. "May I introduce myself, please—my name is Vasilios Talides. And I am Greek. I live here now in Bryn Mawr with my mother and sister, and I haf a shop on Clark Street where I work as furrier. May I know your name?"

Taking a deep breath, I quickly made a decision. "I am pleased to meet you, Vasilios. I am Mary Ellen Blevins and I live on Winthrop Avenue, very close to Bryn Mawr. I've just moved there, so I don't have a telephone yet, but I work at the Pair Schools of Business on Wabash Avenue—I'm a teacher."

"I may call you there, yes?"

"Yes, definitely. I have lunch at noon and you can call me there whenever . . ." My voice trailed off into nothingness as I realized I was probably being too bold. I decided to ignore those self-recriminations—and my mother's training—as I gave Vasilios the school's telephone number. "I look forward to hearing from you." *Please, please, please!*

Thus began what I hoped would become "an affair to remember" with my Greek Adonis. Vasilios had Americanized his name to Bill, which was easier to pronounce but did not contain the aura of sensuality I felt whenever I breathed his name—Vasilios . . . Vasilios.

He called me the next day at school, and we made a date to meet after work Friday evening at the Painted Penny. He was extremely polite, a perfect gentleman, and did not make a pass or suggest anything that could be construed as fresh. I couldn't help but think, "Shucks! He doesn't like me."

However, at the end of the evening, he asked for my home telephone number—the phone had been installed the previous day, thank goodness. "And you must call me at my home," he insisted. "My mother or my sister, Toula, may answer, so you say, *'Boro lemiliso to Bill, para kalo.'* That means, 'May I speak to Bill, please.' Can you say that?" Within a short time, I could ask to speak to Bill in Greek whenever I called him at his apartment.

Vasilios was a member of that well-honored Greek tradition in the Chicago of the 60s—he was a furrier. He gave me a tour of his shop one Saturday afternoon. The walls were lined with fur pelts—mink, silver fox, and other luxurious furs that cause a woman's heart to flutter uncontrollably as she drapes herself with the spoils of a war she could never win. I was no exception. I was hopelessly lost in romantic ruminations of a possible future with this Greek hero. But I couldn't help but ask myself, "What does a man who looks like *that* see in me?"

Nevertheless, I prayed he would be the one to remove the symbolic scarlet *V* from my bosom.

His old-world charm affected even my prudish mother. My folks visited me in my new apartment shortly after I moved in, and one day during their visit, the telephone rang while I was at work. Mom decided to answer and take a message for me. Her voice sounded very much like mine as she answered, "Hello?"

Before she could identify herself, she heard Bill's deep, throbbing baritone, "Hellooo dahhling." (I think Mom then had the only orgasm she ever experienced in her life.) Mom never told me what she said to him after that. But I think she had a better understanding of my regard for the man.

I loved my new apartment, even though it was small, but I soon discovered it had a few drawbacks. One morning I was a little late for work, so I dressed in a hurry, quickly slipped into my new patent leather high-heeled shoes, and raced to the elevated train stop that was a few blocks from the apartment. While standing on the platform, waiting for the train to arrive, I felt that my right foot was a bit cramped in the new shoe. Did I leave some of the wrapping paper in the shoe? Leaning against a bench, I nudged the right shoe off with my left toe, the shoe dropped to the platform, and a three-inch-long cockroach raced for freedom. I was so traumatized that from then on, I always shook out my shoes before putting them on—just in case something had decided to take up residence there.

The school had both day and night classes. That meant that two days a week I taught from eight in the morning until two in the afternoon, went home for three hours, and then came back to teach another three hours in the evening. I'd usually take an afternoon nap so as to have enough energy to get through those evening sessions.

I was asleep in the bedroom one afternoon when I heard shouting coming from the apartments across the court. I looked out the bedroom window and saw a scene that might have come from the Hitchcock movie, *Rear Window.* People were standing on wooden landings or leaning out their apartment windows, shouting and gesturing. I got up quickly and opened the bedroom window to hear what the neighbors were saying. My heart stopped momentarily. They were screaming

"Fire! Fire!" The rear of my apartment building was ablaze! Fortunately, I was already dressed so I grabbed what was important—purse, glasses, and my picture of Vasilios—and raced down to join the other residents on the sidewalk.

Apparently, the incinerator at the back of the building had caught fire. Nothing was damaged in my apartment, but I did have to contend with even more cockroaches for a while because of garbage lying by the useless incinerator chute that was waiting for someone with enough skill, or inclination, to repair the device.

The romance with Vasilios was progressing according to plan—almost. Our dates were not as numerous, or as private, as I would have liked and usually consisted of dinners at his home with his family—mother, sister, and innumerable cousins. A couple of times I was invited to attend a picnic on the shore of Lake Michigan with several of his Greek friends. There would be gigantic Greek salads hand-tossed in galvanized washtubs, accompanied by rivers of *retsina*—a wine flavored with pine resin that was, at first taste, acrid and bitter. However, after several glasses it was as smooth as a velvet-covered boxing glove—one that delivered a potent punch.

The group dates with Bill's Greek friends were made even more memorable one sunny afternoon when, after consuming several bottles of *retsina*, a few of the guys pulled out some musical instruments that looked like large mandolins. They began to play and sing Greek music. Everyone was clapping and dancing to this exuberant sound. To my delight, one of the young men suggested they should teach me to dance the *syrtos*—that ancient and passionate Greek dance where, with arms raised, you hang on to your neighbor by a handkerchief and periodically let out an exuberant *"opah!"* Within a short time, I lost my inhibitions (thanks in part to the *retsina*) and was sidestepping, skipping, and dipping with my new *ellinika* (Greek) friends.

Finally, Vasilios asked me if I would like to see the movie, *Never on Sunday*, with him—no friends, just the two of us. The film was shown in a Greek theatre near his home, but it had English sub-titles that allowed me to understand the dialogue. With a hopeful heart, I said I'd be delighted, thinking, "Alone at last!"

After the movie, I was a bit dejected. If only I looked like Melina Mercouri, I'm sure Vasilios would solve my—problem. I thought I must still be daydreaming when he leaned close to my ear and asked, "Would you like to go to my friend's apartment for a drink? I have the key, and we could be alone."

Giving thanks to the Greek gods who must be smiling down from Mount Olympus at this moment, I blushed a bit and said, "That would be nice." Nice? That would be heaven on earth!

Most women probably remember their first sexual encounter, but when Bill left me at my apartment door after a long and lingering goodnight kiss, I couldn't think of a single detail of that evening, except that it was slightly painful and very messy. Oh, well, I did it! "And," I thought gleefully, "I'm gonna do it again! And again!"

Bill also taught me a few other helpful Greek phrases over the next several months, but the one I used as often as I could, without trying to seem too forward, was "*Thosa mou ena fillaiki!*" Translation: "Give me a little kiss." And, while I was cleaning my tiny hovel, which I forced myself to do at least every other month or so, I would sing the entire libretto, in Greek, to the song, "Never on Sunday."

However, my hopes for a future life with Vasilios began to wane slightly, because we were seldom alone. He was extremely devoted to his extended family, most of whom were new arrivals to America. They were lovely people, and they treated me with great warmth and respect, but they still were very "old country" in their beliefs about male and female roles.

For instance, at these frequent family gatherings, I was expected to stay in the kitchen with the rest of the women, stuffing grape leaves with rice and ground lamb and preparing *spanakopita* (a spinach-filled pastry.) Although the women tried to make me feel welcome, the language barrier made this somewhat difficult. I felt like a castaway on a Pacific island inhabited by friendly natives who spoke only Tongan. Actually, I would rather be in the living room with the men in the family, who were smoking, drinking, laughing, and telling lewd and funny stories nonstop. But, I doubted the jokes would be as funny in Tongan.

I couldn't help but feel that the cultural differences between Bill's family's expectations of my behavior, and my own somewhat *avant garde* approach to life, presented a potential obstacle to my future relationship with this Greek god.

# CHAPTER 12

·•◦❀◦•·

# CATCH A FALLING STAR

Then the elevator starts its ride.
And down and down I go . . .
—Harold Arlen, "That Old Black Magic"

One evening as Vasilios and I were saying goodnight after another family dinner and an evening of my feeling like an unnecessary appendage, I decided to confront my lover.

"Vasilios, how do you really feel about me?"

"My dahhling, you are my little love, *agape mou.*"

"But do we have any future together, as man and wife?"

Vasilios took a long time to respond, looking at me somewhat ruefully. "Of course, my dahhling. But we haf to wait a while. I must take care of my mother and my sister, Toula, and I haf a younger brother, Dmitrios, I must bring from Greece and set him up in business, and . . ."

I placed my fingers on Vasilios's lips to stem the flow of useless explanation. "I know, I know. You are the patriarch of your family and your first responsibility is to them. I understand."

It broke my heart to do so, but I reluctantly told Vasilios that I could not see him again. I told him I wished the very best for him and his family.

Although I dated a few other fellows after Vasilios, none of them made much of an impression. I don't even recall their names.

I did have the hope, for a brief moment, that I might have a future in show business. Friends heard me singing around the office and persuaded me to enter the 1961 Harvest Moon Festival, a talent contest for singers sponsored by *The Chicago Sun-Times* newspaper. This contest was somewhat similar, though lesser in scope, to today's *American Idol*.

There were hundreds of singers meeting at the first session, and I had grave doubts that I would be chosen to continue to the semi-finals. The pianist who accompanied me was lukewarm in his encouragement—I think he said "Nice" after I completed my performance. Therefore, I was astonished when I was selected as a semi-finalist. I doubted that I would get much further, but to my surprise—and to the chagrin of several other contestants—I was selected as one of the finalists. (If you want to see a picture, Google "1961 Chicago Sun-Times Harvest Moon Singing Contest Finalists.")

As part of my so-called winnings, I appeared on John Doremus's *Patterns in Music* show on WMAQ Radio, where I was interviewed and sang the song that so bewitched the judges, "That Old Black Magic." When Mr. Doremus asked me about myself, he was surprised that I was a business teacher and not a professional musician. I explained, "Business is my profession, but music is my *life*."

Shortly after my radio appearance, I received a call from the leader of a local dance band. "Would you be interested in singing with our band? Our regular singer is out of town for a while. We heard you on the radio and liked what we heard. We can't promise anything permanent, of course."

I was thrilled! Maybe this was the start of a new career as a singer—my dream was about to come true. I called my mother in Indiana to share the good news, and she immediately shot me down.

"You can't trust musicians! They'll get you into trouble, you're liable to get raped, and before you know it, you'll be a pregnant dope fiend!"

Well, like a dutiful daughter, I listened to my mother, even though I didn't really understand her vehement objection. But her voice continued to ring in my ears, and so I turned down the dance band offer. In retrospect, I've always felt that the moment represented what could have been a major turning point in my life. As Marlon Brando's character said in *On the Waterfront*, "I could-a been a contender, I could-a *been* somebody!"

Although I didn't sing for a band, I did discover a local piano bar (think of it as early karaoke) that I frequented with my girlfriends after work on most Fridays. It satisfied, to some extent, my desire to sing. I didn't have a big wardrobe—only one really nice outfit—and I would wear that dress on the Fridays that we went to the piano bar. One week, my friend Jane and I made plans to go to dinner at the piano bar on Wednesday instead of our regular night. One of the guys in the office said to me, "I see you're wearing your Friday dress on Wednesday." That taught me you never know who is watching what you do—or what you wear.

In 1962, after a year at Pair Schools, I accepted a position as private secretary to the assistant tax manager at Pullman Incorporated, the multi-national holding company for the Pullman Car Company, M. W. Kellogg, and other transportation subsidiaries. Their offices were located in the upper stratosphere of the Borg Warner Building, a high-rise glass and steel building across from the Art Institute and Buckingham Fountain on Michigan Avenue.

It was from those windows during the summer of 1963 that I watched and cheered President John F. Kennedy and his wife, Jackie, while they rode in an open convertible as part of a motorcade down Michigan Avenue. How were we to know that six months later a similar motorcade in Dallas, Texas, would end so tragically?

I was now making enough money to afford a better apartment several blocks farther north, on Winthrop Avenue near the Edgewater Episcopal Church where I was a professional choir singer. My college vocal coach, Jim Angell, had secured a paid position for me there as a soprano in the choir of this orthodox Episcopal Church.

The music we performed was highly challenging; we often sang classical oratorios and cantatas for church services. The choir director at that church preferred singers with absolutely no vibrato. I think he would have hired castrated eunuchs if they were available. So, for ten dollars a service—extra for funerals and weddings—I learned to sing with an absolutely straight tone, at will.

I may have been "just a secretary," but Mr. Reed, my boss at Pullman, Inc., soon recognized my talents (at least at the calculator) and gave me the autonomy to gather all necessary data and to prepare the tax returns for the conglomerate's pension plans. I was learning so many things about big business and discovered that I loved the challenges of corporate life.

Nevertheless, my boss still signed all my work as his own.

Although I was enjoying my idyllic life as a free spirit in Chicago and had good friends and a cute apartment just one block from Lake Michigan, my experiences in love and business made me realize that I would always be "the little woman behind the man" in both the personal and professional aspects of my life. I never would achieve my ambitions without more education.

I made another call to Dean Muse of the School of Business at Indiana State. I couldn't believe my good fortune! Not only did he accept me into the master's degree program the following September, but also he offered me a graduate assistantship, which meant my tuition would be paid and I would receive a small stipend as well.

So, after two years as a single girl in the big city, and despite my disappointment in love and career, I went on to another chapter in my life's adventures—graduate school, an MBA, and the first of four "MRS" degrees.

However, there was at least *one* positive result of my Chicago experience. I was no longer the oldest living virgin in the state of Indiana!

# PART II

---•❊•---

# VERSE

(A badly programmed girl makes poor
choices and suffers in silence)

# CHAPTER 13

---•❈•---

# ALONG CAME BILL

Men marry because they are tired;
women because they are curious.
Both are disappointed.
—Oscar Wilde

Early in September, I waved good-bye to Chicago, where I had
had the time of my life, and drove to Terre Haute, Indiana,
with six hundred dollars in savings in my pocket and high
hopes for the future. The money I'd saved would be enough to rent
a small apartment for one year. With housing and tuition paid and an
assistantship stipend to pay for food and books, I was on my way.

Nevertheless, there were times that year when I would be reduced
to searching beneath couch cushions and car floor mats for enough
coins to buy a fifteen-cent McDonald's hamburger. And if I managed
to find a quarter, I could get a burger *and* fries!

When I first enrolled at Indiana State as a freshman, the school
was called Indiana State Teachers College. By the time I earned the
baccalaureate degree, it was Indiana State College. Now, it was Indiana
State University. But it wasn't only the name that changed. When I was
an undergraduate, women were not permitted to wear slacks or shorts
on campus except to go to and from the library. Single women couldn't

live off campus unless they lived with a relative. Now, there were no constraints—on clothes, living arrangements, or behavior.

As I drove into Terre Haute, I noticed that it still smelled bad. I think that was because of the local fat-rendering plant. I checked with the campus housing office and found an apartment for rent in the home of my former piano professor, Miss Bard, now retired. She had transposed—to use a musical term—two small rooms, a hallway, and a porch into a tiny apartment. There was a living room in front with a private entrance, a dining room with a daybed for sleeping, a kitchen in what was formerly a hallway, and a bathroom in what had been the back porch.

The downside of this arrangement might have been the small size of the apartment, but the upside was that I could hear Miss Bard playing her Steinway grand piano, with a Baldwin baby grand snuggled next to it, through the connecting door. Occasionally, she would have musician friends over for a Sunday afternoon musicale of dual pianos and string quartets, and I would relax in my miniscule home, surrounded by heavenly harmonies.

My curriculum would lead to an MBA (master of business administration). Among the courses were Marketing Research (for which I was the graduate assistant), Business Law, and Income Tax Procedures (two semesters). The first time I walked into the income tax class I was overwhelmed. There were rows upon rows of armchair desks reaching up to the ozone layer, all filled with—*men!* I was one of only two women in the class. I couldn't decide whether to embrace the odds—about eighty-to-one—or run away from the course that, to quote my academic counselor, "separated the men from the boys."

For the first few weeks of classes, the men ignored the women because it's common knowledge a man knows more about income tax than any mere woman (she said, facetiously). Then we had the first examination. The two highest scores in the class were earned by—you guessed it—the two women.

Suddenly I was much sought after. Not only was I better at income tax than the men, but also my female competition was—somewhat less attractive. I would never call anybody homely. One of the men approached me after class a couple days later.

"Hi, my name is Bill. You seem to have a better grasp of this class than I do. Would you mind helping me with this next assignment? I'll even spring for a cup of coffee."

How could I refuse such an offer? Besides, he was tall, dark, and handsome. (Rarely have I been known to fall for short, blond, and average looking.) His name was Bill Trowbridge; he was twenty-six years of age, born in Martinsville, Indiana, and he was a veteran of the US Air Force, now attending school on the GI Bill. He was still sporting a GI buzz cut, a crew neck sweater, nicotine-stained fingers, and a shy smile.

A week later I was having lunch at the student union cafeteria and noticed that Bill was sitting at the next table with his friend, Jim. I couldn't help but overhear what they were saying. They were trying to recall the name of an Indiana State undergraduate who'd written a book when she was a teenager. I don't know what came over me. I leaned over to them and said, "Mr. Trowbridge, the book was *The Riddle of the Genesis Tree* and the girl was Lynne Harding." (Name changed, of course.) Before they had time to register surprise, I went on, "The book was panned by reviewers as being a takeoff of *Raintree County*, but she made a big splash, at least for a while." They looked at me as though I had two heads, but they smiled and thanked me.

Shortly after that, Mr. Trowbridge—now just plain Bill—asked me to join him and his buddies after class at a local watering hole frequented by the GI vets. For some reason, his pals always called me "Charlie." I guess they simply thought of me as one of the boys. Or, perhaps it was because I earned good grades in a class that was considered a male domain. We usually ended up there two or three times a week.

After a while, as Bill told me later, his friend Jim teased him: "You're seeing an awful lot of Mary Ellen lately. Are you starting to fall for her?"

"Nah—she's just helping me with the income tax class. You know I'm not ready to settle down to just one."

"You know what they say," Jim reminded him. "A man chases a girl until *she* catches him."

Bill and I went out to dinner together one night, Dutch treat, and a week later I invited him to my apartment for dinner. I bought take-out instead of cooking the meal myself because, to paraphrase Richard Nixon, "I am not a cook!" Of course, we saw each other often during and after class.

Then one day, he asked me out for a real date—a romantic dinner for two on Valentine's Day at the swanky Terre Haute House. Jim told me later that Bill called him the next day and admitted, "Jim, I think you may be right."

Meanwhile, I couldn't give up my music entirely. I took an elective in opera workshop and was awarded the role of Cherubino in Mozart's *The Marriage of Figaro*. Cherubino is a young teenage boy whose part was written by Mozart to be sung by a mezzo-soprano. I had a wonderful time with that part. I got to wear a pigtailed wig and a velvet brass-buttoned coat with knee pants, and I pranced around like a young boy besotted by the women of the household.

At one point in the opera, Cherubino has to dress as a girl in order to escape the wrath of his master, the Don. I was especially pleased with the newspaper reviews of my performance: "Mary Ellen Blevins is a girl who plays the part of a boy who has to dress up like a girl. She played the part as though she had never worn a dress." And this was *before* the Broadway musical and film, *Victor/Victoria!*

During the spring semester Bill and I had another class together, Business Law. By the end of the semester we had set the wedding date—June 6, 1964, the first weekend after the end of classes. We went to the professor to request an early final examination because of the need to be in Fort Branch for wedding preparations. The professor said, "I thought something like that was brewing back there." Perhaps he saw us holding hands under the chair arms.

In May, we rented a duplex for the next year while Bill finished his degree. I would be completing my MBA in August. Our half of the bungalow-style house had a living room, dining room, and kitchen on the first floor; two bedrooms and a bath upstairs; and a small basement with a furnace and coal room. I moved in by myself before the wedding because my parents insisted that it would not be proper for us to live together until after the wedding. (They didn't know *everything* about my Greek god, Vasilios.)

I decorated the apartment with the few pieces of furniture I had brought from my Chicago apartment, as well as several cast-offs from my parents. Bill didn't have much to contribute—the clothes on his back and his ancient Buick. His mother later gave me a beautiful antique sheet-music cabinet that had been in the family for a couple of generations. It still has a place of honor next to my piano.

On my first night in the duplex, I was almost asleep upstairs when I thought I heard a rustling sound coming from below. Despite my fear, I walked to the head of the stairs and turned on the downstairs light. I couldn't believe my eyes! The living room and dining room floors were literally undulating and nearly black. Thousands of cockroaches were scurrying to find cover, some humping each other in the process! It seems the critters had been enjoying free rein in the place because our side of the house had been unoccupied for several months. I screamed and then turned on every light in the house for the rest of the night, praying that the insects couldn't climb stairs. The landlord put out poison the next day and Bill shoveled dead cockroaches by the ton out of the basement. (What is it with me and cockroaches?!)

A woman usually remembers her first wedding—even if she'd rather forget any later ones. In 1964, weddings did not require that parents mortgage their home to provide their daughter with the wedding of her dreams. My parents certainly gave me the wedding of *my* dreams—I never dreamed I would get married! After all, I was almost twenty-five, the traditional age at which an unmarried lady, especially in Indiana, is considered an old maid.

My gown was virginal white. (I chose to forget about my romp with Vasilios.) It was a floor length, slim gown in a much smaller size than I wear today; I probably could fit my thigh into the gown now. The dress had lace-trimmed gossamer sleeves, a long, removable train, and a veil anchored by a beaded tiara. All the men in the wedding party, which included my brother Bill and two friends of my new husband, wore white dinner jackets and black bow ties. The bridesmaids—two cousins and a sorority sister, Ruth—wore matching powder blue dresses and hats, all handmade by my great aunt, Belle. Although I had asked my college roommate, Janet, to serve as my matron of honor, she declined because she was eight months pregnant. My father escorted me down the aisle, and I was as elated as Cinderella on her special day.

We started married life with a broken-down Buick and not much money, so our honeymoon was brief and cheap. We both had to return to campus in a week for summer school. Our wedding night was spent at my in-law's house in Columbus, Ohio. Bill was an only child, born when his mother was in her late thirties and had given up hope of having a baby, so his parents were always overly protective. Bill was coddled as a child—his mother didn't let him ride a bicycle until he was sixteen. So, I shouldn't have been surprised when, on our wedding night, she came into the bedroom, kissed us both, and, to my horror, tucked us in. It was obvious why Bill had joined the Air Force after two years of college—he probably wanted to get away from home.

So why did I marry him? I have often asked myself that question. He was quiet, but charming. He was not effusive in his lovemaking, yet he was tender and sincere. And we had similar backgrounds, both from small Indiana towns and loving families. After all, his Grandpa Trowbridge drank his coffee from his saucer after he cooled it, just like *my* grandfather.

I did try to be a dutiful housewife and attempt to cook. My husband loved pecan pie, and I was determined that I would bake one for him and that he'd be rhapsodic in his praise. I worked and worked on the pie dough using the recipe my mother had given me, the one that had been passed down from her mother and grandmother. However, every time I tried to put the dough in the pie pan, it would tear. So, out it would come onto the breadboard, and I would work on it some more, kneading and kneading it over and over. I worked on that dough until it was grey. I suppose the pie tasted okay, but I never attempted to bake another one. Thank goodness for frozen pie dough!

After we were married, Bill still had a semester to complete before earning his bachelor's degree, so I accepted a position as a public school teacher for the school year 1964-65 at a nearby high school in Clinton, Indiana. My first day at the school was like a chapter from the book, *Up the Down Staircase.* I was descending one of the stairways to my new classroom on the lower floor when an older teacher accosted me, shouting, "Use the other staircase!" I froze momentarily, until

I explained that I was the new business teacher, teaching beginning and advanced typing, shorthand, and office practices. He grudgingly allowed me to continue.

In my role as business teacher, I was also the faculty sponsor of the school newspaper, *The Wildcatonian,* which was typed by our student reporters on stencil masters, run off on hand-cranked mimeograph machines, and the copies stapled together before being distributed to the student body. I was quite proud of the students' journalistic abilities.

We had one very talented young man who drew delightfully unusual pictures for the cover of the paper. However, I had to replace him when his drawings became a bit too horrific for my taste. For Christmas that year, he drew a gruesome picture of a skeleton being dislodged from a chimney. The skeleton was wearing a Santa Claus suit. I don't know where his abilities took him eventually, but he had the talent to draw cartoons for *Mad Magazine.*

What I loved about the job was the students; what I hated about the job was the school rules for teacher behavior. Teachers were prohibited from being seen smoking in public, entering a bar, or even buying alcoholic beverages in the store. This amused me somewhat, because every week in the attendance report teachers were told that some young female student wouldn't be attending for the rest of the year. The unspoken reason was that she was pregnant (can you say "double standard?").

My most embarrassing moment as a teacher occurred in the beginning typing class. I had told the students that the space bar must be struck with the right thumb. I really don't know, to this day, why that is; perhaps it has something to do with the alignment of the right thumb with the keyboard. I was wandering around the classroom watching the students during a practice session, and I noticed one young man using his left thumb to strike the space bar.

I went up to him and reminded him, "Lenny, use your right thumb on the space bar."

He held up his right hand, "But I don't have a right thumb!" He had lost his thumb in a farming accident.

Without missing a beat, I chirped, "Okay! *You* can use your left thumb."

Apparently the Clinton school board thought I had done a good job because they offered me a contract for the next year, but I declined. Bill had been accepted by the US Navy and would be attending Officer Candidate School in Newport, Rhode Island, immediately after graduation. I couldn't visit him during his schooling, but I did drive to Newport to attend his graduation and a formal commencement dance at the officer's club at the Newport naval station, where I wore the new evening gown that I had sewn on my mother's old treadle sewing machine.

I know that OCS was both physically and mentally challenging for Bill. After all, he was older than the average cadet. However, he managed to avoid falling on his shiny new navy sword, and in November 1965, he was commissioned an ensign and assigned to Brunswick, Georgia, the Fleet Anti-Aircraft Warfare Training Center, abbreviated FAAWTC and called by the acronym, "fawt-see."

So, we packed up the sword, the newly acquired cat, and our few meager possessions and headed south. It looked like fair skies and clear sailing from then on! I just didn't realize how *far* south we'd be going and how stormy the seas would become.

# CHAPTER 14

---

# ANCHORS AWEIGH

Remember that it is not the billows but
the calm level of the sea from which all
heights and depths are measured.
—James A. Garfield, 1881

When I was an undergraduate at Indiana State, I attended a presentation by a US Navy recruiter, and I immediately changed my career goal—well, my parent's goal—of public school teaching. Instead, I wanted to join the navy and, as the posters proclaimed, "See the World." I didn't think that goal ever would come to fruition. After all, Indiana is relatively land-locked.

Therefore, when my husband Bill decided he would be happier in the military after graduation, rather than teaching history in a small southern Indiana high school, I was thrilled. When the Air Force turned him down for officer training but the navy welcomed him, I was ecstatic! Finally, I would be able to see more of the world than was visible from the banks of the Wabash River.

After OCS, and before assignment to a billet on board a ship, Bill had to attend another navy school, the Fleet Anti-Aircraft Warfare Training Center in Brunswick, Georgia, where he would be trained as a combat information officer.

So, we left our Midwest roots and headed for the Deep South. As we drove into Brunswick, what do you suppose I first noticed? Was it the stately pine trees draped with Spanish moss or the sandy earth with scrawny tufts of grass here and there? Was it the nearby ocean lapping at the shore? *No!* It was the incredibly noxious stench of what must have been tons of rotten garbage that had been stacked up for months! Was the entire waste disposal system of the southern half of the country out of commission? Actually, it was the wood-pulp plant for which Brunswick was famous. Despite the locals telling me, "You'll get used to it," I never did.

Brunswick also is the home of the outer islands—most notably, St. Simons Island, Sea Island, and Jekyll Island. Some of the islands were relatively deserted at that time, but they have since become highly developed. Jekyll Island was once one of the playgrounds of the rich and famous. In 1964, it was a great place for young navy families to go on weekends. We would visit some of the old mansions, have picnics on the beach, and collect driftwood to polish and display in our temporary homes. I still have a driftwood candleholder Bill made for me.

Most of the population of the city was navy personnel and their families. Housing units had been hastily built to accommodate the military and their dependents. Our apartment was on the second floor of one of those matchbox constructions, where the walls were so thin you could hear everything that was said or done in the next apartment. This made for a few embarrassing moments.

One day, Bill and I were sitting at our kitchen table having lunch when we distinctly heard the young wife of the FAAWTC student next door tell her husband, "There's not enough here for a whole sandwich."

Bill and I looked at each other for a second and then spoke loudly to the wall, "Then give him *half* a sandwich!" There was dead silence. I don't think that couple ever looked us in the eye thereafter.

The apartment building did not permit pets, and I was not going to relinquish my beloved cat, so "Turd" had to live in our car for the two months we were in Georgia. Although we had first called the cat "Tom," he was always getting into trouble and Bill would say "Stop that, you little turd," so the name stuck. The cat was quite comfortable in the car with his litter box, food and water bowls, and chewable toys, and I would visit him often throughout the day. However, Bill had to carry a lint remover with him at all times or he would look as though his uniform had grown hair overnight.

In 1965, race relations in the United States were just beginning to undergo change, and the people in the South were probably the most resistant to that change. I never thought of myself as either conservative or liberal, and certainly not prejudiced against people of color. Of course, in my small hometown in southern Indiana, there were no people of color—unless you counted the rednecks.

One afternoon in Brunswick, I received a delivery at home, a care package from my mother. The deliveryman was a mature black man who spoke so slowly and with such a heavy drawl that at first I couldn't understand him. To make matters worse, he would not look at me.

"Ah got uh box hyar fr Trubrge."

"What?"

Again, I heard a garbled mumble directed at the floor, not at me.

"Sir, would you mind repeating that? Perhaps if you looked at me I could understand you."

I guess I hadn't realized what a liberal Yankee I really was and how out of touch with the current reality of the South I must have been. Sadly, I think I might have hurt the fellow more than helped him with my "Stand up and be a man!" reproach.

Bill was paid—but not much—while he was attending classes, so we had to live very frugally. A portion of his pay was deducted to reimburse the navy for the cost of that swash-buckling sword. (However, I had strong doubts that he would ever buckle any swashes.) The first Friday of every month, the local Howard Johnson's restaurant offered an "All You Can Eat for $3.95" fish dinner special. That was a favorite dining-out occasion for many of our young navy friends. One night, when the waitress plunked down Bill's third serving of clam strips, she told him, "The manager says that's *all* you can eat for $3.95."

After completing the course at FAAWTC, Bill was officially qualified to push the red button in a war against invading aircraft. Somehow, that didn't exactly fill me with confidence. After all, I recalled his repugnance in the cockroach war—remember our duplex in Terre Haute?

Bill was assigned as the assistant combat information officer of the *USS Dewey* (DLG 14), a destroyer-leader, guided-missile frigate home-ported in Norfolk, Virginia. That was the sleekest, most beautiful floating craft I ever saw. The ship was slightly larger than a destroyer, and it positively bristled with guided missiles and ASROC (anti-submarine rocket) launchers. In a way, I felt that I, too, had joined the navy and soon would be seeing the world.

The wardroom on board—the mess hall for officers—was only slightly larger than a breakfast nook. However, the service was as elegant as a queen's table at the palace. Philippine waiters in crisp white uniforms served the meals. Charger plates and tableware in heavy silver, huge white linen napkins, and silver napkin rings engraved with each officer's name and rank graced the tables. I guess it's a fact—when a man receives a commission in the military, he is officially "an officer and a gentleman," even if he's simply a good ole boy from southern Indiana.

The captain's wife was a hard-drinking, fun-loving party girl. When the *Dewey* was out at sea, she would take me along with her to the officer's club for dinner or to play cards. I think she thought she wouldn't be tempted to stray too far if I were along. I learned a great deal from her, and not just about protocol and the expected junior officer's wife behavior. After all, she taught me to play duplicate bridge, and eventually I would win several master's points.

Our cat, Turd, was still with us when we moved to Norfolk, and he really lived up to his name. We rented a two-story townhouse in a brand new complex, built by the US Navy for navy personnel. Turd was so happy to be released from the car. He loved to roam the neighborhood, seeing what mischief he could get into. He had never been neutered. I always imagined what it would feel like to have one's sex organs chopped off, so I just couldn't do that to him. However, on one of his meanderings, he walked past the open door of a neighbor's house, and what did he see? A beautiful, simpering, snow-white female Persian cat was sitting in the doorway. He pounced, did his thing, and a purebred registered feline was ruined forever. I don't understand why we weren't offered any of the half-breed kittens; we were certainly told, in no uncertain terms, about Turd's misbehavior!

After two years on the *Dewey*, Bill was assigned as assistant combat information officer on the aircraft carrier *USS Forrestal* (CVA 59) following the devastating fire of July 29, 1967. I believe that fire destroyed more aircraft than the Viet Cong had done during the entire war and killed so many sailors. The fire started while the ship was moored at Yankee station in Vietnam. A Zuni rocket accidentally fired from an F-4 Phantom parked on the starboard side of the flight deck. The missile hit the fuel tank on a parked A-4D Skyhawk, which spewed fuel and then exploded, spreading flames over the entire surface of the ship. The deck was fully loaded with armed aircraft, and when the flames hit them, they exploded in a fiery inferno. Berthing spaces below the flight deck became death traps for more than fifty men, while others were blown overboard by the explosions.

I didn't know the full story at the time, because when Bill was assigned to the *Forrestal*, the carrier had been restored to its former glory with no sign of the previous devastation. Immediately after the ship was repaired, all the wives and families of the officers and crew were invited to the ship for a dependent's cruise, a short sail out of Chesapeake Bay. The ship provided an air show, with fighter planes taking off and landing, and visitations to special places on the ship: crew's quarters, officers' quarters, mess hall, hospital, and the Combat Information Center, where Bill was assigned. While the ship was underway, most of the other wives stayed below, feeling a bit queasy, but I was on the deck, wind in my face, finally achieving my long-held desire of sailing aboard a navy ship and seeing something of the world outside Indiana.

At the first organized luncheon of the *Forrestal* wives, I was introduced to the captain's wife, a grandmotherly type. She looked a great deal like the wife of the first President Bush, but of course I didn't know that at the time. This captain's wife also adopted me—but for different reasons. She asked me, and I agreed, to write a newsletter for the ship's wives, both those of the "black-shoe navy" and those of the "brown-shoe navy."

Bill was a member of the black-shoe navy, meaning he was an officer of the line, i.e., ship's operations. Officers of the line wore black shoes with their navy blue-black uniforms. The officers who were assigned to the squadrons flying off the carrier were called brown-shoe navy. Those officers wore brown shoes with their khaki-colored flight uniforms.

Whether I liked to admit it or not, and no matter how much I tried to defy the rule, a navy wife *does* bear the same rank as her husband, at least informally. One of the squadron wives said to me at our November *Forestal* wives luncheon: "Is your husband flying home for Christmas? Oh, that's right, you're a black-shoe lieutenant, and only the brown-shoe commanders get to fly home." I looked at her and replied, not as meekly as I should have, "I'm *not* a lieutenant and my husband *is* flying home with one of his friends, Commander Bailey." Now that I think back on it, I don't recommend outspokenness as a way to win friends and influence wives of superior officers.

Going from the *Dewey* (a small, friendly puppy of a ship) to the *Forrestal* (a gigantic, soulless, behemoth) was, in a way, a perfect reflection of my life so far. I had gone from being a small-town, naïve country girl to a big city woman of the world—well, perhaps not quite of the *world*, at least not yet.

The *Forrestal* was deployed, on the average, about ten months of the year. When the ship was in port, it would anchor away from the pier, because of its size, and the officers and men would be required to go from shore to ship on launches, or tenders. I called them "little boats." I would drop Bill at the pier every morning before heading to my job on base, and pick him up every evening before going home. One morning—I don't know what came over me—I think I was influenced by Jane Fonda's character in *Barefoot in the Park*. When Bill got out of the car and headed toward a group of his fellow officers and crewmen waiting for the little boat, I ran up to him, threw my arms around his neck, gave him a big kiss, and said, "Y'all look me up next time you're in town, ya hear?" Then I quickly jumped in the car. I can only imagine how he explained that to his men.

The job I went to after dropping my husband at the pier was another great adventure for me. When we'd arrived in Norfolk, I knew I wanted to work, preferably on the naval base, so I took the federal service examination—a requirement for anyone who wanted to work as a civilian for the US Navy. I scored well enough on the exam to be given a fairly high GS (government service) rating, and I applied for a job on base that required that rating. When I think of it now, after many years in the business world, it seems incongruous that I was hired, without question, solely on the basis of my GS rate, as the public relations officer for the US Navy Public Works Center for the Atlantic Fleet. Small town girl makes good!

My assignment was, single-handedly, to photograph newsworthy items, conduct the research, write, and type articles and press releases, construct the layout, and publish *The Center Post*, the newspaper for staff and personnel of the Navy Public Works Center. The NPWC was the home of the navy Seabees—the construction battalion—based at the Norfolk naval station. The head of the base was a navy admiral, a delightful, lovable character who always called me "Scoop." My immediate civilian boss was Katherine, an immaculate, uptight, upright woman of Virginia who was a great boss. She let me do my job to the best of my creative ability, and she saw to it that I had the help I needed when the task overreached my ability.

I was given one assignment that did test my ability, at least my ability to think of safety first and story second. The aircraft carrier, *USS John F. Kennedy* (CVA 67), had just been commissioned and outfitted with the latest, state-of-the-art avionics equipment. I thought the story would make a great front-page spread, together with pictures of all this new equipment. The shipyard workers were so pleasant and helpful to me, and when I mentioned that I wanted to get a long shot of all the avionics gear lined up on the flight deck, one of the workers suggested, "I'll lift you up on a forklift and you can get the money shot!"

He put a wooden pallet on the forklift tines, and I climbed aboard. However, as I snapped the picture I must have shifted my weight, because the pallet tilted. The worker had not fastened the pallet to the tines, as it should have been, and I took a nosedive onto the flight deck, making a perfect one-point landing! My nose was broken, and so was the two-year safety record at the shipyard. But I saved the camera, and it was a heck of a picture! It graced the front page of the next issue of *The Center Post*.

Bill was gone an average of ten months every year that he served on the *Forrestal*, so I soon learned to take care of everything on my own—car, pet, job, and home. I decided that our small patio needed a facelift. I bought a decorative privacy fence and had that installed. Then, I built a small wooden deck—a sort of platform—and installed that myself, putting an umbrella table and four chairs on the deck. I finished off the unpaved portion of the patio with flagstones surrounded by white gravel: Very nice, if I do say so myself.

Our townhouse was rented, so I couldn't deface the walls in any way. I wanted bookcases for my growing library collection, but we couldn't afford stand-alone floor-to-ceiling bookcases. I decided to build them myself, and I put my high school algebra and geometry to good use. I calculated that the sides of a hand-built bookcase could not be the full eight feet tall (the height of the room) or it would not clear the ceiling as I lifted it into place.

So, with the Wizard of Oz scarecrow whispering in my ear, I recited the geometry theorem: "The square of the hypotenuse is equal to the sum of the squares of the other two sides." I knew the hypotenuse of the side (upright) board of the bookcase should be eight feet (ninety-six inches) and the depth of the bookcase would be ten inches. What, then, should be the length of the board, in inches? Freshman algebra to the rescue! The equation: $96^2 = 10^2 + x^2$. Solving for x: $x^2 = 9216 - 100 = 95.4777$ inches. *Voila!*

I went to the lumberyard and ordered four ten-inch by eight-foot by one-inch boards cut exactly to 95.4777-inch lengths, plus the shelves in four foot lengths. I built the two bookcases on the floor, lifted them up to the walls, and they just kissed the ceiling as they settled perfectly into place. But of course, when Bill came home from his cruise, I had to pretend to be the helpless little wife again.

He did admire the bookcases and patio, however.

While we lived in Norfolk, I was very physically active, so I was slender and looked fairly attractive. I was the hit of the wetting-down parties (the celebrations on the occasion of an officer receiving a promotion) probably because I would sing and dance until the last dog died. But I was never in any danger. The officers in Bill's circle were, indeed, gentlemen.

However, as I was soon to discover, not every man is, by definition, a gentle man. Bill had a TDY (temporary duty) assignment at Cape Kennedy in Florida. The base originally was called Cape Canaveral. Then the name was changed to Cape Kennedy to honor our slain president. But in recent years, it's been renamed Cape Canaveral. At that time, during 1967, we were driving a real muscle car—a white Buick Wildcat convertible with red leather interior—that required nearly a city block to park.

Because the TDY was only for two weeks, I accompanied Bill and stayed in a nearby motel while he was on base. We would see each other when he had off-duty evenings on alternate nights. The motel where I stayed had a cocktail party every afternoon at five in the afternoon. I was young and feisty (and thin) and I didn't see any harm in a little flirting. (It seems that I never feel like flirting when I've gained a little weight.)

Perhaps it was the Wildcat convertible, or the fact that I was a navy wife and therefore fair game, but one man began paying me an inordinate amount of attention. He was rather ordinary looking; he might have been another good ole boy from the Midwest. But his wit was his charm, and I found him delightful fun—dopey me! One night, he followed me from the cocktail party to my room and attempted to push me into the room. Remember, I am a strong-willed country girl and not easily intimidated. I braced my hands and wrists on the outside of the door so that he was unable to overpower me and force me into the room. He finally gave up in disgust. I had the bruises on my wrists for weeks. Bill never noticed.

That was my first inkling that men want what they want and do not necessarily have a woman's best interest at heart. I had learned, for the moment, how to say "No." Too bad the lesson didn't imprint permanently on my psyche; I could have avoided a lot of pain and heartache later.

# CHAPTER 15

•❀•

# OVER THERE

Thus he will travel five hundred miles in a
few days as a distraction from his happiness.
—Alexis de Tocqueville, 1835

The winter of 1968-1969 was especially memorable to me. I quit my job at the Navy Public Works Center to be free to join my husband in Europe, when his ship was in port, for a couple of months of his ten-month deployment on the *USS Forrestal*. While the *Forrestal* was circumnavigating the Mediterranean, I was circumnavigating Europe with my friend Myrna, another officer's wife.

We flew to Frankfurt, Germany, in an airliner that was deadheading back to Europe as a special flight for military dependents. The cabin was filled to capacity with women and children. Tots were sitting in their mother's laps, and infants were hanging from the overhead in canvas baskets. The plane was an El Al airliner from Israel, and the entire crew was Israeli. The food served on board was strictly kosher. The flight attendant was stunned when I asked for cream in my coffee to accompany the lamb stew. She gave me an emphatic, "No!" I thought she had some sort of superiority complex. It was several years later I learned that kosher rules do not permit dairy products and meat products to be served together in the same meal.

The flight landed in Frankfurt. It was my first time outside the United States and it seemed as though the air in Europe was a strangely lighter, hazier hue than the air at home. Both of us had purchased Eurail passes and, armed with the book *Europe on $5 a Day,* we immediately boarded the train for Munich for the start of our low-cost trek across Europe: Germany, Austria, Switzerland, Italy, Monte Carlo, France, and Spain. We really did manage to do it for five dollars a day, plus the cost of souvenirs.

All of us "seagulls"—wives who were following the *Forrestal*—would be waiting at the dock when the ship came into port, usually about every two weeks. Bill and I had some wonderful times seeing Europe's famous ports. First, there was Genoa, Italy, where Bill commented about the city's walls. As I recall, he said, "This place is really *old.*"

During the next two weeks, about fifteen of us, mostly wives of the squadron aviators, rented a villa in the south of France while we explored the countryside. "Villa" is rather overstating the accommodations; it was more like a huge ramshackle farmhouse. Because I was a black-shoe wife, my accommodations were less fancy. The squadron wives made me sleep on the couch.

After the *Forrestal* docked at the port of Gulf Juan in southern France, Bill and I rented a car and drove up the coast to Monte Carlo, where I lost twenty-five francs—less than a dollar—in the famous Casino Royale.

At Christmas, Bill had a week's leave and we took the train to Zurich to spend the holiday in a picture-postcard winter setting. Sadly, Bill caught a cold and we spent Christmas snowbound in a *pension.* The owners took pity on us and invited us to share their yuletide repast. We did manage to attend a movie in Zurich: *Chitty, Chitty, Bang, Bang,* starring Dick Van Dyke and Julie Andrews. We could hardly see the picture for the sub-titles that covered the screen (Italian, French, German, and Dutch.)

Bill and I had worked out a deal with the hotels at many of these ports. When he would stay overnight with me, we paid for a double occupancy, but when I was staying alone, I would notify the concierge and receive a cheaper rate for that day. I sometimes wonder what the man at the front desk of the Genoa hotel thought when I called him every other evening and said, *"Mi mari e non con mio questa sera."* Translation: "My husband is not with me tonight."

I always try to communicate in the local language when I visit a non-English-speaking country, but I am not always successful. When traveling through French-speaking Switzerland on the way to Geneva, I was worried that the train seemed to be late in arriving and I would miss my connection. So I approached the conductor and asked him, in my carefully rehearsed schoolgirl French, *"A quelle heur arriver nous en Geneve?"* ("What time do we get to Geneva?")

He replied in French, *"Huit heur et cinq minuit."* ("Five minutes after eight.")

I mentally translated his response for a second and then responded, *"Merci."*

Then he said to me in perfect English, "Did you understand?"

*"Oui, merci!"* ("Yes, thank you!") I walked away in a huff.

Most of the people in the countries we visited in Europe during that winter were either very sympathetic or antipathetic to Americans. There didn't seem to be a middle ground. In Italy, of course, the men thought we would enjoy being pinched on our plump American bottoms. We didn't. (But perhaps we shouldn't have been wearing those leg-revealing miniskirts.) In Germany, an older woman on the train was cautious and reticent to engage in conversation, even in German. Perhaps she had bad memories from World War II. But the young couple with her seemed delighted to learn that my girlfriend and I were Americans, and they wanted to know all about us.

People in Austria were especially friendly and helpful. When Myrna and I were unable to secure a hotel room upon our arrival in Vienna, an Austrian lady who had been seeing her daughter off to school at the train station overheard our dilemma and invited us to stay at her home, in her daughter's room. We accepted her gracious offer and paid her what we would have paid a hotel. She even cooked breakfast for us. Afterwards, we admitted we were a bit insane to have done that—we could have ended up in pieces in the Danube River!

On another occasion, we were trying to find the famous Spanish riding school that trained the Lipizzaner horses—Arabian horses that can actually dance. They would leap up from a standing position with all four feet in the air and perform amazing stunts, even marching sideways. We stopped a lady on the street and asked for directions to the riding school. Without hesitating, she said, "Follow me," and then walked with us to the school's entrance.

An elderly gentleman on the train in Spain (and yes, we were staying mainly on the plain) was complaining about the Franco government and the poor condition of the public services, especially the trains. He was curious to know about our experiences with European train travel, and he was especially appalled when I told him what had happened to me at the border crossing between France and Spain.

As we came into Spain, the train ground to a halt and everyone was required to disembark. We were then shuffled off into a large warehouse where we had to show our passports and have our bags inspected by Spanish soldiers in uniform. They were quite unfriendly to those of us who were Americans. I found it difficult to be truly intimidated because they sported huge black patent leather bows on their uniform hats. I would have giggled if they hadn't searched my bag so diligently. I had packed so as to utilize every inch of space, and when the guy with the patent leather bow on his hat scooped up my shoes, my hair curlers jumped out and bounced all over the inspection hall. It was all I could do to keep from laughing as I chased the errant, jumping-bean curlers. I'm positive I saw a hint of a grin on the soldier's face.

While Myrna and I were sightseeing around Barcelona before heading to the next port of call for the *Forrestal*, we saw a beautiful building that looked as if it might be an ancient palace. There were guards posted at the sides of the great open archway leading into the courtyard. As we started to enter, the two guards suddenly leaped in front of us, guns raised as if to fire. We quickly backed off. I mumbled under my breath, "Generalissimo Franco must be at home."

I particularly enjoyed the island of Palma de Majorca, Spain, with its vineyard-covered hills and quaint shops. That was to be the next stop for the *Forrestal*. Myrna and I almost missed the experience, however. We arrived at the embarkation port for the ship from Barcelona to Palma after the ticket office had closed. We stood at the base of the gangplank; I looked up at the ship's deck officer and gave him my most pitiful look while I begged, *"Por favor?"* (Please?) He allowed us to board and pay for our passage.

After the *Forrestal* docked, my husband and I had a beautiful week of sunshine-filled days, tours of the cultured pearl factory, afternoon siestas, and delicious seafood *paella*. We especially enjoyed the food— although Bill and I became victims of Montezuma's revenge. (And I thought *he* only operated in Mexico!)

After two months living the luxurious life of a jetsetter (albeit on a five-dollar-a-day shoestring), it was time to return home and go back to the mundane, leaving the fun and excitement of Europe behind. But the memories of the people and places I had experienced would stay with me forever.

How was I to know that forever sometimes lasts only a couple of years?

# CHAPTER 16

·•❀•·

# CALIFORNIA, HERE I COME

The coldest winter I ever experienced
was a summer in San Francisco.
—Mark Twain

When I finished high school, I had three wishes: to get a pair of prescription sunglasses, to own a real fur stole, and to live in California. I achieved the first wish while I was an undergraduate at Indiana State. The second wish came true when Bill was on the *Forrestal's* ten-month cruise in the Mediterranean Sea. He brought back a Stone Marten fur stole from Thessalonica, Greece, to dry my tears of loneliness. That fur still languishes in the back of my closet, because wearing a fur today is a politically incorrect no-no.

The third wish came true a few months later.

Before Bill returned from that Mediterranean cruise, I went to Ames, Iowa, to be with my brother, Bill, and his wife, Barb, at the birth of their first child, Kristina Ann, in April 1969. I don't know why I thought I could help. I'm like Butterfly McQueen in *Gone with the Wind*: "I don't know nothin' 'bout birthin' no babies!" But I could keep Barb's mind off things while she was waiting for the blessed event, and I could wash dishes and call the pizza parlor when someone was hungry.

After the baby came home, I thought she was the most beautiful infant I ever laid eyes on. I wanted to hold her, feed her, change her diapers, and do anything to be close to my niece. On one of her first days home, I was changing her diaper when—horror of horrors—the umbilical cord came off with the diaper! I was convinced I had ruined the child forever. Twenty years later, when Kristi was a student in a class I was teaching at Purdue, she begged me, "I don't mind if you tell the class I'm your niece, but *please* don't tell them the story about my umbilical cord!"

The summer of 1969, my husband received orders to transfer to the Pacific Fleet, to the *USS Mataponi,* a navy tanker then moored near the naval station on Treasure Island in San Francisco Bay. Treasure Island lies between San Francisco to the west and Oakland to the east, anchored by the Bay Bridge. The entire island was occupied by the US Navy and had no special assets to boast of at that time, other than a terrific view of Coit Tower and a PX that undersold every store in California.

We had acquired a second car while we lived in Norfolk—my MGB sports car—so we each drove a car as we traveled from the East to the West Coast. The navy moved our furniture, and we deposited the cat, Turd, with my parents in Indiana to keep until we had a permanent home.

At one point in the trip, we pulled off a toll road for lunch at a pre-appointed stop. We didn't have cell phones in those days and communication between cars could only happen at our stops. As I exited the toll road at the head of our two-car convoy, I heard a loud *bang!* I said to the attendant at the tollbooth, "What was that noise? Did something explode in my car?"

The attendant chuckled, "No, there's a firing range over in that field. That's what you heard—gunfire."

My husband, Bill, was immediately behind me at the exit, and when he rolled up to the tollbooth, the attendant was laughing. He pointed to my departing car, "That lady thought something was wrong with her car 'cause she heard the gunfire from the firing range."

Bill looked at him, and with a straight face, he said, "That was no lady; that was my wife." (Isn't it great when life gives you opportunities like that?!)

We were breezing along the famous Route 66 through New Mexico, approaching Albuquerque and the Sandia Peak in a torrential downpour, when the alternator went out on my MGB, and the car lost all electrical functions. I had to reach outside and wipe the windshield with one hand and keep driving with the other hand on the steering wheel, because I knew if we stopped, the car would never start again. Thankfully, we made it to a Motel 6 at the edge of the city and were able to get the car fixed that night during our stopover. And believe it or not, back then the Motel 6 cost only six dollars a night. I guess that's why they called it Motel 6.

During our westward-ho journey, we visited many natural wonders and tourist sites along the way. I never had been west of Oklahoma, so I was thrilled by the Painted Desert, the Petrified Forest, the Grand Canyon, Meteor Crater, Big Bear, and Liberace's home in Palm Springs. It was shaped like a grand piano!

After we arrived in California, we rented an adorable three-bedroom house high on a hill overlooking the Pacific Ocean in Pacifica, a quaint beach town south of San Francisco. I immediately asked my mother to ship my cat, Turd, to California via airfreight in the large wooden crate I had purchased from the airlines. When the cat arrived, we picked him up at the San Francisco International Airport. Apparently, he had held everything in for the entire trip, because when we let him out of the crate in the car, he was so glad to see me that he jumped up, put his paws on my shoulders, and pooped in my lap!

I became active in the local community arts commission and made some great friends. Most of the people in our neighborhood were young, upwardly-mobile professionals—the first *yuppies*—and we partied—and partied—and partied! There were, of course, the TGIF (thank goodness it's Friday) parties celebrating the approach of the carefree weekend. But we also had regular "hump-day" parties on Wednesday, which celebrated the fact that the workweek was now half over and the weekend would be coming soon. And we usually got together on Sunday afternoons for one last party before the workweek began again. Several of the neighbors played musical instruments and I would sing. I must admit I was happy in that carefree existence. Just picture bell-bottoms, kaftans, headbands, guitars, and sangrias!

San Francisco had much to offer, as well. In addition to the typical tourist sights—Fisherman's Wharf, Ghirardelli Square, Coit Tower, Nob Hill, cable cars, Alcatraz, and the Golden Gate Bridge—just living and working in the city was thrilling. Soon after we arrived, I answered an ad in the *San Francisco Chronicle* newspaper and was hired as an assistant to S. Marshall Kempner, an elderly, well-to-do gentleman who managed the financial affairs of some of the wealthiest people in the world. His office was in the area of San Francisco known as the West Coast Wall Street. Because we were trading on the New York Stock Exchange in real time, our workday started very early. I couldn't believe I was involved in trading stocks and making purchases amounting to hundreds of thousands of dollars. It didn't seem real to me—it was just arithmetic. Unfortunately, I didn't learn how to *make* money in the stock market, only how to spend it.

There was one tradition on that West Coast Wall Street that I found delightfully strange, and which probably annoyed the heck out of the San Francisco city workers. On the last workday before New Year's Eve, everyone in all those high-rise buildings would empty their page-a-day desk calendars out the window. Those pages floated to earth like giant snowflakes, covering the streets and sidewalks in knee-high drifts, which kept the street cleaners busy on January 2!

Bill did *not* have smooth sailing on the *Mataponi*. It was 1970 and the ship was assigned to support the navy gunboats in the war in Vietnam. It wasn't only the jungle climate and the tensions of the war that got him down. The captain of the ship was either affected by the heat or was mentally deranged. He would make all the ship's crew, even the officers, stand at attention on deck for hours while he conducted inspections. On one occasion, he decided that one officer's cover (hat) was not polished sufficiently, so he threw it overboard into Cam Ranh Bay.

When told he would be re-assigned to serve on the *Mataponi* on another deployment to Vietnam, Bill resigned his commission and went into a depressive funk. He tried, unsuccessfully, to sell products for a pyramid-type cosmetics company, but he didn't seem to have the aggressiveness required. And he obviously didn't know much about wearing makeup!

I thought things were looking up when Bill got a job as a warehouse manager for an automotive parts firm, Maremont, headquartered in the City of Industry in southern California. The firm was listed on the New York Stock Exchange and seemed to have a lucrative future. We moved to Anaheim and rented a two-story town house to be close to Bill's new employment.

For a while, we had a good time in southern California. After all, no one could be bored when there is Disneyland, Knott's Berry Farm, Newport Beach, La Brea Tar Pits, Farmer's Market, and all of Hollywood to explore.

However, Bill lost his job at Maremont after a year or so. I think he had a fight with his boss. Perhaps his being an only child made it difficult for him to deal with ordinary interpersonal conflict, especially with superiors. It also made him reluctant to have children. I believe the reason we never had children was that *he* wanted to be the only child in our household.

Soon after we arrived in southern California, I secured a position as registrar and director of admissions for Western State University College of Law, the largest law school in California. I didn't want to leave that job nor move again, so I told Bill not to worry about me, just to do what he wanted and take care of himself. And, I'd take care of me. (My "voice" was beginning to rise above a whisper for a change.)

We did not divorce immediately, but we divided our household possessions and went our separate ways, seeing each other from time to time. He started selling things at swap meets. I'm not confident of the legal ownership of some of those items—but I didn't ask.

Finally, he worked as a caretaker at an apartment building in return for a free apartment. This man who had a college degree in social studies, who had been an officer in the finest navy in the world, was now repairing toilets and changing light bulbs.

Recently I read the following passage in Agatha Christie's book, *Appointment with Death*, (© 1937, Dell Publishing Co., New York, NY) about a couple in a similar situation: "A man who respects himself strikes out on his own and makes something of his life. He doesn't just sit around and twiddle his thumbs. No woman ought to respect a man who does that." If it weren't for the fact that Ms. Christie wrote that in 1937, I would've thought she was describing my husband and me.

As Oliver Wendell Holmes so wisely declared, "To reach a port we must sail sometimes with the wind and sometimes against it, but we must not drift or lie at anchor."

A few days before Christmas, 1972, my neighbor, another divorcee, came over for coffee. I directed her to the kitchen and asked her to pour the coffee for herself while I finished wrapping the gift for Bill, my ex-husband.

She stepped back in disbelief, "You got a present for your *ex-*husband?"

"Yeah, we're divorced, but he's not dead. We actually like each other." I didn't bother to explain that we simply had different goals. He wanted to do nothing, and I wanted to do—everything.

# CHAPTER 17

---•◉•---

# LOVE AFFAIR(S) TO REMEMBER

Love is only a little foolishness and a lot
of curiosity; no really self-respecting
woman would take advantage of it.
—George Bernard Shaw

Please remember that during this time, the early 1970s, I was divorced, in my early thirties, a professional law school administrator, and living in Southern California. My life as a single woman epitomized a life style once labeled as that of the "gay divorcee." And the word "gay" in those days meant something far different from today, at least for me. I'm afraid I wasn't as gay, sophisticated, and worldly wise as I would have liked.

One of my friends, Pat, also recently divorced, loved to mingle in the singles scene. She coaxed me to go with her to one of the local clubs, called "meat markets," every Saturday night to drink, dance, and look for men. Those hot spots were popular during the loose and lascivious seventies, and Pat was an outgoing, good-looking young woman who always received lots of attention from the fellows. I was not as outgoing, I suppose, or I was still smarting from the disappointment of my recent divorce, but I didn't find those evenings as enjoyable as she did. I usually spent the time at our table balancing my checkbook while she danced and flirted. I suppose that schizo personality was rearing its confused head; part of me wanted to break out of the traces, and the other half was still a nerd.

Pat actually took me along on these excursions for insurance. If she was pursued by a man she didn't particularly care for, she used me as an excuse for saying, "No, thanks," when he invited her out afterwards for more fun and games. She'd tell him she had to take me home—even though the fact is that I always drove us to the club. On the other hand, if she felt like accepting his invitation, she'd give me a high sign and leave with the man of the hour.

I was a bit surprised one night when a tall, slender, handsome young man with a head of adorable curly hair came up to me, introduced himself, and asked me to dance. As we were dancing and trading verbal *repartee*, he suddenly looked at me carefully and said, "I think I know you from somewhere."

"I can't imagine where—I don't really get out much."

"This is not a line. I'm positive I've seen you before." He kept looking at me carefully, frowning a bit in concentration.

"Well, unless you've seen me performing with my quartet . . ." He shook his head. I continued, "Or unless you attend Western State University . . ."

"Oh my God! You're Ms. Trowbridge! You interviewed me when I was applying for admission. Oh my God!"

I told him there was no problem. After all, he was already admitted and I had nothing to do with assigning grades to students, so I didn't think that dancing together would constitute any breach of administrator-student decorum.

Dennis and I began dating regularly, and I found him charming. He was a fabulous cook, a talent I have never possessed. We loved to dance together—among other things. However, I knew that he was twelve years younger than I was (remember, I had access to his records) and that difference made me uncomfortable. I was *not* a "cougar."

We stopped dating after several months, and I didn't see or hear anything of him until I saw an article in *Parade* magazine six years later. The lead story featured Maureen Reagan, the daughter of President

Ronald Reagan, and showed pictures of her California home and her new husband. Yes, it was Dennis, the former student I had dated who was twelve years younger. The article gave Ms. Reagan's age, and lo and behold, she was my age! I told my friends, "I must have whetted his appetite for older women." (Of course, *she* was rich and famous!)

There was another brief affair with one of the WSU students, also younger. He was a blond-haired, muscular, beach boy type who worked as an oil well rigger in order to pay his tuition. It was a dangerous job and it seemed he was always getting hurt. He nearly gave me a concussion one night during our mattress calisthenics when his cast-encased arm bonked me on the head. That affair didn't last long. Passion does not sustain a long-term relationship when there is little else in common—and when one partner is constantly sporting plaster casts.

One of the assistant deans of the law school (name withheld for obvious reasons) was a character with a reputation as a ladies' man who fancied himself God's gift to women. He was always pursuing me, but I knew he was married and I wanted nothing to do with that can of worms. I suppose he was insulted by my rebuff, because one day he walked into my private office, closed the door, and unzipped his trousers. He stood there against the door, grinning and waiting for my reaction. I just kept working at my desk, looked up for a second, and said, "Did you have something important to show me? Oh, I see—it's no big thing." He zipped up, slithered out, and never bothered me again.

Jeannine, one of the young girls who worked in my office at Western State University, said to me one day, "You're always singing around the office. My mother's best friend belongs to a group of women who love to sing. Maybe you'd like to meet her?"

I agreed, and soon made arrangements to meet Helen, her mom's friend, who took me to a rehearsal of her Sweet Adelines group, the Rio Hondo Chorus of Whittier, California. The chorus was preparing for a double quartet contest. A double quartet is, obviously, eight people who sing four-part barbershop harmony, two people singing each part. One of the songs they were singing was "The Boy Next Door" from the film, *Meet Me in St. Louis*. I knew the melody, although not necessarily their arrangement of the song. Someone coaxed me to stand up and sing with the other members, and before the night was over, I had fallen head over heels in love with *real* barbershop harmony (not the pseudo barbershop of my high school days.)

I immediately signed up as one of the lead singers of the double quartet contestants. That was 1972, and from that day to the present, more than forty years, I've been a member of Sweet Adelines, an international organization of women singers who sing four-part barbershop harmony *a cappella.*

One of the WSU students had given me tickets to "The Living Art Pageant" in Laguna Beach—an exhibit in which people bring famous paintings to life by re-creating full-sized, three dimensional pictures, complete with color, lighting, furnishings and costumes. However, I wasn't dating anyone at the time and had no escort to the event. My new friend, Helen, offered her son as escort. He was (you guessed it) twelve years younger. Chris was a very sweet, bright, and funny young man with the long hair that was fashionable on men in the 1970s. We had a terrific time, and when he brought me home, I thanked him for a wonderful evening and extended my hand. He said, with an exaggerated long face, "Oh no! A handshake instead of a kiss!"

I told him, "Your mother would kill me for debauching her son if I did." Then I kissed him on the cheek. I think he went to Canada shortly thereafter, probably to avoid *me*, not the draft.

One of the highlights of my years at WSU, and one in which I fell instantly in love, was a graduation ceremony with Bob Hope as the commencement speaker. I'm not sure how the president of the class pulled that off, but we had the most well attended graduation ceremony of all time, thanks to Mr. Hope. I was the one who called out the names of each graduate in the ceremony, so I sat on the dais with the college president, the dean, distinguished faculty, and our guest speaker.

Bob Hope was as delightful in person as he was in films, although we did have a moment of panic when, shortly before he was to speak, he whispered to the dean, "I left my reading glasses in my jacket." Someone was dispatched to search for the glasses, but they were nowhere to be found. Just before he stood up to speak, Mr. Hope said, "Oh—here they are, in my shirt pocket." Even the mighty are human!

I met another somewhat famous person—accidentally—when he was a student at Western State University. I was pulling into the faculty parking lot one morning, driving my adorable little MGB sports car with the personalized plate, "M.E. FIRST." I suppose I took that message to heart and simply assumed I would be allowed to go first, when a student pulled into the parking lot through the student side entrance and plowed directly into my car. The driver was Bob Chandler, the quarterback for the Buffalo Bills. He attended law school classes during the Spring Semester when football was not being played. Because the accident occurred on private school property, I wasn't able to obtain satisfaction through legal means (according to the law professors) and the famous quarterback did not offer to pay for the damages. Needless to say, I never rooted for the Buffalo Bills after that.

We offered both full-time and part-time programs of study at the Law School, day and night classes, so we had students who were working adults attending school every other semester, such as the football star, or in the evenings only. There were two commercial pilots, Jerry and Wayne, who attended night classes and scheduled their airline flights around their class schedules. Interestingly, although they were Americans, they flew for Iran Airlines. At that time, the US and Iran were allies, and Iran Airlines was one of the largest international airlines, second only to Pan Am. That changed, of course, after the Islamic revolution of 1979.

Jerry was tall and slender, with red hair, freckles, and a wicked smile. Wayne was tall, a little heavier, with a droll sense of humor. They both were witty and erudite and would often come into the registrar's office to tease me. Jerry showed me a cartoon once that he said described me perfectly: "She does not suffer fools gladly." I said it depends on the fool.

I was quite pleased when they invited me to dinner at the apartment they shared. Before long, I began to have inklings that these two were not the he-men that they appeared to be, especially when Wayne came out of the kitchen in his ruffled apron to show me the perfect Yorkshire pudding he had prepared. Oh well, it was, after all, California in the 1970s.

My one very traumatic experience with illegal substances occurred with a man I had met at one of the "meat markets." He picked me up at my condo for a dinner date, and on the way to the restaurant, he offered me a puff from his cigarette. (I had smoked for a brief time after my divorce.) It seemed to me that the cigarette was odd looking and strange tasting, and when I remarked about that, he said it was South American cannabis. I thought he meant it was a rare tobacco—little did I know it was marijuana!

As we approached the restaurant where we were to have dinner, I saw several young men standing around outside. For some reason—the result of the joint, I suppose—my brain told me they were hoodlums waiting to capture me and have their way with me. I begged my date to keep driving past the restaurant and take me home. I was so agitated I suppose he decided it would be best to humor me. As we were going back to my place, I was wringing my hands in terror. Suddenly, I screamed at him, "Take me to the hospital! I can't feel my hands!"

He just laughed and said, "You haven't had much experience with that stuff, have you?"

By the time we reached my house, I was feeling a bit better, but I was now ravenously hungry. By the way, anything else you may have heard about marijuana increasing appetites—both culinary and carnal—is completely true. I stopped smoking any and all kinds of tobacco immediately.

One other affair comes to mind that was not mine, but I was connected to it, indirectly. My Sweet Adelines chorus at that time, the Mission Viejo Chorus, often performed for various events, even producing an annual show. One of our members was involved with a very familiar fellow, one whose character I enjoyed immensely on television. It was Doc, of *The Love Boat*. Yes, my friend was dating Bernie Kopell, and she had invited him to our chorus show. I was delighted to meet him. I can always brag, "I entertained Bernie Kopell one night."

My friend Pat and I had dinner one evening at a nearby supper club that boasted a terrific restaurant, including a bar and dance floor. A tall, not-so-dark, but very handsome, sandy-haired man came to our table and, surprisingly, asked *me* to dance.

By the end of that dance, I was besotted. He was witty, romantic, and simply oozed sex appeal. He had me laughing hysterically at his endless stories, some of which were true and some, as I was to find out later, not so true.

# CHAPTER 18

---•❂•---

# HOW COULD YOU
# BELIEVE ME

Fraud and prevarication . . . grow out
of the necessities, and always out of
the habits, of degenerate spirits.
—Edmund Burke, 1797

The thirty-six months from May 1973 to the summer of 1976 included some of the most euphoria-producing yet misery-inducing experiences of my life—thanks to one man.

I met him on May 2, 1973, at the Golden Pheasant Supper Club in Anaheim, California. After dinner, my friend, Pat, and I decided to stay awhile and listen to the live band and the adorable male singer. The mood was mellow, the lights were low, the wine was flowing, and the guy was crooning, "Tie a yellow ribbon 'round the old oak tree."

A tall, slender man with sandy-colored hair came up to the table, leaned over my shoulder, and whispered in my ear, "Let's dance." He was loose-limbed and lantern-jawed, wearing tight blue jeans and a tan suede jacket with leather elbow patches. I thought he might be a famous author or a walking dream. We talked and danced and I fell in lust at first sight.

His name was Carlton Hunt Brannen. He was the grandson of George W. P. Hunt, the first governor of Arizona when it became a state on February 14, 1912. He was the son of Governor Hunt's only child, Virginia, and Carlton Brannen, a prominent civil engineer who designed many of the famous Arizona highways. He had one married sister who lived in Phoenix with her husband and two children, and he had spent many of his younger years playing in the governor's mansion in Phoenix, Arizona. All of that was true.

He was single, owned several horses at his ranch outside Anaheim, California, and had recently sold some of those horses to the King Ranch in Texas. I found out later that *none* of that was true.

Hunt, named for both his father and maternal grandfather, was an artist working for Interstate Electronics Corporation. His job, in addition to creating posters for the Employee Relations Department, was drawing realistic renderings of the electronic devices that the engineers invented. He was so talented that his drawings looked like photographs. But he couldn't resist including a little joke in the picture. One drawing of a huge industrial computing component showed an unusual spot visible on the side. On closer examination with a magnifying glass, one could see it was a coin slot with the words "Insert five cents" printed above.

His cartoon style of drawing and painting was a combination of beauty, realism, and quirkiness. One of his larger artworks depicted an antique railroad train wending its way through the mountains of the Southwest. Colorful buttes and mesas in shades ranging from red-gold to magenta were the backdrop for the foreshortened train. The cars seemed to disappear into the distance, and the final car was an open flat car, on which a long line of people meandered toward the back, where they lined up in front of—an outhouse.

Within a couple of weeks after we met, Hunt talked me into going with him to San Diego, one of my favorite destinations. He made reservations for us to stay on the beachfront at the Hotel Islandia on Harbor Island. I was thrilled to see that he signed the register as Mr. and Mrs. Hunt Brannen. (What else could he write, "Me and my tootsie?") I couldn't help thinking, and hoping: *Was this an omen of things to come?* The passion that weekend would certainly indicate that. We received a call from the front desk saying the people in the neighboring room had complained about the loud television in our room. But we never turned on the TV set. Oops!

He took me camping at California's Kern River in August that year. We drove there and stayed overnight in his truck, a fairly new Dodge Ram with a complete camper shell installation. There was a door in the rear, a kitchenette on one side, a small table and bench on the other side, and a bed over the truck cab roof. He mesmerized me so much that I didn't mind the primitive accommodations or the fact that we spent three days in the dust, rocks, and dirt of the wilderness. This was not my idea of luxury living.

In September, we drove to San Francisco, another one of my favorite places: I think I left my heart there in 1970. We visited all my special haunts from the years I'd lived there with my first husband, and we stayed in a downtown motor inn. While we were there, the television show, *Streets of San Francisco*, was filming and the entire cast and crew were at the same hotel. When Hunt and I went to breakfast in the inn's dining room, I was astonished to see the actress, Mariette Hartley, at a nearby table. I was thrilled seeing her in person, but I maintained my cool and only watched her, awestruck, from a distance. Apparently, her co-star, Michael Douglas, was not due to film that day. (Shucks!)

Soon after we met, Hunt took me to Phoenix to meet his mother, Virginia Hunt Brannen Freund. She and Hunt's father, Carlton Brannen, had divorced when Hunt was a child, but they had an amicable relationship, even going on trips together with their respective spouses. Hunt's mother was a lovely, gracious lady, who exemplified her upbringing. She had been educated at a finishing school in Switzerland and traveled globally with her famous father, George W. P. Hunt, who was the ambassador to Siam before he became governor of Arizona. Virginia was everything a girl could want in a mother-in-law—she was funny, smart, and hated housework: my kind of woman!

Shortly thereafter, we traveled to Kingman, Arizona, to meet his father and stepmother, a round dumpling of a woman who reminded me of my precious Grandma Blevins. Hunt's father was ill and dying of cancer, but he stole my heart from the moment we met. It was clear that Hunt's acorn of charm didn't fall far from the tree. When Hunt led me into his father's sickroom and introduced me, Mr. Brannen took my hand, looked at me with a wry grin, and said, "Why, she's as pretty as a speckled pup." I don't think I ever received a higher compliment. Sadly, we had to attend his father's funeral just a few months later.

Despite my rigorous upbringing—or perhaps because of it—I permitted Hunt to move in with me that fall. I was so crazy about him that I believed everything he told me. Also, it didn't hurt that he was from a prominent Arizona family.

The façade of lies began to crack when he received a birthday card that was signed by Mike, Karen, and Cole. He had told me about Mike and Karen—they were the children of his ex-wife from her first marriage—but I didn't know about Cole.

I asked him point blank, "Who is Cole?"

After some hesitation, he offered, "Oh, he's their dog."

I persisted, and finally he admitted that Cole was his son by his not-yet-ex-wife, Linda, and that he and she were still married, but separated. Convinced there was still more to be told, I continued to question him, despite his attempts to wriggle and equivocate. The story that ensued was tragic, and to someone schooled in psychology, it might explain his behavior.

He finally confessed that he had been married before. He and his first wife had lived in Phoenix and had two children, Hunt Junior and Cheryl. Little Hunt had died when he was a toddler, and his death had negatively affected the marriage. The couple had divorced, and Hunt had left Arizona.

Hunt's second wife, whom he had met in a bar after he moved to California, had had two children from a previous marriage, Mike and Karen, and two with Hunt—Scottie and Cole. Scottie, sad to say, had also died as a toddler. It seemed that Hunt carried a genetic disorder that caused each of his first-born children to die of heart defects before they were five years of age. Consequently, he had had a vasectomy after little Scottie's death so that he would never again pass on the defective gene. I was disappointed that he and I would never be able to have children, but as things turned out, it was a blessing.

The loss of his children had jolted his moral compass and had left him with a truly amoral attitude toward all things. We were having brunch in a popular restaurant one Sunday when the hostess guided a large group of people, obviously churchgoers, to the table next to us. They said a prayer before eating, and this must have triggered Hunt's anger, because when we got up to leave after our meal, he leaned over their table and said in a loud voice, "God sucks!" I was stunned and mortified! I wished a hole would open and I'd go through the floor.

After confessing the true state of his marriage, Hunt left my condo and moved into a boarding house with Don, another worker at Interstate Electronics, also a gifted artist. Don once gave us a large oil painting of a Navajo Indian boy. I still have that painting in my Arizona home. Hunt said he was going to seek a divorce from his wife, and then we could be married. But I never knew what was true and what was not. I was so out of my mind with lust and jealousy. Sometimes I would see his vehicle—or one that looked like his—and follow it all over Orange County.

At Easter, 1974, Hunt came with me to visit my family, bringing his eight-year-old son, Cole, with us. There was some constraint on my parents' part in meeting Hunt, but my folks adored his son. My father took me aside and told me why my mother was not very welcoming. He confessed that Mom's mother, my Grandma Dorsam, had been seduced in 1919 by the eldest son of the family she worked for in Oklahoma, and she had become pregnant. The man, Paul Smith, was a musician in a dance band.

Mr. Smith, my birth grandfather, had impregnated my grandmother, married her so as to give the child (my mother) a legitimate status, and then abandoned her. My grandmother returned to her home state of Indiana and married a well-off but brain-damaged farmer, my step-grandfather Dorsam. According to Mom's story, his mentally ill mother had deliberately dropped him on his head from a second-story window when he was a baby. My mother had sought out her birth father only after her mother's death.

Aha! Now I understood!

Knowing all this helped me realize the motive behind my Mom's attitude whenever I had the opportunity to engage in any behavior that seemed to match what had happened to her mother. It explained her agitation and proscription against my singing with the band in Chicago.

She obviously didn't want her daughter to suffer the same fate as her mother. Again, she was ruled by her concern with what everyone else might think. She didn't see that society had evolved and the old "norms of behavior" had changed—somewhat.

Hunt obtained his divorce and moved back in with me in the fall of 1974. His son, Cole, would visit us most weekends, and we had lots of fun with him, building model railroad cities and playing games. One of our favorite television shows was *Monty Python's Flying Circus*. When the movie *Monty Python and the Holy Grail* came out, we took Cole to see it. We were all laughing hysterically, until the castle scene—the one with the grail-shaped neon sign on top. The young virgins of the castle were being very unhelpful, giggling and cavorting, when Sir Galahad became angry at their behavior and threatened to spank them. The head virgin then clapped her hands and said, "Oh goody! First the spanking, and then the oral sex!"

I was aghast! I couldn't decide whether to clap my hands over Cole's ears or simply ignore the scene, hoping he wouldn't understand. No such luck. That innocent little face looked up at me and said, "What's oral sex?"

Thinking rapidly and scrambling for a G-rated explanation, I said, "Oh, it just means kissing." That seemed to satisfy him. Once again, I felt empathy with—and sympathy for—all mothers.

Hunt would leave me now and then, claiming that he needed his space, moving back into the boarding house with Don, his coworker friend. Finally, I told him that I could no longer accept things the way they were and I was never going to see him again. (My "voice" was getting a little stronger.) I went home to Indiana to visit my brother, Bill, his family, and my parents at Christmas, 1974.

By this time, my brother was enjoying success at Purdue and had a lovely home in the country outside Lafayette. His second daughter, Melissa Marie, was a beautiful child who was now in her terrible twos. When she came in from playing outside, my sister-in-law, Barb, told her, "Hang your coat in the hall closet."

Melissa, whom we all called Missy, gave the typical two-year-old response, "No!"

Her mother gave her "the look," and Missy dropkicked the coat into the closet like a Green Bay Packer. All mothers seem to know how to use "the look." Do they learn that from a manual?

Hunt called me at my brother's house and said he couldn't live without me, and we could marry as soon as I returned to California.

We married on May 23, 1975, at the home of my boss, Kenneth Klofkorn (the administrator of Western State University), on a hilltop overlooking Irvine, California. It was a non-traditional ceremony, typical of the 1970s. Hunt drew the pictures on the hand-made invitations, which included a verse of the song "Wildwood Flower": "I will twine and will mingle my raven black hair, with the roses so red and the lilies so fair."

He depicted me wearing a homespun-type dress and playing a guitar, and he drew himself dressed in backwoods garb of overalls and patched shirt, playing a fiddle. I wrote the words on the invitation, as well as our wedding vows: "Please join us in an evening of music and laughter, joy and happiness, as we twine and mingle our two lives into one by celebrating our marriage."

A Sweet Adelines barbershop quartet, The Matchmakers, sang "One Song," and a young man from the college, Mike, played guitar and sang, "Follow Me." My friend, Helen, was matron of honor and Hunt's friend, Don, was best man. The dress was typical of the seventies: I wore a long, off-white dress—to exemplify my less-than-lily-white status—with flowers twined in my hair, which was brown, not raven black. Hunt wore a tan corduroy jacket and tight blue jeans, rather like the outfit he was wearing when we met. (It reminded me of the old joke: "How can you tell if it's a formal wedding in Montana? The groom wears clean blue jeans.")

One of the best things that Hunt did for me was to teach me to play the guitar and the auto-harp. At our wedding reception, we entertained the guests by playing and harmonizing together such songs as "Wildwood Flower," "The City of New Orleans," and "The House of the Rising Sun."

All the faculty and staff of Western State University were happy for me, but I suspect they had some premonition of things to come. One of the attorney faculty members wrote this on his good-luck card: "Please accept the enclosed as a token of my best wishes for your wedded bliss. I was going to give you a copy of the latest edition of the casebook on community property, but you can always check that out of the library!"

We had a spectacular honeymoon in Mexico City, visiting the ancient pyramids and Indian ruins, the museums, the formal gardens, and the *Ballet Folklorico*. Hunt would disappear mysteriously from time to time. Later, I often wondered what he did when he disappeared. Did he pick up some woman, even on our honeymoon?

Hunt's officemate and good friend, Bob, and his wife invited us to dinner one evening. The other guests included the wife's girlfriend and her date, Stafford Repp, the actor who played the part of Police Chief O'Hara on the television show, *Batman*, starring Adam West. By the way, Mr. Repp did *not* speak with an Irish brogue in real life. I was so nervous meeting him that I spilled the dessert strawberries on the white linen tablecloth. Once again, my behavior was so typical of my nerdiness.

The couple needed extra money for some reason, so they sold their piano to me, a Baldwin Acrosonic that I still have today. Friends have told me it's one of the best spinet pianos ever made and I've been offered a great deal of money for it, but I'm reluctant to let it go. I'm saving it for the children of my nieces—provided they have inherited the music gene and develop an interest in piano playing.

I continued to have some suspicions that Hunt was not a faithful mate. He would still disappear from time to time with no explanation as to his whereabouts or activities. One weekend, he said he was going to see his stepmother in Kingman, Arizona. I believed him, against my better judgment. Come to think of it, there was very little better judgment in the entire relationship.

Because the marriage seemed to be in trouble, I suggested we see a marriage counselor. We had a joint session, and then the counselor asked to see Hunt alone. After that session, the therapist saw me by myself and told me that Hunt was, in his expert opinion, a pathological liar. The doctor suggested that the best thing I could do was seek a divorce.

The next Friday evening Hunt did not come home from work. He also didn't come home on Saturday. I was frantic, and checked with the police and local hospitals to see if he'd been in an accident and rendered unconscious. I even called his widowed stepmother in Kingman to see if he'd gone to see her again. Mrs. Brannen said she hadn't seen him since his father's funeral two years before, and she begged me to ask him to come visit her. (Aha! Another lie!)

Hunt finally dragged in Sunday evening looking exhausted, his hair and clothing disheveled. I was in tears as I related how I'd tried to trace his whereabouts, convinced that something must have happened to him. He then admitted that he had stopped for a drink at his favorite watering hole after work on Friday and met a woman who invited him to come home with her. He'd spent the weekend with the woman, and he seemed incredulous that I was so upset.

The next morning after he went to work, I packed all his belongings in a few plastic trash bags, put them beside the driveway, and then changed the locks on the doors. I called him at his place of work and told him not to bother coming back except to pick up his things that were in front of the house. (My "voice" had appeared momentarily!)

I filed for divorce *in pro per*, meaning that I would represent myself in the divorce proceedings. The professors at the law school helped me with the paperwork, so I was prepared for my divorce hearing. The bailiff swore me in, the judge asked the expected questions, and I gave the textbook answers.

The judge finally asked me, "Would seeking the advice of a marriage counselor be of help in saving this marriage?"

I replied, "The marriage counselor is the one who advised me to get a divorce."

The judge banged his gavel and decreed, "Divorce granted. See the bailiff."

When I stopped at the bailiff's desk to pay the required fee, he sniffed the air and said, "Mmm, Shalimar perfume! You won't be single for long."

As I was writing this chapter, I began to think that my experience might serve as an example for other women. What pithy lesson could I provide for those who might find themselves in similar situations? How about this: "If the man cheats on someone else while wooing you, expect that eventually he will cheat on *you* while wooing someone else."

To celebrate my freedom, I booked passage on the *Pacific Princess* for a cruise to the Mexican Riviera. I was assigned a roommate, Shirley—a forty-something recently widowed lady from Seattle whose children had given her the cruise to help her recover from her grief. I couldn't decide if I wanted to recover from grief or celebrate emancipation.

My roommate and I were assigned to a dining table with four twenty-something single girls who were loads of fun. We went everywhere together, and other guests on the ship soon identified us as "the girls." The ship would fix box lunches for us to take as we explored each of the ports: Cabo San Lucas, Mazatlan, and Puerto Vallarta. One young, single Burmese man (very short and not at all handsome) who was an architect from San Francisco attached himself to our group and followed us around like one of Bo Peep's sheep.

There were very few single men on the ship—at least, none over four feet ten inches—but the ship's British officers did their duty and saw to it that we had escorts for dancing. I must confess I did have a momentary emotional breakdown when the band played that schmaltzy song that was so popular at the time, "Feelings." But, if you listen to the words to the song, you begin to realize that you don't *need* to have those feelings—it's a choice.

When the cruise was over, Shirley thanked me for being her roommate and for getting her to laugh and have fun. She said, "You've helped me see that perhaps life is worth living after all."

All six of us vowed to stay in touch with each other after the cruise, but as such things usually happen, we did not. Except—the short Burmese architect kept writing to me. Since he only came up to my nose, I didn't encourage him.

Did the experience with Hunt finally convince me that men were no damn good and I should buy a chastity belt? I certainly felt that way at the time; I was sure that true love was not in my future. But I still had my cat, and the belief that, as Shirley had said, "Life may be worth living, after all."

# CHAPTER 19

⸱⸱❀⸱⸱

# UP, UP, AND AWAY . . .

I love weddings, especially honeymoons.
The trouble is, as soon as the honeymoon is
over, they want to come in the house!"
—Roseanne Barr, Comedienne

First, I must apologize to Robert Fulgham, the author of *All I Really Need to Know I Learned in Kindergarten* (© 1989, Ivy Books), because I say, "All I really need to know I learned in a flying lesson." Unfortunately, it took me too long to learn my lessons.

The first time I married, I married for love. However, love went south (and east and west), so the next time I simply married for good old-fashioned lust. That husband was the greatest lover I ever had encountered. Once I woke up to the fact that he was also a great lover to every woman on the block, I decided I needed to marry for security the next time.

Another bad decision

I had reached what I felt was the pinnacle of my career. I was the director of admissions and records of the largest law school in California. I had a huge staff of young men and women who were hard working, fun loving, and conscientious. We were the pioneers of automated educational record keeping, and our innovations in computing were featured in IBM's national magazine. I was invited by Big Blue to share

140

our experiences in a speech at a national seminar for IBM System Three users, held at the company headquarters in Atlanta, Georgia. The IBM executives gave me a gift to commemorate the occasion—a delicate, life-size crystal apple on a small pedestal with an engraved inscription on a brass plate, "An Apple for the Teacher."

I was finally enjoying career success; I owned a condominium in Anaheim, California, overlooking Interstate 91, and currently I was unencumbered by romance. At night, I could imagine that the traffic on the interstate was actually the surf pounding on my shore.

One day, shortly before Valentine's Day in 1978, one of the young women in our admissions office came into my private office and announced, "There's a gentleman at the counter asking to see you. He says he's a personal friend."

Curious, I walked into the outer office and saw a dark-haired gentleman of a certain age and of medium build, who stood as though he had a ramrod fused to his spine. It was George, the ex-husband of Shirley, one of my former barbershop quartet members. I was surprised to see him, especially since I'd heard that he and his wife had divorced after a contentious battle and he'd moved away. We chatted for a while, and he asked me to lunch the next day. I didn't think there would be any harm in that. He was considerably older than I was and he didn't necessarily "float my boat." Nevertheless, a free lunch is a free lunch.

*Lesson: Maybe it's true that no flight lasts forever, but it's a good idea to try out a few airlines before you settle on one that lifts your flaps.*

The next day was Saturday, and George picked me up at my house, well before noon. He asked me if I liked Mexican food. I retorted, "Doesn't everybody—especially in California?" He drove to Fullerton Airport, and led me to a sleek Cessna 172 airplane.

I asked, "Where exactly is this Mexican food—Tijuana?"

He smiled smugly, "San Diego."

I had mixed feelings. Sure, I wanted to go to San Diego and eat Mexican food for lunch, but I wanted all my body parts to be in their original location while I did so.

The flight was without incident, the lunch was delicious, and I was beginning to change my idea about security not being a reason to hitch my wagon to a star, even one that was burning a little low. George was thirteen years older than I was, but he had two pensions—one from the US Navy and one soon to come from Interstate Electronics. He had no alimony to pay, possibly because his ex-wife had left him for another man—or else he had a great lawyer.

And yes, George met my ex-husband, Hunt, at Interstate Electronics one day when Hunt was visiting George's officemate. My picture was on George's desk, and when Hunt saw it, he asked, "Is that Mary Ellen?"

"Yes—how do you know her?"

"I was once married to her." (It's a small world after all.)

We'd been dating for about six weeks when George approached me with his plan: "I think we should date for six months, live together for six months, and then get married."

"No, I've been down that path before. I'm not going to live with anyone without making it legal."

We were married the next month, on April 28, 1978, in the chapel at El Toro Marine Base. The wedding party was small, but the ceremony was quite lovely, as could be expected in a military wedding. My friend, Helen, was matron of honor (yet again), and George's brother-in-law, Dick, was best man. I could bite out my tongue, but the chaplain insisted on using the ritual in the English Book of Common Prayer, and I gagged a little but I did promise to honor and *obey*. (That first-grade Scotch tape was still on my mouth!) I'm sure God will forgive me, under the circumstances.

For the first few months, we lived in my Anaheim condominium. My cat, Turd, had survived two marriages and five homes, but he must have known more than I did about what was about to happen in this one, because one day he disappeared, never to return. I always had the suspicion that George may have had something to do with Turd's disappearance.

George owned some property in northern California near a small community, Brownsville, about a mile high in the foothills of the Sierra Nevada. A group of ten retired flyers had purchased acreage, then built a dirt runway and clustered their doublewide mobile homes around the landing strip. I almost recanted my marriage decision when, in describing the property, George said, "I'm going to set up an inner and an outer perimeter to protect us against the black hordes that are likely to attack from Los Angeles." I guess George came by his redneck bigotry honestly; he was born and raised in Texas.

I was reluctant to give up my career at Western State University in order to move to Brownsville, and I wanted to seek a similar position, at the same or better salary—perhaps at the University of California at Sacramento. George said I didn't stand a chance. (Never tell a Capricorn she cannot do something!) I applied for the position of director of financial aid at UC Sacramento and after a highly successful interview, I was offered the job—at a higher salary, I might add. However, I turned them down when I realized the daily commute from Brownsville to Sacramento was much too long. Nevertheless, I think I showed George that he should never tell me I couldn't do something!

On the other hand, shortly after we moved to Brownsville I learned that I should be very careful in defying George. One day while making our bed, I discovered a gun under his side of the mattress. Suddenly, that vow to "honor and obey" took on an entirely new dimension.

Each house in our little community boasted a hangar instead of a garage enclosing at least one, sometimes two, private airplanes, ranging from hand-built vintage mini-planes to sleek twin-engine aircraft. George had three planes: a Smith mini-plane, a V-tail Beechcraft Bonanza, and part ownership of a high-wing Cessna 150. All the husbands were pilots, either private or retired military, and had kept their certifications current. The wives nicknamed the husbands the "Brownsville Air Reserve Force," or BARF, for short.

> *Lesson: No matter how great you think your life is going, inevitably some things just make you want to throw up.*

Speaking of throwing up—George insisted that I cook Thanksgiving dinner for our new neighbors the first November we lived in Brownsville. Now, there were two problems with that. First, you may remember that, to paraphrase Richard Nixon, "I am not a cook!" Second, we were living at the time in a small travel trailer while our house was being built, and the only cooking appliance I had was a travel-size stove and an oven the size of a breadbox. I was in the miniscule trailer kitchen, and the guests were gathered in the small plastic covered, screened-in room that George had erected next to the tiny trailer and heated with a woodstove in winter.

The turkey seemed to be done, so I carefully lifted it from the oven. However, as I did, the trailer heaved a sigh, moved slightly, and I momentarily lost my balance. The turkey decided to fly into the afterlife, landing on the carpeted floor with a soft thud. Embarrassed, I quickly peeked into the anteroom to see if anyone noticed. They didn't. So, I scooped the turkey off the floor, made sure there was no lint clinging to it, and plopped it on a platter on the table. We had a great dinner, and I never bothered to explain the stain on the carpet.

Because we were often in the air, and because he was considerably older, George insisted I learn to fly our Beechcraft Bonanza. After all, I should be able at least to land the aircraft if he were to suffer some sort of nasty attack while at the controls—heart, stroke, gastro-intestinal, or random act of kindness (which would have been rare, indeed.)

I was absolutely against the idea of flying lessons. I wasn't sure which would be worse—dying in a plane crash or suffering the humiliation of taking lessons in the air from my husband. But George assured me that learning to operate an airplane was no more complex than learning to operate a sewing machine.

My witty, snappy response was, "Yes, but when I make a mistake on my sewing machine I don't risk spreading my brains over three counties in Northern California."

Despite my kicking and screaming, I found myself one morning at the dual controls of the Cessna 150. George approached the plane with a quick-time swagger, reminiscent of the bantam roosters strutting in my grandmother's chicken coop. The tasks of run-up, taxi, and takeoff were accomplished without incident. (Well, to be honest, George did that part.)

When we reached cruising altitude, George handed the yoke (control wheel) to me. "Watch the little airplane," he shouted, "Keep it level!" The little airplane was the attitude gauge and it indicated whether you were climbing, descending, or on a straight and level course. The noise in the cockpit made shouting a necessity. Of course, George remained calm throughout—that was one of his most irritating qualities.

"Shut up!" I whispered back to him, choking the yoke and vowing that one of us was going to die before sunset. "I'm more interested in keeping this *big* damn airplane level and in one piece." Those wedding vows to honor and obey meant nothing at six thousand feet.

> *Lesson: All too often, we spend too much of our time keeping an eye on the little airplane, the nitty-gritty irksome details of daily life, when we'll get a much better view and enjoy the ride a lot more if we keep our focus on the big airplane picture.*

"Keep your eye on the horizon. There's an aircraft at three o'clock," shouted George.

"What do I care?" (Dare I say it?) "It's only nine-thirty!"

It probably comes as no surprise that George and I divorced after fewer than four years of marriage—and three flying lessons. After all, not many marriages can survive a husband-wife/teacher-student relationship, especially if the teacher is a private pilot. Remember that delightful joke about the difference between a cactus and a cockpit, and the location of the pricks? (With a cactus, all the pricks are on the *outside*.)

One of the few things I did enjoy while living in Brownsville was the opportunity to star in a community theater production of *Frankie and Johnny*, in which I played a bordello madam. (No comments, please, about typecasting.) At the cast party dinner following the final performance, I was soaking up the accolades and feeling the special thrill that always accompanies a well-played performance, when George tapped me on the arm and announced, in a loud and indifferent voice, "Your mom called while you were at the theater. Your aunt Bertha died."

I couldn't believe any person could be so cruel as to make such an announcement in so heartless a fashion. I was heartbroken, not only by my dear aunt's passing, but also by the sure knowledge that this was the meanest man who ever drew a breath. I managed to get through the event without sobbing, but I had a feeling that this was the beginning of the end.

In December 1981, I went home to visit my parents in Indiana for the Christmas holidays; George refused to go with me because he hated my parents. That was hard for me to understand because George was closer to my mother's age than to mine. But I soon discovered the real reason for his decision to stay at home. Shortly before I returned to California, I received a call from my neighbor, Wanda.

Wanda sounded hesitant when she said she had something to tell me, and she didn't know how to put it delicately. Finally, she blurted out, "George has run off with Arlene!" Arlene was another flier's wife in our small, close-knit community.

Hardly a heartbeat of time passed before I blurted out, "Thank God!"

They always say the wife is the last to know. Apparently, George and Arlene had been having an affair almost under my nose for the previous six months or more.

At the time, I belonged to the San Jose Chorus of Sweet Adelines, commuting there every Tuesday and staying overnight with one of the members. Two friends from the chorus, Joyce and Liz, accompanied me to the courthouse for the divorce court appearance. George had engaged in so many underhanded shenanigans, such as hiding money and attempting to cover up his unfaithfulness, that I was glad I'd engaged the services of a competent lawyer. However, my only objective was freedom. Not only did the judge grant my freedom and declare my income from the sale of my Anaheim townhouse condo as my own personal property, but he also added six months of spousal support and one-half interest in our Brownsville house and property. I was delirious. I exited the courtroom, did a perfect heel click, and said in a voice that rang throughout the courthouse, "Champagne for everyone!"

To this day, one of the things I hate about flying is the cavalier and sometimes God-like attitude of private pilots. Their favorite cry of triumph upon landing a plane is, "Well—cheated death once again!" A private pilot's definition of a landing is "a controlled crash," and a good landing is described as "any one you walk away from."

George didn't quite walk away from one of his landings, however. A few years after the divorce, my friend, Helen, told me he'd crashed his Bonanza on takeoff and was severely burned about the groin and buttocks. I couldn't stop my quick response, "How terrible! George has completely lost his identity, because his ego was in his crotch and his brain was in his butt!"

Alexander Pope said, "A little knowledge is a dangerous thing." Well, I learned just enough about flying to be dangerous, at least to my own equanimity. When I'm flying as a passenger on a private plane now, I watch the gauges like a cat stalking a cockroach, and I question the skills of the pilot when I see any abnormality. I've become especially obsessed with exhaust gas temperature. Although I'm not quite sure what a too-high exhaust gas temperature signifies in terms of potential danger, I'm convinced it indicates imminent death if it deviates from the norm.

When I fly on commercial flights, of course, there's no opportunity to remind the pilots of their duties in the cockpit, but I do work from my own in-flight checklist. I note how well the pilot follows the approach pattern to the airport, whether the landing gear is lowered at the appropriate point, and if the flaps are extended at the correct angle on approach. Upon touchdown, I count how many times my teeth rattle to judge the smoothness of the landing. As I exit the plane, often the pilot will come out of his little tin hut and say to me, "I hope you enjoyed your flight."

My response: "And I hope you keep an eye on your exhaust gas temperature."

*Lesson: Never smart off to a commercial airline pilot. He has the right to divorce you from your life as a free woman.*

The Beechcraft Bonanza is a fast airplane. Flight instructors drone endlessly to student pilots, "Think ahead of the airplane." In life, we tend to get bogged down in what's happening at the moment, or at least what is on our to-do list for the day. Our lives go by at speeds even greater than that of a Beechcraft Bonanza, and we often arrive at destinations we didn't plan for, or at least sooner than we anticipated.

*Lesson: Failure to think ahead of the airplane could result in a crash and burn farther down the skyway of life, because we might get there before we're ready.*

It should come as no surprise that never again did I get behind the yoke of a private plane. By the way, I also gave up sewing—both are too dangerous. However, I did not give up on husbands and was fortunate enough later to fall in love with and marry a man whose idea of flying high was to order another glass of champagne at Sunday brunch!

Just one final word of caution:

*Lesson: Never forget to check your exhaust gas temperature—you never know when someone else will be aware of it.*

*Footnote*: In 2005, George's ex-wife, Shirley—who had retired to Arizona with her wonderful new husband—called to tell me that George had passed away. During our conversation, we shared similar tales of woe concerning our marriages to the man. She revealed that after she had walked out on him, he had picked up her small Chihuahua dog and threw it against the wall in anger, killing it instantly. In retrospect, my feelings of George as evil personified were justified.

# PART III

---●◈●---

# REFRAIN

(A sadder but wiser girl reprograms
herself and finds her lost voice)

# CHAPTER 20

⚬❋⚬

# HAIL, HAIL TO OLD PURDUE

Perplexity is the beginning of knowledge.
—Kahlil Gibran

I had been knocked for the proverbial loop when my third husband, George, abandoned me in northern California, running off with my next-door neighbor in the middle of a winter snowstorm, leaving me penniless and homeless. (Cue the violins playing "Hearts and Flowers"!)

Two of the gals in my barbershop quartet, Jean and Kathy, were members of the San Jose Chorus of Sweet Adelines and quickly assured me, "Don't worry! Our director, Pat L., has a spare bedroom and will take you in until you decide what to do."

Of course, Pat didn't know me, other than as the lead in the quartet, the West Coast Connection, that she had sometimes coached. But she opened her heart and her home to me without hesitation. I didn't want to mooch off her, so I agreed to stay with her *only* if I could serve as her *au pair*—a maid/cook/dishwasher/child minder.

As I've said before, I'm not a very good cook, but Pat had a closet full of family-tested recipes, so I attempted to prepare edible meals for the family. Pat's son, Kevin, her only child still at home, was fourteen years of age and really didn't need any minding. Kevin was always in

151

and out of the house with his friends and his dog, Prudence, a lovable German shepherd.

One day I dashed out to the grocery store for some last minute items for dinner, locking the front door behind me. I thought Kevin was in his room doing his homework. But as a matter of fact, he was outside with Prudence, working in the back yard. What happened next was worthy of a television sitcom script.

When Kevin tried to enter the house, he found the door locked. Being a resourceful teenager, he climbed onto the lower roof of their split-level home in an attempt to enter the house through one of the upstairs bedroom windows. A neighbor spied him on the roof and called the police, thinking a thief was burgling her neighbor's home. Kevin was unsuccessful in finding an open window, so he climbed back down and ran around the side of the house, directly into a .357 Magnum pointed at his nose. (I really don't know what type of gun it was—Kevin simply said it was *big!*) The policeman holding the gun made him "assume the position," hands on the wall, and feet spread apart while he was searched and questioned.

Kevin kept insisting, "This is my house! I live here!" But his pleas fell on deaf ears. He finally pointed at Prudence and said, "That's my dog! Here, Prudence; here, girl!"

Prudence promptly sat on her haunches and tilted her head to one side as if to say, "Who are you? I don't know you."

Kevin somehow convinced the policeman that this was, indeed, his home—and his dog. When I returned, Kevin was sitting on the front steps of the house with Prudence, both of them grinning from ear to ear, eager to tell me the story—which they never have let me forget to this day! That's okay, because I never will forget Pat and her family. They brought a total stranger into their home and made her a lifelong friend and devotee.

Sophie Tucker once sang a wonderfully bawdy song, "Life Begins at Forty." Well, I was forty-one, contemplating what to do with the rest of my life, staring at middle age. What do you do when you are perplexed and don't know which way to turn? I don't know about most people, but I go back to my roots. So I hightailed it to Indiana to spend Christmas with my brother and his family. My parents made the trip north from their retirement home in Cherokee Village, Arkansas, and we all spent the holidays at my brother Bill's home outside Lafayette, Indiana.

While we were enjoying a delightful Christmas together, Bill—now a full professor at Purdue—said to me, "You always wanted to get your doctorate, and Purdue has a world-class school of management, so why don't you enroll there? And by the way, Mom and Dad, the house next door is for sale."

Barb, Bill's wife, bundled me up and drove me through the usual Indiana winter snow in her four-wheel drive Chevy Tahoe so I could immediately submit an application to the PhD program at Krannert Graduate School of Management. That same weekend, Mom and Dad made an offer on the house next door.

I returned to Pat's house after Christmas to contemplate my options. Should I return to Indiana and work for a doctorate at Purdue? And was there any future for me in California? Pat, who was born and raised in Kokomo, forty-five miles east of Lafayette, had earned her undergraduate degree in engineering at Purdue University. She spoke highly of the university, but she preferred that I attend nearby Stanford University for my doctoral degree. Perhaps she really wanted me to stay close so I could continue working as her *au pair.*

Meanwhile, my quartet, West Coast Connection, was performing regularly for audiences in and around San Jose and Santa Cruz with a great deal of success. The other gals—Kathy, Opal, and Georgina—were good friends, great fun, and excellent singers; and they didn't want me to leave them or the quartet. Pat thought we had a good chance to win the Region 12 Quartet Competition coming up in March. So, once again, not exactly taking control of my own life, I decided to let fate determine my destiny. If the quartet should win the contest, I'd stay in California. Otherwise, I would go "back home again to Indiana." The West Coast Connection quartet sang beautifully in the contest—and came in *second.*

The next week I received a telephone call from Purdue. I was accepted into the doctoral program in organizational behavior at

Krannert Graduate School of Management, with the offer of a graduate assistantship that would pay my out-of-state tuition plus a monthly stipend for living expenses. Mom and Dad's offer on the house next door to Bill was accepted, and I had to admit that "somebody up there" must have been directing things, for a change.

Between Christmas 1981 and May 1982, my target date for returning to Indiana, I remained with Pat and her family in San Jose. In order to earn some money before starting my doctoral studies, I took a part-time job with Kelly Girls, a firm that supplied temporary office workers. I suppose I was more experienced than the average Kelly Girl because, at every assignment, the firm where I was working temporarily asked me to join them permanently.

One of my assignments was at a large engineering company in the Silicon Valley—the name given to the area of California that was home to many computer and electronics firms. When my boss asked if I would be interested in working for the company full-time, I replied, "Thank you, but no. I'm going to begin my doctoral studies in organizational behavior at Purdue in a few months."

The man drew back in mock horror. "*Please* don't tell them about *our* organizational behavior!"

I received that reaction wherever I worked, whenever the staff discovered I would be studying for a doctorate in a behavioral science. Apparently, we all know our behavior needs help—we just don't know, or don't care, how to fix it. Lucky for me, I would soon enroll in an educational institution where I would be taught by learned people who *did* know how to fix behavior, and the behavior that was in the greatest need of fixing was—*mine!*

# CHAPTER 21

---•❈•---

# ON THE ROAD AGAIN

You're the mate that fate had me created for.
—Song, "That Old Black Magic"

When George left me, I packed up my own furniture and personal belongings, and friends helped me move them into a storage facility in Marysville, California. When I was accepted to Purdue's doctoral program, my sixty-six-year-old father swallowed his fear—it was his first airplane flight—and flew to San Francisco to help me move. With the help of my friends, we packed all my household belongings into a rental truck, attached my Ford Granada to the truck, loaded the car with my clothing hung on a rod in the back seat, and headed east.

Daddy and I stayed the first night in a motel in Sacramento. During the night, thieves broke into the truck by smashing the side-vent window on the passenger side. They stole a large metal box, similar in size to a moneybox, which was lying on the front seat. I'm sure the crooks were surprised when they got back to their thieves' lair and broke open the box to find that it contained, not money, but my entire collection of barbershop quartet cassette tapes. Fortunately, they must have thought the car held only clothing, because they left it untouched. They didn't see the color television set that was buried under the clothes.

I made a quick call to the rental firm to report the incident, and then we continued east to Salt Lake City, where the company had a repair facility. They quickly replaced the broken window, and we were soon on the road again to Cheyenne, Wyoming.

After spending the night in Cheyenne, we headed east once more, climbing upward toward the Great Divide of the Rocky Mountains. Halfway up the mountain, the truck inexplicably stopped. My father had a heart condition, so I tried very hard to avoid hysterics and thereby cause him to get overexcited.

I told him, "Don't worry. There's an exit just ahead. I'll walk up there and find a telephone to call a repair shop."

Daddy looked at me, his eyes filled with unspoken anxiety. We both were thinking of the news report we'd heard the night before, about a couple who had been assaulted and killed when their vehicle broke down on this same Interstate highway.

I started walking up the hill. I hadn't gone more than fifty yards when a large semi-tractor-trailer pulled off the highway beside me. The driver leaned out the side window and asked, "You havin' trouble, ma'am?"

I told him that my father and I were going to Indiana and our rental truck had broken down. I pointed to the top of the hill. "I'm going to that exit and call the highway patrol for help."

He said, "Hop in and I'll take you up there."

My mind raced between thoughts of thankfulness and visions of violent mayhem. "Uh—thanks, and please don't be offended, but I don't feel comfortable getting into a vehicle with a stranger."

He smiled to show he had no hard feelings. "I understand completely, ma'am. Tell you what I'm gonna do. I'll radio the dispatcher for help."

I smiled, thanked him profusely, and walked back to relay the trucker's plan to Daddy—who by this time was white around the gills with fear.

Soon we saw the trucker headed back down the hill toward Cheyenne, after having turned around at the exit. He waved and gave us a thumbs-up sign. In less than an hour, he was driving up the mountain again and stopped by our truck to relate his good news.

"The company is sending up a tow truck to take your rig back to Cheyenne, and the highway patrol is gonna pick you up and take you to the nearest motel." And sure enough, we could see the tow truck and police car in the distance.

I couldn't find the words to tell him how grateful we were for his help. I just looked at him with tears in my eyes and said, "God bless you."

"My pleasure, ma'am. Take care, now." And with a blast of his horn, he rumbled onward, up the hill and over the Great Divide, like the Lone Ranger on his mechanical silver steed.

We did make a pretty picture on the way back to Cheyenne: a huge tow truck, towing a large rental truck, towing a clothing-filled four-door sedan, followed by a highway patrol car with two refugees in the back. By the way, in case you were wondering, there are *no* handles inside the doors in the backseat of a police car, at least in Wyoming.

The company fixed the truck problem overnight, and we were on our way the next morning. Surely this was the end of our troubles!

We stopped for lunch at a truck stop somewhere in Nebraska the next day, and after we had eaten and paid the bill, I inquired about a public telephone so that I could call ahead for motel reservations at our next overnight stop. I was directed outside to the rear of the restaurant where a pay telephone booth was perched in lonely isolation in the middle of a large patch of dirt and gravel. I put my purse up on the ledge inside the booth, made the call and the motel arrangements, and then walked back to the truck where Daddy was waiting. We headed onto the Interstate, feeling pretty good that everything seemed to be going well.

A few miles down the road, I reached for my purse to apply my lipstick after lunch, and was horrified to discover that my purse was gone! "Daddy! I must've left my purse in the restaurant. We've got to go back!" I was especially worried because I had more than one thousand dollars in travelers' checks in that purse.

It's a miracle my father didn't have a heart attack right then or leave me in the plains of Nebraska to fend for myself. But silently, and with his usual good humor, he turned around and drove back to the restaurant. I explained to the waitress that I must have left my purse at our table.

We looked there; no purse. I searched the women's restroom; no purse. I went outside to the telephone booth; no purse. I was just about to commit *hari kari* when my father pointed and said, "What's that?"

My purse was lying on the ground at the back of the telephone booth. We discovered that there was no glass in the booth's back wall, and when I'd put my purse on the ledge, it fell off through the open back and onto the ground, where it sat like a lonely prairie dog waiting to be rescued. Everything in the purse was intact. Once again, the guardian angels were hard at work.

We made it to Lafayette without further incident, and I moved my belongings into the house that Mom and Dad had purchased, next door to my brother's family. My parents had to wait a few months before moving in; it took that amount of time to sell their home in Arkansas and move their belongings to Lafayette.

Meanwhile, they insisted that I set up a studio apartment in the master bedroom suite and they would sleep in one of the other bedrooms. I furnished the space with my couch that made into a bed at night and a light bridge over the couch with side cabinets that served as bedside tables and lingerie drawers. I had a desk and two bookcases, an easy chair and floor lamp, two closets for my clothing, a built-in vanity and sink, plus a bathroom with shower. It was a *big* room. Best of all, there was space under the vanity sink to hide my wine purchases; Mom and Dad were teetotalers.

The rest of my California furniture was added to that which my parents brought from Arkansas, and we filled the house: three bedrooms, two bathrooms, living/dining room, family room/breakfast nook, kitchen, and, within the year, a sunroom that Daddy added to the back of the house. As one of the neighbors explained, "Somebody left a bunch of lumber at the back door and Bud just organized it into a room." A year later, Daddy built an adorable two-story red-painted barn beside the house as a workroom and storage shed.

Although my classes would not start until the fall of 1982, I audited a summer course in master's level statistical analysis because the dean of my program noted that I had no background in statistics. As I'm sure you know, research and statistical analysis are integral parts of any doctoral program of study.

That first day of summer school, I was feeling a bit anxious to be returning to school at my age. I parked in the students' parking garage and entered the elevator leading into the classroom building. Another student jumped into the elevator as the doors were closing. She had multi-colored hair and was dressed in a long, unevenly hemmed skirt that looked as though she'd pulled it hastily from the dirty laundry basket. I thought I was dressed appropriately in a knee-length slim skirt, white blouse, and gray blazer, carrying a leather briefcase—a farewell gift from my California friends. We looked each other over, head to toe. A cartoonist might have drawn a thought balloon over *both* our heads: "How disgusting!"

This event, and other things that were soon to happen, made me feel that I must be the oldest living graduate student at Purdue. Oh, there probably were students who were older—but they were no longer living! I'm sure their bodies were cluttering up the stacks at the library.

At first, I was a bit overwhelmed in the statistics class I audited that summer. I told the professor I wanted to take all the examinations and receive a grade, even though the official grade would be, "Audit." I worked hard. I took copious notes in shorthand—every word the professor said—and typed all my notes. When I stopped the professor after class one day to clarify a point he'd made, he saw my typed notes, complete with Greek *mu*, the symbol for mean or average. Taken aback, he raised his eyebrows in astonishment, "You *type* your statistics notes?!"

On the way out of the classroom, I overheard one of the younger students comment, "I hate older students—they are such brownnosers."

I should have turned to her and said, "I'd rather be a brownnoser than a red-neck, green-eyed monster." But I didn't. The Scotch tape was still on my mouth—metaphorically.

One of my first classes in graduate school was Strategic Management. After the mid-term, the professor, who was younger than I was (come to think of it, most of my professors were younger than I), called me to her office. Dr. Cynthia Lengnick-Hall spoke somewhat reluctantly: "Your test scores are excellent, and your case studies are superb. However, you never talk in class or enter into the discussions. I cannot give you an A grade for the course unless you begin to participate." Obviously, she hadn't noticed the Scotch tape on my mouth.

She didn't realize it, of course, but it was as though she had opened a door to my soul and given me permission—even encouragement—to speak. Finally, I started to join in the class discussions and even injected some of the humor I used in my quartet performances. The professor was trying to help us understand the principle of incrementalism, so I offered this story as a definition: "It's like that joke about the farmer who had a pig that could actually talk, but the pig had one leg missing. When asked what had happened to his leg, the farmer explained, 'Well, you wouldn't wanna butcher a pig that smart all at once, would ya?'" Incrementalism!

Some of the other students looked at me with that same you-have-two-heads look Bill Trowbridge and Jim R. had given me in the student union building at ISU in 1963.

As a graduate assistant, I worked with a tenure-track assistant professor, helping him with his research as well as teaching the recitation sections of his organizational behavior classes. He would give a lecture on Tuesday to all 240 students, and I would teach six sections of about forty students each on Thursday and Friday. The students, who were mostly nineteen-year-old Indiana farm kids, thought I was a bit strange. I suppose my years in California had changed me substantially from my midwestern upbringing.

On the first day of class, one of the students challenged the usefulness of the class, saying, "Isn't organizational behavior simply good, common sense?"

I responded with my usual cheekiness: "I agree that effective organizational behavior makes good sense. Unfortunately, it's not very common."

One of my fellow students in the organizational behavior program had just married in November, and he and his wife gave a party to which they invited several fellow graduate students and every single person they knew—that is, every person in their acquaintance who was not married. The hosts wore nametags labeled "Role Model." The party had a theme, "The Après Ski and Kite Club." All invited guests were requested to bring a bottle of champagne—and a kite. It was late

February, and everybody with a kite was in the field next to the house, champagne in hand, and flying high!

I couldn't help but be reminded of the story W.C. Fields once told about his ancestor: "My great-great-grandpa could have discovered electricity before Benjamin Franklin. But he was so poor he didn't have enough money to buy a kite. He had to go out and rent one. So there he was, out in the rain, hirin' a kite!" (It's funnier when you *hear* the story, rather than read it.)

I knew only two or three people at the party, and I am by nature a shy person, so it took a great deal of courage for me to introduce myself to a tall, dark, handsome man—six feet, four inches tall, with thick, wavy black hair, an Ernie Kovacs mustache, and twinkling brown eyes. He was surrounded by and towered over a group of women in the middle of the living room. I approached him, waited for an opportune moment, and introduced myself, "Hi! My name is Mary Ellen, and I'm a graduate student in the organizational behavior program at Purdue."

He grinned mischievously, "I'm Mike, I'm an engineer at Delco Electronics, and I have my own theory of organizational behavior. When someone asks me to do something, I say 'No!'"

Was this the man I had been waiting for? He was good looking, smart, *and* funny. But I had been down that road before. Perhaps, despite the saying about third time being charm, it was the *fourth* time that would be the charm.

# CHAPTER 22

---
·•✥•·
---

# MICHAEL ROWED
# THE BOAT ASHORE

I've had eight husbands . . . four
of them were mine.
—Mae West

I'd been studying diligently for more than four months and had
successfully completed my first semester with all As: Strategic
Management, Human Resources Management, Experiential
Learning, and Statistical Analysis for the Social Sciences. I was living
with my parents in my own private suite in their red-brick, black-
shuttered, ranch-style house under the oak trees in the country outside
Lafayette, Indiana, next door to my brother. Life was going well—for
a middle-aged broad with three ex-husbands.

One of my classmates had invited me to a party at his house, but I
thought I probably should study for my mid-term exams instead. My
parents, however, encouraged me to go to the party. Mom said, "You've
been working so hard, you deserve to give yourself a break." I couldn't
believe that Mom and I actually, finally, agreed about something. So
I decided to take an hour or so out of my study schedule to attend the
party.

As I left the house, Daddy called out, "Happy hunting!"

"Oh, Daddy, I'm not hunting anybody any more. I think my bait has gone bad."

But when Michael looked at me at the party and said, "I have my own theory of organizational behavior. When someone asks me to do something, I say 'No!'"—well, I was the one who was caught—hook, line, and sinker.

Later on during the party, someone suggested a sing-a-long might be fun, and the hostess asked, "Does anybody know how to play the piano?" I tentatively raised my hand, looked around, and saw I was the only one to offer. When I sat down on the piano bench, Michael plopped down beside me. As I played the music from the books on the piano, I'd nod to Michael and he would turn the pages for me. People were singing at the top of their lungs—just as though they might be close to the correct pitch.

When the party began to break up, most people were leaving in pairs, even though they might have arrived singly. Michael asked me to go out for coffee with him. We agreed to meet at the Sheraton Hotel bar, where we had a glass of wine instead, and we made a date for lunch the following Tuesday.

Michael came to my folks' house to pick me up for lunch, and I introduced him to my parents. Daddy told him how he'd said, "Happy hunting!" to me when I left for the party.

With a triumphant gesture, this handsome hunk responded from his six-feet-four-inches, two hundred twenty pounds, "And look! She bagged a moose!"

For our first date, Michael took me to lunch at the TGI Friday's restaurant in Indianapolis. My brother thought it was idiotic to drive an hour just to have lunch. That shows you the difference between someone who lives in rural Indiana and someone who had lived on the West Coast. In California, we thought nothing of driving sixty miles for lunch—it took longer than that to get from Orange County to Los Angeles County. And remember, for my first lunch with George, husband number three, we flew an airplane from Fullerton to San Diego for lunch!

The next day, Steve (the classmate who'd given the party) asked me if I had enjoyed myself and if I'd hooked up with anyone. I answered hesitantly, "Um—Yes, I think so." He told me he thought there were

163

several couples created at that party. I found out later that he counted Michael in at least two of them. A friend of Steve's wife had met Michael in a local bar the previous week and invited him to the party; she claimed him also.

Well, Michael must have made his choice quickly, because we had another date two days later, and from that day forward we were together at some point every day—or at least we talked to each other by telephone if we had to be separated for any reason.

Michael's fourteen-year-old son, Scott, was living with him in his loft apartment. Even though his ex-wife, Bobbi, and her new husband had legal custody of Scott, he was such a disruptive influence in her new marriage that she sent the boy back to live with his father.

We would often have dinner at Michael's apartment, and after dinner Scott would either do his homework or listen to music on his boom box, with earphones, so the adults could have a conversation without shouting. We discovered that if we wanted to go upstairs to the loft bedroom and "canoodle," Scott's earphones offered some measure of privacy. Like Pavlov's dog, the boy quickly learned his conditioned behavior. As he likes to tell the story, he would automatically put on the earphones as soon as I came into the apartment.

It was February when we met, and the romance progressed quickly. We were sitting in his living room after dinner—another great meal cooked by Chef Michael—sipping champagne and discussing our possible future, when Michael took my hand, looked me in the eyes, and said, "Our relationship will last as long as the champagne."

"Well, that doesn't exactly fill me with confidence, because we've been putting it away at a pretty good clip."

"Follow me." Michael led me to the storage closet at the back of his apartment. He opened the door with a flourish and pointed at the contents. There, in bubbly splendor, were cases and cases of champagne in boxes, stacked floor to ceiling. (Scott told me recently that he almost got a hernia carrying all those cases of champagne into the house.)

I could feel that hook, line, and sinker beginning to imbed itself in my heart.

"Michael, we need to do something I just learned about in my Human Resources class. We need a realistic job preview."

"A what?"

"A realistic job preview. It's how a company ensures that the people it employs won't be disappointed after they're on the job for a while and become dissatisfied with the deal they made on being hired."

"And this means what for us?"

I felt as though I was the professor enlightening my students. "I'll tell you what you can expect from me as your wife, and you will tell me what I can expect from you as a husband. We can agree to take each other as we are. That way, we won't be disappointed later because things turned out to be different from what we expected. In other words, there won't be any unmet expectations that we had created in the glow of romance. It's important that you know that I am going into the world of academe, which has a publish-or-perish paradigm, so I won't have time to be a normal housewife, cooking and cleaning and doing the laundry."

"That's okay. I love to cook, and I think I do the laundry as well as any woman."

I couldn't believe this man was real. "Honey, I'm yours!"

We were married two months later, on April 30, 1983. My brother's wife, Barb, was my matron of honor and Michael's son, Scott, was his best man. His daughter, Shari, was there with her husband, Joe. Shari was especially happy for her father—she'd been afraid he would marry some girl younger than *she* was. My mother had baked and decorated the traditional multi-tiered wedding cake, and my Sweet Adeline friends from the Lafayette chorus sang traditional wedding songs. Of course, I wore the traditional off-white and ecru.

At the reception following the ceremony, I sang a song from the musical, *Cabaret* (© 1963, The Times Square Music Publications Company), a song that seemed to summarize my love life up until then, "Maybe This Time":

> Maybe this time, I'll be lucky, maybe this time he'll stay,
> Maybe this time, for the first time, love won't hurry away.
> He will hold me fast. I'll be home at last,
> Not a loser anymore, like the last time and—the time before.
> by Fred Ebb and John Kander

Michael and I rented a two-story townhouse in the same apartment complex where he and Scott had lived. It had three bedrooms, three bathrooms, a living room, a family room with a corner fireplace, a dining area, a kitchen plus a breakfast bar, and a laundry room, so it would be large enough for the three of us. I furnished the apartment with all the furniture I had moved from California, minus a few pieces that looked better in Mom and Dad's place. Michael brought his few possessions: one couch, one bed, one dresser, one dining table with four side chairs, a lamp, a TV, and a toilet bowl brush. He loved to mimic the scene from Steve Martin's movie, *The Jerk*. He'd put on a silly grin and say, "All I need is this lamp and this toilet bowl brush." (By the way, I still have the lamp, but the toilet bowl brush is history.)

The two of us had many traits in common. For instance, we were both goal-oriented and penny-wise, which could be interpreted as frugal—or *tight!* We were both born under the same sign of the zodiac (Capricorn) so we were both determined in our approach to problems (some might say *stubborn*). I wanted to learn more about our deep-seated personalities. In Group Dynamics class I'd been introduced to David Kolb's learning style inventory—based on Carl Jung's personality assessment—so I was eager to try my hand at some psychological research.

Administration and analysis of the inventory revealed that Michael was oriented in the world of abstracts and rules and was likely to take immediate action in solving problems—a trait common to engineers or accountants. I, on the other hand, was more concrete or real world in orientation, and more likely to gather lots of information and then explore every possibility before taking action—so typical of teachers or human resource managers.

According to the learning style inventory, Michael was a converger: "There is only one answer and I have it." I was a diverger: "There are many paths to the correct answer and I take my time to study them all before deciding which one is best." Usually, what happened was this—while I was contemplating a problem and its possible solutions, Michael had done something already—his way, of course.

I wasn't as bright at being a stepparent as I was in the classroom, however. One of Scott's friends stopped by one morning so the two could walk to school together. They disappeared into his bedroom. I was working in my home office across the hall from Scott's room when I smelled something burning. Where had I experienced that peculiar odor before? Suddenly, it dawned on me: Marijuana! Scott was smoking marijuana in his bedroom! I didn't know what a stepparent should do in this situation, so I called Michael at work and told him what Scott and his buddy were doing. He demanded, "Put Scott on the phone."

I knocked on Scott's door. "Scott, your father would like to speak to you."

When Scott came to the phone, Michael simply told him, "Get to school, now! I'll deal with you later."

Apparently, there had been a few incidents even before I met Michael that caused this to be the proverbial straw that broke the camel's back. Scott had run into a pedestrian while riding his unlicensed motor scooter, given to him by his mother over Michael's objections. Also, the Purdue campus police had stopped him one night for being out after the curfew for teenagers. Subsequently, Michael and I were summoned, with Scott, to appear in family court to answer these charges, which, fortunately, were suspended.

Calling upon my one semester of behavioral study, I deduced that the boy was probably suffering the effects of his parents' divorce and his mother's remarriage, not to mention his being shuttled back and forth between the two. I bought and read several books about how to be an effective stepparent. Trying to learn how to be a stepparent from a book is tantamount to trying to learn any skill—say, mountain climbing—by reading about it. Unfortunately, you have to do it, and sometimes fail, in order to learn the skill.

Finally, Michael couldn't take any more of Scott's rebellious behavior, so he sent him back to live with his mother and stepfather, an action of which I disapproved. I was sure that acts of loving kindness would bring him around. Was I naïve or simply stupid? As it turned out, this was probably a good move for Scott, because his older stepbrothers could be better role models for him than his Lafayette schoolmates. On the other hand, I can't say the same for his mother as a role model. Her avaricious nature eventually resulted in Scott having eyes that were bigger than his purse; he always wanted, and bought, things that were more expensive than he could afford.

Michael and I quickly settled into our routine of work, study, and more work. His humor, as well as his never-ending encouragement of me, was instrumental in helping me complete my doctorate. Purdue paid my tuition plus a monthly stipend throughout the fall and spring semesters, but not during the summer. There were a few grants available, but they were very competitive and I didn't feel that I had any research idea worthy of a grant. Michael urged me not only to apply for the David Ross Grant, but also to write it as a two-part research project so I could get a grant for the following summer, as well.

Michael's faith in me was rewarded. I won the David Ross Grant two consecutive summers, studying group behavior in performance venues, using various Sweet Adelines choruses as subjects.

In gathering data for the study, we had to travel to Detroit in October 1983 to attend the international competition of Sweet Adelines. However, we had not made advance reservations. When we arrived at the hotel, we were told there were no more rooms available. Michael pulled out his General Motors business card and we were immediately assigned one of the best suites in the house. (Obviously, that was before GM's subsequent difficulties.)

Anyone who has suffered through four semesters of statistics will relate to some of the angst I experienced. My first introduction to PhD level statistics was in the class taught by B. J. Winer, the most-cited statistician in the world at that time. His students lovingly dubbed him "b sub j" Winer. I was terrified of him; his voice was gruff and he never smiled. He would require each student to meet with him individually after each exam. Many of them came out of his office in tears.

When it was my turn, I knocked on his office door with my heart in my mouth. He hardly looked at me as he said, "Good job," and handed me my test results. An A! He taught me so well that, at the end of the year, my fellow graduate students were calling me the SPSS Queen. SPSS is the acronym for the computer software—Statistical Program for the Social Sciences. (Sadly, Dr. Winer passed away a few years later, alone in his bachelor apartment.)

In Multiple Linear Regression Analysis, however, I was perplexed for a few weeks. The instructor, Professor Pilai (discoverer of the Pilai trace, an obscure statistical marker which bears his name), spoke with a thick, singsong East Indian accent. I was puzzled as he was explaining an equation on the board, saying, "As you can see . . ." Well, I didn't see what he was babbling about—something called the "resa jewels." I was frantically leafing through the book, looking for the meaning of "resa jewels," when it suddenly dawned on me. I exclaimed out loud, the Scotch tape now completely gone: "The re-*sid*-uals!" I noticed there were several faces reflecting thankfulness for my outburst, rather than annoyance. They hadn't understood him, either.

After two years in graduate study at Purdue, I'd completed all the required classes for my doctorate, with only my dissertation to research and write. However, I wanted to get out of student mode for a while, so I applied for and was hired to a position in the School of Health, Social Science, and Education (HSSE) as an admissions assistant. My task was to create the brochures and recruiting materials for all the departments in the school and correspond with Indiana high school guidance counselors about Purdue's liberal arts programs. In addition, I would set up college fairs and answer students' inquiries about the university and our programs in the social sciences.

While working full time, I also conducted the laboratory research that provided the data for my doctoral dissertation. Lest you think I was playing Igor to Dr. Frankenstein, the research was a simulated group work project that the students actually enjoyed. Each subject was placed in an isolated, soundproof booth and given instructions through a headset for tasks to complete on a computer. They were given feedback to simulate various work situations—individual or group tasks, directive or non-directive leadership—and then asked to complete a survey about their experiences. I analyzed the results and drew conclusions for my dissertation, entitled, "The Technological Imperative for Focus of Feedback."

To my mind, the results were not unexpected; workers want directive leadership when the job is complicated, and they want to be left alone when the task is self-explanatory. And nobody enjoys working in groups where their individual effort is not noticed. I suppose that's the purpose of scholarly research—to affirm what we already know very well.

After I'd been with HSSE a year, a tenure-track faculty position became available in the School of Technology at Purdue University, in the Department of Supervisory Management. I applied, together with about a hundred other hopefuls, one of whom was a man in my department at HSSE. Much to my coworker's chagrin, I was selected as one of the final six applicants. He claimed gender bias, as in affirmative action; I claimed superior credentials.

The Supervisory Management Department chairman called me and asked when I would like to schedule my interview. He gave me a choice of morning or afternoon, Tuesday through Thursday of the week of interviews. I thought for a moment, remembering what I had learned so far about human behavior.

"Dr. Barnes, I would like to be interviewed in the morning of Thursday, the last day, because people will be relatively alert in the morning, and the recency effect of being seen on the final day will work to my advantage."

He chuckled approvingly and assured me that my request would be honored. The faculty of the entire department interviewed me as a group. Everyone was quite pleasant and interested in my research, except for one older professor, who nodded off during my presentation. Was I that boring? It turned out he was due to retire within the year, and I suppose he was simply not interested—or really old. I was hired as an assistant professor, ABD (all but dissertation.)

In the meantime, my major professor—the one who had to sign off on my dissertation—failed to achieve tenure at Purdue, so she accepted a position at one of the colleges in California, to begin the next school year. However, she assured me she would return from time to time for meetings to counsel me and critique my work. I had heard of sixteen-year dissertation horror stories, and I was determined this was not going to happen to me.

Michael told me to buy a personal computer to speed up the process. They were fairly new at that time, but I was thrilled with the speed with which I could write, make editorial changes, and print the revised copy using a PC. So, while my major professor completed her final year at Purdue, I wrote like a madwoman. I would submit one version, the professor would make hundreds of changes, and I would rewrite it and submit a revision to her by the end of the week. This went on until the final revised version looked considerably like the original I had submitted. But I guess I wore her down, because I completed my doctoral dissertation during my first year of teaching at the School of Technology. I defended it to my committee, and received my doctorate on May 18, 1986, "with all the honors, rights, and privileges appertaining thereto."

Now, I could focus on my next major project—buying my dream house. Michael and I looked at so many houses, and made so many offers that were not accepted. I came to think our dream house was just that: a dream. As usual, when I was discouraged about something, Michael would say, "Let's go feed the ducks." We would walk from our townhouse, down the hill, and over to the lake in Vinton Woods, where the ducks swam and waited for the smorgasbord of goodies provided by gullible humans.

On the street that led to the lake, there was a neat, one-story Cape Cod house, white clapboard with deep blue shutters, situated on a peninsula of land directly across from Vinton Woods. We had admired the house for three years, on every one of our walks. As I was moping my way toward the ducks, I couldn't trust what my eyes were telling me! There was a For Sale sign in front of my dream house! We memorized the real estate agent's phone number, raced back to our townhouse, and called the agent for an appointment to view the house the next day. The inside was just as charming as the exterior. We offered the asking price, got a bank loan approved, and purchased the house within a week. The owner told me at the closing, "I can't believe you didn't dicker about the price. We should have asked for more money."

Michael and I had such fun decorating the house, and we seemed to agree on every aspect—colors, carpets, and wall coverings. There were pussy willow bushes growing in the back yard, so we hung pussy willow wallpaper in the dining room and entry hall.

The house itself was snug and well built, but situated on a bit of a hill. In the winters in Lafayette, that uphill driveway could be very treacherous, despite spreading sand and salt on the icy drive. I soon learned to approach the house while pressing the automatic garage door opener, and then hit the driveway at thirty-five miles per hour, slamming on the brakes as I crested the hill and entered the garage, halting just inches from the back wall.

One day we were driving down one of the streets in Lafayette and saw a bay window sitting in the lawn of a newly renovated house. Michael stopped the car, and we ran up to the house to make inquiries as to the intended plan for the old window. We bought that bay window then and there. Our house had a covered patio just off the kitchen, so Michael built a breakfast nook in what had been the patio, installing the newly purchased bay window above a new window seat, raising the floor to house level and installing carpeting that matched the rest of the house. The carpet layer said he had never seen the floor of a home-built addition match so well. Michael put in a sliding glass door that led to the new concrete patio that he and Daddy poured and smoothed to perfection. Here was a man who was just as handy as my father!

Before we built the breakfast nook room, there had been a chipmunk living under the patio's concrete floor. One day we were sitting in our new bay-windowed room, admiring the patio and the umbrella table and chair set we had purchased to complete the view. Just then, the chipmunk came dashing across the patio, having just stuffed his cheeks with new maple seeds from the neighbor's tree. Apparently, the little fellow forgot that we had just built a room on top of his daily route home. He ran into the sliding glass door with a splat! He peeled himself off the glass, shook his head, and quickly found a new path to his home under the concrete.

After Scott was graduated from high school in Illinois, he went through colleges like the proverbial dose of salts, flunking out of first one, then another. I think partying was his major course of study. After the third unsuccessful collegiate experience, he was working as a winter caretaker at a summer camp in southern Indiana, living in an unheated cabin and caring for the camp's livestock. When Michael and I visited him that winter, Scott asked me if I could get him admitted to Purdue. I said, "Yes, I can get you in, but *you* have to get you out."

I was soon to rediscover the joy of stepparenting, but this time the stepchild was a drop-dead gorgeous self-reliant twenty-year-old, and I was older and wiser—well, older anyway.

# CHAPTER 23

———————— •◦❊◦• ————————

# I Did It My Way

There is only one success . . . to be able to
spend your life in your own way, and not to
give others absurd maddening claims upon it
—Christopher Morley (1922)

M ichael's son, Scott, lived with us for a while in Lafayette
during his first semester studying political science at
Purdue. I thought that was wise because I could help him
with his studies, if necessary. He was not a little kid anymore, so I
thought it was perfectly acceptable for him to come and go on his own
schedule. I had only one admonishment for him. He was good-looking
and the girls were absolutely gaga over him, so before he would leave
for the evening, I'd call out, "Remember, Scott. No glove, no love!"
This would be the first of many times that his parents' loving and caring
behavior caused him inordinate embarrassment.

I set up my computer on the dining room table to be convenient for
Scott to use. One night after coming home from a date, he was working
at the computer, writing a paper for the next day's class. Michael and I
were in bed. Suddenly, Michael got out of bed—wearing only his tee
shirt and under-shorts, of course—and came out to the dining room
to confront Scott. "Get to bed! All that clickety-clack on the keys is
keeping me awake!" Michael hadn't noticed the girlfriend Scott had

brought home to help him with his homework. That may have been the reason Scott decided to move out the next semester to share an apartment with one of his classmates.

I think the proudest moment of my life occurred when Scott was enrolled in Human Relations in Business, the class for which I was the professor in charge of sixteen sections of the course. All the sections used a study guide I had written. The first day of class, the young man sitting next to Scott saw the name, Dr. M. E. Stepanich, on the front of the guide and asked Scott, "Is she related to you?"

Scott replied, "Yeah, that's my Mom." So, for a brief moment, I was able to experience a form of maternal pride.

One evening, I came home after a full day of teaching at the university followed by consulting at Alcoa, teaching a night class for new supervisors. I was completely exhausted, and my tail was dragging. As I slowly crawled out of my car, the door from the house to the garage was flung wide. Michael was framed in the doorway, posing with one arm raised and the other across his chest. He snapped his fingers and cried, "Behold, the flamenco dancer returns!" This man knew how to make my day!

On most Sundays we would have lunch at my parents' house outside Lafayette. I remember one Sunday we stopped to talk to my brother, Bill, who was next door working in his barn, attempting to repair his automatic clothes dryer. He was trying—unsuccessfully—to insert a small coiled spring into the mechanism that caused the dryer drum to revolve. Every time he would insert it, the spring would pop out. Michael watched his struggles for a minute or two and then said, "Use a bread twist tie."

My brother looked at him with skepticism. "How would that help?"

"Insert the twist tie through the coil, compress the coil, twist the tie once to keep the coil compressed, insert the coil in the space, and then yank out the twist tie."

Bill followed Michael's instructions, and when he yanked out the twist tie, the coiled spring popped perfectly into place. My brother looked up at Michael with an expression that was half admiration, half disgust. "You son of a . . ."

Michael then performed the gesture I had seen him do so often. He tapped the side of his right forehead with his index finger, as if to say, "It's all up here."

Actually, he had a lot up there. One of Michael's greatest influences on technology and our society was in the 1960s, following President John Kennedy's promise to the American public that we would "send a man to the moon and bring him back safely within the decade." Michael was an important member of the Delco Electronics team that created the inertial guidance system that took the Apollo spacecraft—and Neil Armstrong—to the surface of the moon on that hot July night in 1969. Michael enjoyed boasting, with his characteristic humility, "Well, they didn't have to make a midcourse correction, thanks to us." I think he actually said, "Thanks to *me*."

He was also very accurate in describing small-town, midwestern lifestyles. In 1987 my hometown of Fort Branch had a parade and festivities in celebration of Heritage Days. Each high school class had a float and/or an automobile representing the year of graduation, with the class marching behind its entry. Our class of '57 marched (well— ambled) behind a 1957 Chevrolet. All the townspeople were out on the sidewalks along the parade route, cheering us on. Younger people stood and waved special Heritage Days flags, and elder citizens sat in their lawn chairs, enjoying seeing old friends and neighbors. At the end of the parade, my classmates all retired to the local VFW post for refreshments. Michael's observation of the event was dead accurate: "The people in this town must have nothing more exciting to do than watch a bunch of old farts walk down the street."

I had a great deal of success at Purdue, and I loved every minute of my time there. I was rewarded for my efforts by being promoted to associate professor, with tenure, after two and one-half years as an assistant professor. Tenure is a guarantee of lifetime employment at the granting university. Once you have tenure, you have to do something really terrible to lose your job, like sleeping with the entire football team. And even that might be forgiven, if the team beat Michigan State.

My students were very special to me, and I received high teaching ratings from them every semester. Thanks to those ratings, I won two

Excellence in Teaching awards, and was invited to speak to several student groups, such as Delta Sigma Pi (a business fraternity), a couple of social fraternity groups, and the annual agribusiness conference.

Many of my students worked part-time at local restaurants. It was so convenient to be able to say to one of my students in class Friday morning, "My husband and I are planning to have dinner tonight at Chi-Chi's." Our favorite table would be waiting for us, as well as the special spinach enchilada that Michael loved.

Teaching does hold a lot of responsibility, primarily because so many students believe every word the teacher says. One day, I saw that a student had left a notebook in my class, and in searching for the owner's name so as to return the book, I noticed he had written down my comments almost word for word, including a mild expletive! When I was teaching a supervision class to juniors and seniors, most of whom were working at part-time and even full-time jobs, one of the young men told me after class: "My boss should have taken your class—he doesn't know the first thing about being a good supervisor. So, I quit yesterday!"

"Oh, dear! I appreciate your frustration, but I wish you had waited. It's always been my motto, 'Never quit a job before you have another one lined up.'"

Although I thoroughly enjoyed teaching, I was not going to give up music. I had joined the Lafayette Chorus of Sweet Adelines soon after I arrived in Indiana. The first night at chorus, as I was being introduced to the group, I noticed three ladies hovering together, looking at me as though I were a plump partridge ready to be gobbled up. They approached me, somewhat tentatively, and asked if I would like to sing in a quartet with them. "Of course!" Thus began Cabaret, one of my favorite barbershop quartet experiences that continued throughout my tenure at Purdue. (Read more about Cabaret in the next chapter.)

In addition to teaching, I served on the Dean's Council of the School of Technology as well as the Faculty Senate of the university. These groups managed the academic and administrative issues for the school and the university, respectively. Also, I was appointed to the Human Subjects Research Committee. This committee had oversight on the research that involved human beings. I believe their objective was to prevent some mad scientist from harming our young students with his monstrous experiments.

Purdue had an impressive record of world-class research leading to innovations in many fields, including managerial, medical, and astrophysical engineering. Some of our most noteworthy graduates included: Lillian Gilbreth, civil engineering; Amelia Earhart, aviation; astronauts Neil Armstrong and Gene Cernan, aeronautical engineering; authors Jan Lancaster and Donald Bain (the writer of the *Murder She Wrote* mystery series); and Chesley "Sully" Sullenberger, the pilot who landed a damaged US Airways aircraft on the Hudson River and saved the lives of 155 people.

Throughout my education and professorship, I was a member of a number of honorary fraternities. When I was an undergraduate, I was selected for membership in Sigma Alpha Iota, a music honorary (I think I treasure that one most), and Kappa Delta Pi, an education honorary. During my doctoral studies I was elected to several honoraries, including Phi Kappa Phi for overall academic excellence, Beta Gamma Sigma for business acumen, and Sigma Xi for research in science. There is also a certificate on my office wall for "Outstanding Contribution to the Professional Program of Delta Sigma Pi Fraternity." I received that one for speaking to the group and helping them find humor in management—not an easy task!

I was fortunate to catch the eye of one of our distinguished faculty, Jim Windle, who had his own consulting firm that kept him so busy, he could devote only half time to teaching. His consulting practice was both lucrative and time consuming, so he asked me to take a job that he did not have time to accept. Probably he was not as interested in that one—it involved performing a job analysis for a large manufacturing firm (*boring!*). But I accepted the task with eagerness, and I must have done it both to his satisfaction and that of the client, because I soon found myself consulting one day a week on behalf of Jim's firm. At that time, one day per week was the amount of consulting time that Purdue allowed full-time professors.

In one of those consulting tasks, I worked for and with the president of Shenandoah Industries, a firm that manufactured the injected plastic molded parts for automobiles, especially Ford, Chrysler, and Dodge.

I was amazed (and somewhat dismayed) to learn how much of an automobile is plastic! The president was pleased with my proposal to increase their performance through shop floor training, and asked me to meet with his executive staff—the vice presidents of finance, sales, human resources, marketing, and manufacturing. After I had worked with this group for an entire morning, one of the younger vice presidents said to me, "You are really smart—you should get a PhD!"

One of his colleagues looked at him disbelievingly. "You obviously didn't read her proposal. She *has* her PhD—from Purdue!"

Another consulting job I enjoyed immensely was supervisory training for Citizen's Gas and Electricity, the public utility company serving Indianapolis, Indiana. I drove to Indianapolis every Wednesday for two years, until I had trained nearly everyone from the top executives to the pipe fitters and ditch diggers. I was so well known by the employees that they would wave me into the employee parking lot without question. On my last evening with them, I received many gifts and hugs of appreciation.

In Lafayette, I had a long-term relationship with Alcoa Inc. (Aluminum Company of America), again training new supervisors. When I left there after the task was finished, I received a letter of appreciation signed by all my students and a strange metal contraption, whose purpose is still a mystery to me, engraved with a brass plate, "Alcoa, Lafayette Works, 1938-1988."

Similarly, I trained the employees at Eli Lilley's Lafayette plant, for which I received a six-foot-long banner signed by every employee—and a chocolate cake!

Each year, the Conference on Intercollegiate Cooperation (CIC) selected one upwardly mobile professor from each of the universities in the Big Ten conference to attend a number of weekend seminars. The program was designed as a training experience for a tenured faculty member who had the credentials and expertise to become one of the deans of his or her school. I was flabbergasted when I was selected to represent Purdue! The trainees traveled to several of the Big Ten campuses throughout the year to attend three-day training sessions.

In early February 1989, I was returning from the CIC seminar at Ohio State University in Columbus, Ohio, by way of Chicago. At

O'Hare International Airport I had to rush to the terminal for smaller aircraft in order to catch the puddle-jumper that would return me to Purdue in West Lafayette. As I was hurrying down the concourse, I looked up and saw—Michael! He had driven to Chicago to intercept my journey and take me back home in the brand new, cherry-red Buick he had purchased as my Valentine's Day gift.

Wow! I had a handsome loving husband, a tenured faculty position at one of the most prestigious universities, the home of my dreams, a lucrative consulting practice, my family living nearby, and a barbershop quartet and chorus that satisfied my need to sing and perform. How could life get any better?

# CHAPTER 24

──•❈•──

# PLAY THAT BARBERSHOP CHORD

The Lord respects me when I work,
but He loves me when I sing.
—Anonymous

The one constant in my life, throughout husbands, homes, and hard times, was Sweet Adelines and barbershop music. I joined the organization after my divorce from husband number one, and it was still a big part of my life throughout my marriages to husbands numbers two, three, and four.

Thank goodness that Michael, number four, supported my singing and performing—unlike some of the others. Hunt, number two, was more interested in himself and his own performance with the ladies than he was in my chorus and quartet performances. George, number three, viewed my absences to sing with my quartet and chorus in San Jose as a perfect time to engage in his affair with the next-door neighbor.

When Michael and I married, I was directing the Star City Chorus, a small chorus in Lafayette, Indiana, and singing with my dear friends Kay, Diana, and Judy S. in a comedy barbershop quartet, Cabaret. We were sought out for performances, even winning a third-place regional medal, primarily because of bass singer Kay's droll sense of humor. She was a country veterinarian in Attica, Indiana, treating the local farmers' cows, horses, and dogs—anything on four feet. She could make a person laugh with her look of naïve, puzzled innocence, and she always told stories that were outrageous, but somehow you believed she could make it happen:

"Isn't that a swell buffet? We were told we could stay after our performance and eat with all of you, but I can't. I've got a hot date tonight, and I've got to lose sixty pounds by ten o'clock."

Sad to say, Kay passed away in 2009.

I have attended chorus and quartet competitions, as well as regional seminars, every year since 1972. When I was married to Michael, he went with me to each competition and seminar, and he would drive me across the width of the state of Indiana so I could attend rehearsals with my new quartet, The Right Arrangement (Deb, Denise, and Judy B.). I'm sure my friends paraphrased that famous golfing joke when describing Michael's devotion: "Go to contest, drag Michael; sing at a show, drag Michael."

However, one year when I was making arrangements for the annual competition weekend, he told me, "I don't think I'll go with you this year. It's really boring for me and I know you like to spend the time with your quartet and chorus."

"Okay. That's fine with me."

As I was packing the car on Thursday morning, getting ready for the competition weekend, Michael was watching me sadly, a lost puppy dog look on his face. "You know, I wish I were going with you."

"I thought you'd feel that way. I made a reservation for the two of us at the hotel. Get your stuff and hop in."

Another year when my chorus won the regional competition, Michael had gone out of the auditorium at one of the earlier breaks between contestants to get a drink. He didn't get back into the auditorium before the doors were closed and locked. That was done so as to avoid any noise or interruption for the next contestant, which happened to be my chorus. Michael tried to listen through a crack in the door. When we were finished, I rushed out to the lobby to see him:

"Did you hear us? Weren't we great? What did you think?"

"From what I heard through the door, you killed 'em!"

He then explained what he had done. I couldn't decide between mayhem at the moment or a quiet homicide at home.

One somewhat exasperating trait that Michael possessed was his reluctance to answer the telephone. He claimed the only calls we received were for me or from telemarketers, so he refused to pick up the phone when it rang. I suppose he was right about that—most of the calls were from my students or Sweet Adelines.

My Indiana quartet, The Right Arrangement, did not let his antipathy to the telephone deter them. The three of them would set up a conference call, telephone our house, and when the answering machine came on, they would shout, "We know you're there, Michael! Come on; get off the john! Answer the phone!" And he would.

When I was a candidate for the international faculty in the mid-90s, I had to submit a videotape of myself teaching classes at choruses and regional meetings. Michael would go along with me and film every session. I would tell the audiences, "That's my husband behind the camera. Pay no attention to him—I never do!" He then would laugh as loud as the women at the meetings.

At many of my quartet performances, I would tell the mushroom joke:

"I've had four husbands, but that really wasn't my fault. My first husband died suddenly one day—he accidentally ate some poisoned mushrooms. My second husband, coincidentally, also died from eating poisoned mushrooms. My third husband died of a skull fracture—he wouldn't eat his mushrooms!"

After one of those quartet performances, the girls came to dinner at my house. Michael had prepared a scrumptious meal of barbecued steaks smothered in—sizzling sautéed mushrooms!

Eventually, Michael did stop accompanying me to Sweet Adelines events, but he was like a dog that has been left alone by his family. Every time I came home, I found that he had destroyed some plant life. In Lafayette, Michael chopped down a crabapple tree in mid-blossom. In

Arizona, I had babied, pampered, and trimmed three oleander bushes until they grew together into a perfect hedge shape, with blended flowers of red, white, and pink. I came home from a Sweet Adelines weekend to find that Michael had chopped them down. He always had an excuse: "Too much trouble to maintain." But I knew the real reason: "Don't leave me alone, or you'll be sorry!"

These words would come back to haunt me all too soon.

# CHAPTER 25

---•❖•---

# TAKE THIS JOB AND . . .

Look up and not down, look
forward and not back.
—Edward Everett Hale, 1871

A member of my former chorus, the Mission Viejo Chorus of Sweet Adelines, surprised me with a telephone call in September 1986. "Mary Ellen, this is M.A." Her name was Mary Ann but her husband had always called her by her initials.

"My goodness! I haven't seen or heard from you in years. How's everything going with my favorite chorus?"

"We're in trouble. We're going to regional competition next April and nothing is going right. Stan, our director, is fighting with the section leaders, who are fighting with the members, who are fighting with the board of directors, who are fighting with the choreographers, and everyone is up in arms. I'm afraid it's affecting our performance. Can you come out to California and do your team-building thing? We'll pay you, of course."

We made the arrangements, and I flew to California for the chorus retreat weekend in the winter of 1986. After all, winter in California is better than winter in Indiana any day of the week. I pulled out my kit bag of team-building materials, and we had a very productive weekend that culminated in a more cohesive, goal-oriented group. Of course, I had to convince a few star members that being placed other than center on the risers meant their voices would reinforce those of weaker singers, thus improving the total sound. (Thank goodness, they bought it!) I cannot take all the credit, of course, but the chorus did win their regional competition in the spring, which qualified them for the Sweet Adelines International competition in Phoenix, Arizona, in October 1988.

In June 1988 there was another telephone call from California: "Mary Ellen, this is M.A. again. Can you come to Phoenix and be with us when we compete at International? I think the chorus will perform better if you give us a refresher session just before we go on stage."

I agreed, primarily because I had seen Arizona only briefly when my first husband Bill and I made our westward-ho journey in the '60s. I was looking forward to seeing more of the state, and Michael had never been to Arizona. The chorus paid all my expenses and fees, and I paid Michael's expenses so he could accompany me.

Maybe it was because Michael had grown up in the asphalt jungle of New York City, where the skyscrapers hid the sun and sky most of the day, but when he deplaned in Phoenix, Arizona, he fell in love with the place. He was mesmerized by the seemingly endless sky, the warmth of the sun, and the almost humanoid-shaped saguaros against the backdrop of purple mountains.

After my duties were completed—and the Mission Viejo chorus won international third place medals—we rented a car and took some time to explore the area. One of my fellow professors at Purdue had retired and now lived in Sun City West. He was the one who fell asleep during my initial interview for the faculty position at Purdue. We called him, and he was delighted to show us some of the local attractions.

On the way back to our hotel downtown, we were traveling on Bell Road, one of the major east-west thoroughfares in the Valley of the Sun. Suddenly, we saw a strange sight: a man dressed as a duck, waving a big board displaying the words "Westbrook Village" with an arrow pointing northward. What the heck? We looked at each other in amazement. Without saying a word, Michael turned and followed the direction of the arrow. We came upon a new housing development, with manicured golf courses, swaying palm trees, and mirror-like lakes surrounded by lovely stucco houses capped by red tile roofs.

We drove to the model homes, which we buzzed through quickly, enthralled by the simple beauty of the southwestern décor. We stopped at the sales office—me, to gather information, and Michael, to follow his own agenda. Within minutes, the saleslady, Paulette, had hooked us. Michael could see himself living the life of Riley here: basking in the sun and soaking in the pool. I was delighted because the recent Keating/ savings and loan debacle had lowered prices and the developers threw in many extras at no additional cost.

Before I knew what was happening, Michael had lured the checkbook out of my purse and onto the sales desk, and we had made a down payment on a house that would be built in 1989. We drove to the lot that eventually would contain Michael's dream retirement home, and I took a picture of Michael pointing to—our very own weed! He was so proud.

We did not plan to move right away. My career was going like gangbusters at Purdue, and General Motors and Delco did not want to lose Michael to retirement just yet. He was especially valuable because he not only understood both electrical and mechanical engineering, but now he had me feeding him tips on improving the organizational and behavioral issues at Delco. So, instead of offering Michael early retirement, they promoted him! Fortunately, there were many people who wanted to sample life in Arizona, and our new house was continuously rented for more than enough money to pay the house payment. We did visit our Arizona home once or twice a year, staying in the vacation rental houses in Sun City West.

In 1990, several things happened to change our long-range plans. First, the couple renting our Arizona house decided to move to California. This meant we would have to make *two* house payments— one in Indiana and one in Arizona. Then, General Motors offered Michael a very lucrative early retirement package, possibly a precursor to the ultimate dismantling of Delco Electronics, which occurred a few years later. Finally, my brother and his wife divorced, leveling a blow to Mom and Dad's ideal life next door to their son, daughter-in-law, and grandchildren.

I told Michael I would not move without first securing a job in Arizona. Leaving Purdue and my career in higher education was not at the top of my wish list. I applied to several positions advertised in the *Chronicle of Higher Education*, and within a few weeks I was notified that I was a finalist for the position of division chair of business programs at Estrella Mountain Community College, one of the Maricopa County Community Colleges in Phoenix, Arizona. I was told to report to the office of a personnel consultant in Chicago for an interview.

I prepared exhaustively for the interview, researching the college and searching out any information I could find about the position. When I arrived at the consultant's office, I saw two chairs, a desk, and a video camera on a tripod. The gentleman seated me in the chair facing the camera and took the seat behind the desk. He told me that he would be videotaping the interview:

"I will ask you several questions, and you will have twenty minutes to respond to all the questions. If the time expires before all questions are answered, you will not have an opportunity to finish. I will not respond to your answers or to any questions you may have during the taping."

Well, that was encouraging—*not*. I put on my best performance face, looked directly into the camera, and the interview began. When the interview was concluded and I had answered all the questions in the allotted time, the consultant asked me, "Did you have a copy of the questions prior to the interview?"

"No—I simply prepared for every conceivable question you could possibly ask." I didn't tell him, but I had a large three-ring binder full of my research and all the questions and answers I had prepared for the interview. By the way, that's the same procedure I used in preparing for the three-day doctoral-degree oral examination at Purdue. I am a great believer in the Scout motto: Be prepared!

In September 1990, I was notified that I'd been selected as one of the six finalists, and was invited with my husband to meet the dean and other administrators of the college for the final interview. We flew to Phoenix where we were given accommodations at the luxurious Wigwam Resort in Litchfield Park. The Wigwam was once the official rest-and-relaxation posh perquisite of the executives of the Goodyear

Corporation. While meeting with the college staff, the assistant dean revealed why I was chosen: "Your video was remarkable. All the other candidates looked as though they were being interrogated by Attila the Hun, but you actually seemed to enjoy the process." (I guess it was the "star" in me coming out!) I was hired to begin my position on January 2, 1991.

We put our Lafayette house on the market—and it sold, at the asking price, the first day. It broke my heart to leave my professorship at Purdue. I was poised to become a department chair, or even an assistant dean, in just a few years. My consulting practice was so lucrative, I was actually earning more as a consultant than I was earning as an associate professor. But, I was born in the culture that decreed the wife follows the husband, and not vice versa. And Michael was going to Arizona!

Even more difficult was leaving my dream house. We had loaded all our possessions and furniture into a U-Haul rental truck and stayed at my parents' house until the house sale and closing was finalized. I made one last walk-through of the house and stood in the driveway, weeping, closing the garage door with the remote control one last time. It was as though the door to my life was also closing.

My parents were so traumatized by both my brother's divorce and my leaving the state that they made a deal to buy a house back in our hometown of Fort Branch. This action actually resulted in a better life for them. They returned to their roots, their old friends, and a new stone home that they loved.

As far as I was concerned, I was moving from an ideal location, in the green and verdant bosom of my friends and family, to a desert where the average annual rainfall was less than one inch and the average temperature was ten degrees below boiling. People would say to me, "But it's a dry heat!"

I would answer, "So is an oven, but I wouldn't want to stick my head in one."

Michael caught a cold while loading our furniture in the U-Haul truck in the rain, so Scott came with us to Arizona and drove the truck the entire trip. I followed behind the truck, driving my car. Michael's car was left in Indiana because he had to return and work one more month before retiring. I stayed about one car length behind the truck, keeping an eye on the taillights and at the same time on a book I was holding on the steering wheel. I think I read an entire book on that trip.

After unloading our possessions, Scott and Michael flew back to Indiana—Scott to finish his degree at Purdue and Michael to finish his career at General Motors. I quickly set up the house, and started my job at Estrella Mountain Community College.

Four weeks later, at about nine-thirty in the evening, I heard a car pull into the driveway. I was a bit frightened, because I hadn't met nor made friends with any neighbors as yet, so I couldn't imagine who it might be. Once again, Michael surprised me. He had driven night and day from Indiana to start his retirement in Arizona as soon as possible.

The job at EMCC was not a good fit for me. I was accustomed to the culture of academic freedom at a large university, but the culture of the community college seemed more focused on how much time you spent at your desk in your seat, rather than doing the job for which you were hired. As division chair of Business, my primary duty was to develop connections with local enterprises so as to ensure that our programs of instruction met their needs. However, the assistant dean complained that I was out of the office too frequently. Apparently, she thought I should have performed my duties over the phone, rather than meeting those people at their places of business. I think the real issue was that she had a friend at the district office who wanted my job. We parted company after one year. And no surprise—her friend was immediately hired as the division chair of Business.

For a while, I toyed with the idea of returning to school at Arizona State University and acquiring a degree in clinical psychology. After all, I would need only a few courses to qualify for state certification as a therapist. However, when I thought about the clientele I would be dealing with—drug addicts and teenagers who cut themselves as a coping mechanism—I thought I wouldn't be well suited to that career. I'm afraid my response to those patients would be, "That's stupid! Don't do that anymore."

I wasn't exactly happy with my job options in Arizona, but Michael was really enjoying his retirement. He went to the community pool every day and made several friends at the recreation center and in the neighborhood. I joined him at the pool one afternoon, and Michael introduced me to one of the members of the group he called Ladies of the Milk Bottles. (They would use empty gallon milk bottles to provide resistance during their water aerobics.)

The woman smiled up at him with what I like to call goo-goo eyes, and then looked at me, "My name is Rosemary. I'm a member of the water exercise group."

I responded with a bit of an edge to my voice. "My name is Mary Ellen—I'm the *wife*."

One of the "exit perks" provided by the Maricopa County Community College system was the benefit of the services of an employment counselor. As a result, I received a makeover—hair and makeup—and my picture and an interview were featured in an issue of *Arizona Woman*. Now I had something more than academic credentials that would really impress potential employers: cheesecake!

# CHAPTER 26

---•◈•---

# I LOVE YOU, ARIZONA

Sing the song that's in your hearts,
Sing of the great Southwest,
Thank God for Arizona,
In splendid sunshine dressed.
—Margaret Rowe Clifford

Eventually, I learned to love my yard of gravel, my cactus and succulents, and my deadly oleander. Add to that the scent of night-blooming jasmine, orange blossoms in the spring, and the desert that always has something beautiful to offer, and within a few years I became a confirmed "Zonie."

A friend of mine who taught botany at the community college told me about one of her class field trips to the desert. A student looked at the vast stretches of prickly pear cactus, creosote bushes, palo verde trees, saguaros, and aloe vera and asked her, "Who planted all this?"

What else could she say? "God."

For our first several years in Arizona, Michael and I behaved like perfect tourists. Every free weekend we explored another of Arizona's special attractions: Grand Canyon (of course), Tombstone, Meteor Crater, Tucson and the movie studios at Old Tucson, Montezuma's Castle, Flagstaff and the San Francisco Peak, Sedona and Oak Creek Canyon, as well as Lake Havasu and the English Village. But we also loved to explore the quaint and less-publicized areas such as Globe, Strawberry, Payson, Eloy, Arcosanti (an artists' colony), and Sunset Crater, the site of a prehistoric volcano.

Shortly after leaving the community college, I applied to Western International University in Phoenix and was hired as a full professor of Management to teach strategic management and organization development in the executive MBA program. I was named Management Department chair within three months, and associate dean in two years. Most of my students were from foreign countries and were a delight to teach, especially the men and women from Thailand and Taiwan. The Asian cultures seem to revere education and educators.

However, the students from Islamic countries—all men—did not respect women, especially women professors. I felt somewhat threatened when I told one young man that he had not earned the A grade that he expected in my course. For all I know, he may have been a prince in his own country, and he considered a B grade beneath him. There was a cake plate and a knife on my credenza, left over from an office birthday party, and when he looked pointedly at the knife, I immediately terminated the interview—and asked for an escort to my car for several days thereafter!

Several months after we moved to Arizona, Michael surprised me one Friday afternoon by picking me up at the university and sweeping me off to a weekend in Prescott at the Hassayampa Inn. In the back seat of our car, he had placed three of the large stuffed animals he had given me over the years. Michael once sent me a Mother's Day card that was signed by these three stuffed animals: Jingle Bear, Fat Cat, and Ether Bunny. Each one was securely belted in, holding a bottle of champagne. We did get several strange looks from the other patrons in the parking lot.

After touring Whisky Row, Prescott's downtown square full of wooden-floored bars and saloons with spittoons and swinging front doors, we made our way to the hotel. The Hassayampa Inn is full of Old-West charm, and accurately reflects the fact that it dates back to the 1800s. The in-room bathroom had been constructed in what was once a broom closet, and the bed was better suited to the average height of the *women* of the old west—Michael's feet and ankles hung over the bottom edge of the bed. The next day, we sat down to a delicious lunch in the hotel's restaurant. While finishing my salad, I noticed a small black object at the edge of the plate. I whispered to Michael, "There's a dead fly in my salad."

I'm proud to say that Michael called the waiter over and quietly, humorously, asked the waiter, "What's this fly doing in my wife's salad, and please don't say 'the backstroke.'" The waiter gave me a new salad, and we also received free deserts, a free bottle of wine, and a voucher for another stay at the inn.

As often happens to those who move to a new state, I received a summons to appear for jury duty soon after registering to vote. I drove to downtown Phoenix and parked in the multi-level garage near the courthouse. As I headed to the elevator, a poorly dressed and rather filthy man, who seemed like he might have been a homeless derelict, entered the elevator car just ahead of me. I paused at the entrance, my small town upbringing making me a bit unsure how to react. He held the door and asked, "Are you getting on?"

"No—I think I'll walk down instead."

He seemed to bristle defensively. "I'm not going to hurt you!"

"I know. I just think I need the exercise. Thanks, anyway." And I hurried to the staircase, raced down the stairs, and ran over to the Superior Court building. My assertive voice was stronger, but I still chose to avoid conflict.

After waiting all morning, I was called—finally—to a courtroom after lunch, with about thirty other people. What followed was a lengthy series of questioning of all of us, twelve potential jurors at a time. One of the attorneys inquired about our education. When I responded that I had a PhD in organizational behavior, the judge interrupted.

"What is organizational behavior?"

"It is the study of individuals and groups in organizations of work, both non-profit and for-profit, with a view to improving their performance and satisfaction through effective communication and leadership."

The judge looked at me for a moment, as if to make sure I was real, and then responded, "I don't want you organizing my jury. You are excused."

I've been summoned to jury duty a few times since, but I've always been excused from duty. The judge was right. I *would* try to organize the jury!

When Michael and I married, I owned both a Baldwin piano and a Lowry organ. The organ had letters on the keys to indicate the name of each note. It also came with a booklet of easy songs, showing which key to strike for each note of the song. One day while I was teaching at the university, Michael worked for hours on one of the songs. When I came home, he announced proudly that he had learned a song to play for me.

"Great!" I said. "Let's hear it."

He proceeded, carefully watching the songbook and the keys as he played: *Pling—pling, pling—PLING pling—plingplingpling—pliiiiiing pling.* "There! What do you think of that?"

"Well, I'm impressed. What *was* that?"

"Jingle Bells!"

"Oh." I didn't want to hurt his feelings. "Well, the notes were good, but I think you need to work a little bit on the timing."

Michael's children, Shari (newly divorced) and Scott (still single), would visit us often in Arizona and always in the winter, of course. Michael would follow them everywhere, video camera in hand. One of my favorite family videos shows the two young people at the driving range at the Westbrook Golf Club. After several minutes, the screen went black—Michael had put the lens cap on the camera. However, the recorder, and the sound, continued. One could hear the *crunch, crunch, crunch* of gravel as Michael walked back to the car. Then came the sound of the car trunk opening. A passerby said something to Michael and his reply sounded clearly, "Yeah, just taking pictures of my kids." Then the trunk closed.

Michael adored his children. Every Sunday, the two of us ritualistically called family; I called my parents and Michael called his daughter and son. They were rarely at home, but he would leave messages, filling them in on our activities.

There was always a bit of competition between Shari and Scott. On one of her solo visits, Shari said she wanted to go skydiving. We took her to Eloy and the skydiving airport. She was a bit nervous, so

Michael told her to take one of the Valium tablets I had unearthed from the medicine cabinet. She took only one-half a pill, because she didn't want to be comatose during the jump. (I didn't tell her they were more than twenty years old and probably lacked potency.) Just before she was to board the plane, she nearly panicked, so Michael said, "Take the other half!" She had a very successful jump and we have the entire adventure on video.

Of course, when Scott came for his next visit, he had to skydive as well. He couldn't let Shari do something that he didn't. There was some excitement during his jump, however. When he landed, the instructor ran to the video-screening room, grabbed the video of the jump from the cameraman, and popped it into the video player. We could all see that the chute did not open when Scott pulled the cord, and it only opened when the instructor frantically manipulated the lines on the drag chute. So, Scott had one up on Shari—he almost died in the sky jump!

When Shari visited the next year, we took her to the glider flying school near Lake Pleasant so that she could have another really unique desert experience. Naturally, when Scott came a few months later, he took a glider flight also, only his flight was an aerobatic one. One-upmanship again! I'm glad I didn't observe that flight; I think my heart couldn't take watching Scott doing loop-the-loops in a glider!

In those days, before 9/11, one could go right to the gate at the airport and greet disembarking passengers. On one of Scott's visits, Michael and I arrived at the airport about an hour early, so we stopped at one of the bars on the concourse to have a drink (or three) before Scott's plane arrived. I don't know which one of us came up with the idea, but we thought it would be hysterical to create a sign to welcome Scott as though he were a visiting dignitary. I took the black Sharpie pen I am never without and wrote on a large napkin: "Welcome, Scott Stepanich." As he came out of the jetway, talking to a beautiful girl (of course), we held up the sign. He turned to the young lady and said something to her. He wouldn't tell us what he said, but it was probably, "My parents—drunk again!"

In 1998, Shari and Scott visited us at the same time. One night, Michael took them to the Lakes Restaurant at Westbrook Village for dinner. I was working at the university that day and planned to meet them at the restaurant later. After the three of them had been seated at our favorite table, Michael turned to Scott and said, "Scott, would you move over to the other chair? Mary Ellen likes to sit here so she can look at the lake." The kids did not tell me this story until after their father's death.

I always said that my Indiana parents had raised me by the Golden Rule: "Do unto others as you would have them do unto you." Michael said that he was raised in New York City by a similar rule, "Do it to them before they do it to you." He often would tell me that most of his high school buddies were either dead or in jail. So, how did I manage to have such a successful relationship with someone who was diametrically opposed to everything that I was and that I believed?

My philosophy is that you simply have to accept those differences as okay. For example, my high school home economics teacher taught me to make a bed with hospital corners. Michael couldn't stand to have his toes hampered by the bed covers. After all, he was almost six and a half feet tall, and he didn't want his toes to be crammed into the tucked sheets. So, we each made the bed on our own side—I tucked in the sheets on my side with perfect hospital corners, and he left his sheets untucked, for his toes. When we married, I already had an expensive, dainty, flatware set that I bought in Chicago in 1962, and he had a set of post-divorce Walmart stainless. He said his hands were too big for my cutlery, so he used his—and I used mine.

The car was another place where our differences were apparent. We each had a favorite route to get to the same place. He preferred freeways and I preferred the less traveled, slower routes. Therefore, when he drove, he went his way, and when I drove, I chose my favorite routes. Again, we had to agree to disagree.

A man, no matter how sweet and accommodating he might be, never likes to be told what to do, especially by a woman, and even less so by his wife. I speak with authority—I've had four husbands!

Michael and I would often drive to California to our favorite destination, San Diego, or to visit my friend and quartet buddy, Judy B., in Temecula. There was a treacherous mountain road on the way to Temecula—at least, it seemed treacherous to me. Michael had an especially heavy foot, and as we careened around the hairpin curves with roadsides that plunged downward to inevitable death, I was terrified. I had learned that to tell Michael to slow down both raised his ire and his speed. So I would say, "Michael, I am not comfortable at this rate of speed." Immediately, his lead foot would ease up on the accelerator. Good old "I" messages—they work every time! (Well, almost every time. In a similar situation his son, Scott, simply told Jennifer, his wife, "You'll be fine.")

On another visit to California, driving up the coastal highway, Michael displayed both his driving daring-do as well as his desire to please me. I captured my feelings about his special talents in the following poem:

The Café on the Cliff
*by Mary Ellen Stepanich*

Speeding north on the coastal highway,
we spot a small roadside café
      perched on the cliff
      awaiting us, as if.
"That looks like an interesting place," I say.

But I quickly change my view, to wit:
*Too bad, we've already gone past it.*
      But Michael is not
      A squeamish sort.
He slams on the brakes, slows not a whit,

makes a 90-degree turn across the street,
careens to a space that's empty and sweet,
      screeches to a halt
      an inch shy of the wall
and grins as he tells me, "Let's eat!"

Michael's cardiovascular system, combined with his diabetes, caused many health problems for him. He had a quadruple bipass surgery in December 1981, just before we met in February 1982. His stitches were still healing at that time, and our lovemaking was often interrupted, not by his cries of passion, but cries of, "Don't touch my chest!" After we moved to Arizona, he had another bipass surgery in 1991. Thereafter, his surgeon told me there were no more veins that could be harvested. His heart doctor tried to insert stents in his heart arteries, but they quickly closed up. I asked the cardiologist, "What's the prognosis?"

The doctor looked at me for a moment, as if trying to decide how to reply. Finally, he sighed and said quietly, "He's going to die." I suppose I chose to deny that.

In 1996, Michael developed a diabetic wound on his foot that would not heal. He was on antibiotic infusions continuously for almost a year. During that time, we had our usual vacations—one to San Diego and the Coronado Beach Resort, and one to the Bay Club Resort on the Big Island in Hawaii. In both instances, Michael did not allow his illness to deter him on our romantic getaways. He carried his infusion stand and antibiotic packets with him to San Diego, and he rode around the Big Island on the back seat of the rental car with his foot propped on a pillow.

I'm ashamed to say that I was not the excellent nurse his condition required. I was so squeamish about giving him the infusions that he quickly learned to do them himself—he probably thought that was safer. He asked the doctor to make the infusion tube longer so he could manipulate it with his left hand while injecting the antibiotic solution with his right.

Unfortunately, the wound did not heal and the doctors said there was no alternative but to amputate the front half of his foot. Michael's foot healed quickly, but his psyche had a wound that was not apparent. He became irritable and withdrawn. He once remarked, "I'm not coming in peace—I'm going in pieces!"

I went to the Cigna Clinic behavioral specialist to find out what I could do to help him. The doctor asked to see Michael by himself, and I said I doubted he would come. But Michael surprised me by showing up at the appointment. When I saw the doctor at the next appointment, he told me, "Michael really loves you. His body is not in the best condition, but his love for you is strong."

No matter what would happen between us, or to us, there was never a doubt in my mind that I had finally found my soul mate. How many more years we would have together was the only question.

# CHAPTER 27

───────◆───────

# WHAT'LL I DO

It is foolish and wrong to mourn the men who died.
Rather we should thank God that such men lived.
—George S. Patton

I took a chance and went alone to the Beach House Grill in Cardiff by the Sea, one of California's jewels strewn along the West Coast. It always had been one of our favorite spots overlooking the Pacific Ocean, where Michael and I would lunch, sip champagne, and just absorb the beauty of nature and each other. I asked the *maître d'* for a table on the open deck where, kissed by the warm California sun but protected from the wild coastal breezes by a clear glass panel, I could once again immerse myself in the view and the memories. It was the second time I had allowed myself this special treat in the four years since Michael had died.

Of course, my pain was not quite as acute as the previous visit with Shari, Michael's daughter. She and I had shared our annual girls week out and had come here to Cardiff by the Sea to discuss "what to do with Michael"—his ashes, that is. As the day slid into evening, the sky's color deepened to turquoise, then mauve and gold, and finally to midnight black.

The waves of the sea at sunset were flat, wide orchestra risers, empty because the symphony had ended, the players having left the stage. The gulls, with moonlight on their wings, ascended to heaven like the ghosts of loved ones.

I couldn't help but relive, for the thousandth time, that horrible day when Mom and Dad's phone rang at lunch while I was enjoying Daddy's famous, mouth-watering chili soup. (I finally convinced him to share the secret of his recipe—he adds a tablespoon of sugar!) After teaching a weekend performance seminar in St. Louis, I had dashed over to southern Indiana for a quick visit with my folks before heading back home to Arizona.

Mom answered. "Hello—Well, I'm his mother-in-*law*." She handed the phone to me. "It's the Peoria police."

Now, there is something about the word "police" that strikes dread in the heart of even the most law-abiding citizen. So I knew it had to be bad news.

"Hello? This is Mrs. Stepanich."

"Hi, this is Officer Foley of the Peoria police. I'm afraid your husband has had what appears to be a heart attack while he was trimming the tree in the front yard. Your neighbor saw him and called 911. The ambulance has taken him to Boswell Hospital."

Why is it that, in the middle of the most God-awful news, our reaction is to immediately make the situation simple, easily solved, and acceptable? "Oh good," I said. "They have all his medical records at Boswell and they know how to take good care of him."

"Does he have any family here in Peoria we can contact?"

"Yes, his sister lives just a few blocks from our house." I covered the mouthpiece. "Mom, can you get my day planner out of my suitcase? I need Rose's phone number." I turned back to the phone. "How in the world did you get *this* number, Officer Foley?"

"Well, I went through your file cabinets—I hope you don't mind—and finally I saw the little Rolodex on your kitchen counter—and a beautiful kitchen it is! I saw the note in front that said 'Mom and Dad's number.' So I called, thinking it was Mr. Stepanich's mother."

I gave him Rose's number and he said he would call back as soon as he knew anything certain.

The four of us returned to our lunch—Mom, Dad, and I, and my Aunt Lucille, Daddy's older sister who was visiting for the weekend. I have often heard the expression about food tasting like sawdust in the height of an emotional trauma, and it's true. What had been a piquant, mouth-watering soup that I have loved since early childhood was now as tasteless as the future that loomed ahead.

A few minutes later when the phone rang again, I answered, tentatively, as though the telephone was a monster waiting to snap off all protruding body parts.

"H-hello?"

"Mrs. Stepanich, this is Officer Foley again. I think you'd better sit down."

I sat.

It is really true that your blood *can* turn to ice water. I looked at my mother, connecting to that invisible but still present umbilicus. "Okay."

"I'm afraid your husband didn't make it. He was pronounced dead on arrival at the hospital. They have taken his body to the Sunland Mortuary. Is that all right?"

I looked at Mom, screamed, and burst out sobbing. "Michael's dead!"

My Aunt Lucille reached across the table and grabbed my hand. "Honey, I'm so sorry!"

Mom took the phone and talked to the policeman while I simply melted into a puddle of agony. She got a number for me to call later to finalize arrangements. Then she turned to me. There was really not a drop of sympathy in her eyes.

"Weren't you expecting this?"

Even though Michael had already had two multiple by-pass surgeries, angioplasty, stents in his veins, two heart episodes the previous month, and a doctor who said there was nothing more that could be done for him, my immediate response was, "No!" I think they call that denial.

Somehow I got through that day, of which I remember very little. Two cousins came over to do laundry, but I couldn't enjoy their banter.

All I could do was weep into soggy tissues and remember my final conversation with Michael when he called me the previous evening:

"Rose and I went to dinner yesterday at the Old Country Buffet." That was Michael's favorite restaurant because you could eat all you wanted. It took a lot of food to satisfy his six-foot-four frame.

"That's great!" I was very pleased that he and Rose had overcome the estrangement that had separated them for twenty years.

"I think I'll trim that African sumac tree tomorrow. It's getting a little hairy."

"Michael, don't you dare! You know you're not supposed to raise your arms over your head. Just wait until I get home and I'll help you."

"Nah, I feel great. No problem."

"Okay, go kill yourself then. I just wish you would wait."

I think—I hope—that the last thing I said to him was "I love you" and not "Go kill yourself."

The sea beckons for his ashes, but I refuse to let them go, as the rocky shore refuses to part with its pebbles.

Just as the waitress delivers the champagne, which I always order in honor of Michael and our first meeting, a seagull delivers his package on the fly and on the slant, hitting the glass panel with a splat! What are you trying to tell me, Michael?

Why is it not as difficult to come here alone now? When I was here with Shari, I had to anesthetize myself with champagne. Tears and champagne mixed together make for a pretty unpalatable brew. Now, I try to visit as an observer, looking for truth and feelings. My writer pose helps me to feel as though I have the right to be here.

Who am I kidding? Dining alone sucks! I still feel Michael near me, or more likely I *wish* he were near me. The only way I can feel good about seeing this astonishing view alone is to imagine Michael beside me. I toast him with my half-empty champagne glass. Is it symbolic of my half-empty life?

There is a group of three guys sitting at a table behind me, ages about thirty—or forty-something. One guy mentions a jazz club he enjoyed in the Gaslamp Quarter. His friend says that his wife and marriage curtail any such activity anymore. The first guy makes a significant revelation: "I've been married seventeen years and I do things I did before marriage with impunity. My wife now just wants me to get out of the house for a while."

Perhaps she, too, wants to be alone—but not forever . . .

# PART IV

❖

# CODA

(A widow survives losses and learns to sing solo)

# CHAPTER 28

•◦✵◦•

# I'M ALL ALONE

None goes his way alone; all that we send into
the lives of others comes back onto our own.
—Edwin Markham (1950)

I n the midst of one of our frequent heated arguments, my third
husband—or as I used to call him, my first husband twice
removed—hurled this curse at me, "You are going to end up
alone!" I remember thinking, "I wish." You know what they say: "Be
careful what you wish for." How was I to know that curse would follow
me into the twenty-first century?

In the first decade of the new millennium, it appeared as though
my ex-husband's curse was coming true. I lost so many people who
were near and dear to me. However, their legacies—the memories and
memorabilia they left behind—comforted me eventually, and I could
begin to cope with the losses.

## Rudolph Michael Stepanich
### (January 3, 1933-November 1, 1999)

Despite doctor's warnings and prognoses, I was not prepared for
the death of my fourth husband, Michael, after only seventeen years

together. I have always been a person who had to be in control of the situation, and I was totally out-of-control when Michael died. First and foremost, I was not there with him; I was visiting my parents in Indiana when he suffered that fatal heart attack in our front yard. Then, I had to take a long drive to St. Louis and a seemingly interminable airplane trip before I could get home to him. The Sweet Adelines chorus I was directing in Glendale, Arizona, had somehow heard the news. The reaction of the members, upon hearing that Michael had a heart attack and died, was disbelief, "You mean *our* Michael?!"

My parents came to Arizona to be with me for Christmas and to see the new millennium dawn in the desert. They also wanted to help me through the first few months of my widowhood. I was not sure if there would be enough money or if I would need to return to work. I had retired from Western International University the previous year, in September 1998, so as to spend more time with my husband. We had only one year to enjoy total retirement together, but we filled it with all the fun we could manage—trips to favorite vacation spots, horseplay in the swimming pool, and dinner parties with good friends. Fortunately, Michael (bless him) had seen to it that his General Motors pension, his IRA account, and full health benefits would be transferred to me immediately.

Anyone who has watched the television series *The Ghost Whisperer* will find the following story credible. Others will scoff and offer a rational explanation.

The summer of 2000 in Phoenix was as hot, if not hotter, than any I had ever experienced. Although the air-conditioning system in our house was only ten years old, in the middle of one of July's scalding days I began to sense the temperature rising—and rising. I realized that the AC was not working. I walked into the hall, stood in front of the thermostat in all my ineptness, and began to cry because I was a mere woman facing a broken mechanical device I knew nothing about fixing. "Oh, Michael, help me! I don't know what to do!"

His voice sounded clearly in my ear. "Shut off the thermostat, wait a few minutes, and then turn it on again." I did as he (his spirit?) suggested, and the air conditioner began operating perfectly. According to the repairman I consulted later, apparently there had been a slight electrical surge and the system had shut itself off and needed to be rebooted.

Michael's voice in my ear helped me cope with one or two other system malfunctions over the next year or two. I suppose what was really happening was that I was recalling times when he had said these things before, but I prefer to think that Michael was guiding me through those first few difficult years without him.

I would often drive over to San Diego, where we had so much fun, good food, and great times. Although I was terribly sad, I wrote down some thoughts to capture my feelings:

At the Beach Café
*by Mary Ellen Stepanich*

At the Coronado Island Beach Café,
overlooking downtown San Diego,
I remember the bay cruise we enjoyed
the year before Michael died.
The tour guide had explained:

"The San Diego skyline is like a tool box . . .
That building is a Phillips-head screwdriver,
And look! That one looks like a chisel!"
I couldn't stop my response: "And there
is the bar where we both got hammered."

The diners at the café are a motley crew:
one elderly couple and three young mothers
with babies in carriages,
two navy officers in sparkling summer whites,
a young high-tech *wunderkind*, and me, a widow.

A handsome, bearded man eats alone,
dark glasses protecting enigmatic eyes,
head, shoulders and hands move erratically.
Parkinson's? Cerebral palsy?
All the patrons suddenly stop eating.

All the diners, whether young or old,
watch, without speaking, a US Navy destroyer,
sailing, gliding through the Mission Bay,
toward the entrance to the Pacific
. . . and whatever lies beyond.


Yes, we are a motley crew.
The elderly couple and the young mothers
       might have loved ones on that ship.
The two navy officers in summer whites
       might be next.
The *wunderkind* probably invented something that
       might destroy the enemy.
The bearded man
       might have been there—once.


And me, a widow, with a broken heart
Who had always yearned to go to sea,
Who has lost her beloved husband
in a different kind of war.

Michael's body was cremated, and we had held a brief memorial service after he died, but I couldn't bear to part with him. I kept his ashes in an urn, and I constructed a miniature shrine in the corner of my bedroom, with his picture, his ashes, his favorite beer mug, and his miniature cedar chest that held his grooming instruments—comb, hair clippers, and nail file.

Was I being a bit ghoulish? Perhaps, but I know that I didn't feel alone. Michael was figuratively, and literally, still with me. It was only after reading about Feng Shui, the Chinese art of harmonious placement within an environment, that I realized I was shutting out any possible future relationship by keeping my dead husband in my bedroom.

Michael had served in the US Air Force as a staff sergeant following the Korean conflict. So, for the tenth anniversary of his death, I planned an interment ceremony to take place at the National Military Cemetery in Cave Creek, north of Phoenix, complete with air force honor guard and flag presentation ceremony.

The ceremony was well attended—his children, Shari and Scott (and their significant others, John and Jennifer), his sister Rose, all of our closest neighbors and friends, and many of my Sweet Adelines acquaintances. I had enticed them to come by saying it would be a dress rehearsal for my own burial. My barbershop quartet, Lilac Crazy, sang "Amazing Grace," "God Bless America," and "We'll Meet Again."

The air force honor guard folded the American flag in an impressive ceremony and presented it to me. One soldier played taps at a distance, family members read poetry I had selected, and I gave the eulogy. It was a beautiful ceremony and I could maintain, for the most part, my emotional equilibrium because it was ten years after Michael had died. My lips did begin to tremble, however, when the young air force soldier knelt in front of me, handed me the flag, and said, "From the president of the United States, and a grateful nation."

There is a saying: "Some people come into our lives and quickly go. Others stay awhile, leaving footprints on our hearts." Rudolph Michael Stepanich was a man who always left footprints. Of course they were size 14D footprints! But they had to be huge, in order to support a man who was larger than life, who had so much to give, and who exerted tremendous influence on his family, his friends—and yes, even on General Motors—in his short time on this earth.

Through this influence, as I told the family and friends at Michael's funeral, "The spirit of Little Rudy, as he was called by his mother, will live on in the hearts of all those whom he loved, and whose lives he touched, as loving husband, doting father, caring brother, loyal employee—and my best friend."

# William Robert Trowbridge
## (August 10, 1937–December 5, 2003)

A couple of years after Michael's death, my mother received a card from Bill Trowbridge, my first husband, saying that his father had died. Mom forwarded the card to me, and I wrote to him offering my condolences. He responded by telling me where he was living (in Escondido) and asking to meet me when I next came to California. Because I was singing with the San Diego Sweet Adelines, I traveled to the coast twice a month. I made arrangements to meet Bill at a popular restaurant off the Interstate in Escondido during my next trip.

When I drove into the restaurant parking lot, Bill was standing beside his car, looking almost exactly like he looked when I last saw him in 1972, when we divorced after nearly ten years together. I think he was even wearing the same shirt—a Norfolk-style leisure shirt. As I pulled up next to him, I lowered my car window and exclaimed, "You have hair!" His father had been bald, and Bill had a receding hairline when I knew him, so I had expected a chrome dome.

We had a pleasant lunch, quickly updating each other on our activities of the past thirty years, sharing pictures and stories. Bill had never remarried and had a very bad job history, to the point that he had to live in his car during one year of unemployment.

As a matter of fact, when I had applied for widow's Social Security benefits at age sixty, after Michael died, the staffer had said, "Let's check the records of your previous husbands." She looked at Bill's data and said, "Never mind."

Bill had subsequently moved in with an old girlfriend who was taking care of him, physically and financially. Before we left the restaurant, we hugged companionably and made arrangements to meet again on my next trip to San Diego. However, his lady friend objected to our continuing to see each other, even on an intermittent, public, platonic basis. I told him I understood perfectly. I probably would have reacted the same way if the situation were reversed.

We corresponded from time to time, and in December 2003 I received a letter from Bill's girlfriend, who forwarded a farewell letter from him, at his request. He had died of cancer only a few months following the diagnosis, and he had asked that my parents and I should be notified. Bill was sixty-six years of age when he died—the same age as my husband Michael when he passed away. That same year, I learned that one of my high school boyfriends had just died of a heart attack— and he was sixty-six. A few years later, my brother was diagnosed with prostate cancer, at age sixty-six. I'm beginning to think that sixty-six is a dangerous age for people of my generation.

## George Beverley Batterton
### (July 6, 1927-Late 2005)

When one of my Brownsville neighbors called me in Indiana at Christmas 1981 to say that George—my abusive third husband—had run away with Arlene, another neighbor, I responded, "Thank God!"

Sometime in late 2005, another former friend and quartet member, Shirley, called me to say that George—who was also *her* abusive ex-husband—had passed away after a long battle with cancer. I kept a firm rein on my tongue and expressed only regret that he had not lived a truly happy life. If one were to examine the circumstances of his early years growing up in Texas, I'm sure there would be clear signals pointing to an explanation for his subsequent behavior. He was the son of an abusive father, and I believe research has demonstrated that abusers beget abusers.

I have given much thought to the question, "What positive legacy did I receive from my four years with George?" He didn't leave any money; he hid resources and absconded with everything he could lay hands on, including my neighbor Arlene's money. He didn't leave good memories; I have managed to erase all traces of him from my home, although I do have a beautiful portrait of the two of us at our wedding. I keep it hidden behind the guest room door.

I suppose I did learn a valuable, although painfully taught, lesson. I fold all my towels in perfect thirds, and I wipe off every faucet after use, even those in public restrooms. During my life with George, I would be severely reprimanded if I failed to do that. There's a scene in the movie, *Sleeping with the Enemy,* starring Julia Roberts, which could have been based upon my life with George.

In 2006, when I was sitting in the hospital waiting room during Daddy's final hospitalization, my niece Kristy, her husband Nick, my mother, and I were discussing heaven and hell. I said, "I know I'm going to heaven, because I've already been to hell—I was married to George."

Nick piped up, "And I've already been to heaven, because I'm married to Kristy." Now *that* is a good man.

## Carlton Hunt Brannen,
### (born sometime in the early 1930s)

Recently, I had the urge to surf the Internet to find out if my second husband, Hunt, was still living, and if so, where. Our marriage had been brief—little more than two years. I found that someone named Carlton Hunt Brannen was living in Fullerton, California, but it would cost $1.95 to get his address and telephone number. I decided he wasn't worth the money

# CHAPTER 29

---·◦❋◦·---

# WHEN THE LIGHTS
# GO OUT . . .

A stroke is God's way of tapping you on
the shoulder and saying, "That's one!"
—Dr. William E. Blevins, 2006

E arly in 2005, my cousin Sharon, who had been something of a
caretaker to my parents, suffered a pneumonia-type infection
and seemed near death. My folks, especially my mother, were
so afraid of being left completely alone in their aged condition that they
allowed my brother, Bill, to convince them to move closer to him. They
reluctantly sold their beloved stone home in Fort Branch and hastily
moved to Lafayette, buying the first house they could find that fit their
budget. Although they enjoyed being close to my brother and to Elma,
my mother's sister, Mom did *not* like the house. She complained that it
was smaller than her stone home, and she had no friends in Lafayette.

I visited my folks in May 2005 to aid them with the move and
the settling in. Daddy was planting some flowers, so I stepped outside
to give him a little help. I remarked that the backyard looked really
nice, with big oak trees and a swing—a perfect place to relax. Daddy
looked around and said, "It's heaven." Any place my father was, it was
heaven.

At Christmas 2005, I flew to Lafayette to visit Mom and Dad for the holidays. Because Daddy's ninetieth birthday was shortly after Christmas—January 11, 2006—I decided to throw a huge celebration for him. I couldn't believe that there were cards and balloons in the stores, preprinted with ninetieth birthday messages! I guess people are living longer nowadays. I invited every living relative in the family, and there were many who were still living. They came from Ohio, all parts of Indiana, and Illinois. Mom and Dad's little retirement home was bursting at the seams, and although I had planned for a mob, we soon ran out of food. They were eating it faster than I could buy replacements. But it was worth it; Daddy had a wonderful time.

I flew back to Arizona the day after Daddy's birthday and drove to San Diego on January 13 to attend the San Diego Chorus retreat. That night, Friday, I had an attack of atrial fibrillation—an irregular heartbeat commonly called "a-fib." It lasted several hours, most of Friday night. I had experienced the condition many times in the past, but I wasn't concerned because I'd been told by a nurse that it was not life threatening. However, this time the outcome was different.

Saturday, I felt tired, but I managed to keep up with the other chorus members. On Sunday morning, while standing on the top row of risers, singing and dancing while preparing for our Spring Chorus competition, I experienced a violently piercing headache. I said to the girl standing next to me, "I'm going to do something I've never done before—I'm going to sit down!"

Trying to be unobtrusive, I squeezed between the ladies, carefully stepping down the risers until I reached the floor, and then I sidled toward some chairs at the edge of the chorus. As I started to sit down, suddenly the lights went out—in my brain, that is. I had a massive stroke. The stroke was caused by a blood clot in my heart that had formed while my heart's left atrium was in fibrillation, i.e., fluttering rapidly and erratically, not beating in rhythm as it should have been. This clot was pumped out into the blood stream when my heart returned to sinus rhythm after several hours and was now lodged in my brain stem.

Fortunately, there were seven nurses in that chorus, and they all rushed to my side, somehow knowing instinctively what was happening. They called 911, and the emergency medical team appeared in short order, did what EMTs do, and bundled me off to the nearby Sharp Memorial Hospital. I was not aware of any of this, of course. I do remember my friend Judy B. taking my hairpiece and jewelry off for safekeeping. In other circumstances, I would have been humiliated to be seen without my hairpiece, but when your brain isn't working, nothing seems to matter. In the ambulance, an EMT repeatedly called my name, but I was unable to see him or respond. I also remember the chorus singing to me as I was wheeled out of the room, but my addled brain doesn't remember the name of the song.

At the hospital, a series of fortunate events occurred—and I believe several heavenly bodies aligned. A doctor from Germany who was an expert on strokes and stroke victims was just completing a sabbatical visit to the hospital. He was called back in to the hospital—it was Sunday morning, after all—and was requested to examine me and give an opinion as to my condition and treatment. He rapidly assessed the situation and recommended a direct infusion of tPA (tissue plasminogen activator, a clot-dissolving drug) into my brain stem via the femoral artery, through an insertion in my groin. All of this—from attack to treatment—took place within the space of two or three hours.

I awoke in a hospital bed to see doctors with anxious faces bending over me. The German doctor was introduced to me, and he held out his two index fingers and commanded in his accented voice, "Squizz my feenghers."

Memories of Michael and the tricks he used to play on his children leaped immediately into my mind, and I innocently asked this famous, wonderful, life-saving stroke specialist, "You're not going to fart, are you?"

The doctors pronounced that I was a living miracle. I had no discernible after effects of the stroke, with a few minor exceptions. I seemed to have absolutely no inhibitions and would say whatever came into my mind. Sometimes, the things that came into my mind were not what I had intended. The nurse had to monitor my intake and outgo of fluids, so she told me to use the hat device in the toilet and to refrain from flushing the toilet after use. I promptly forgot her directions, and when she came to check on me, I apologized, "Oh, I'm sorry! I already flushed the dishwasher." I didn't realize my mistake until I saw the quizzical expression on her face.

I was astonished to awake on my second day at the hospital to see my brother, Dr. William Earl Blevins, full professor and head of radiology of the School of Veterinary Medicine of Purdue University, striding into my hospital room. This was the brother who rarely stuck his head out of his office other than to go home to his ranch. And he had flown across the breadth of this country to come to my aide. I could hardly believe my eyes! I had to face the fact that this aloof academic, my annoying little brother, must love me, after all.

My sister-in-law, Michael's sister Rose, also drove over from Phoenix. She's a retired nurse, so I suppose she wanted to make sure they were taking care of me "according to Hoyle."

Within five days the doctors pronounced that I was miraculously cured, but that I would need to be treated for the atrial fibrillation condition so as to avoid a repetition of the stroke. My brother drove me in my car back to Arizona. We stopped for lunch, and, except for a slight unsteadiness, I was able to walk holding on to Bill's arm.

As we ate, I was discussing the prescriptions for my care that the doctors had suggested: "And I'm supposed to see my major professor as soon as I get back."

Bill looked at me with that you-have-two-heads look, again.

"I meant primary care physician." I was still having difficulty grasping the correct word or expression, a condition that lasted several months.

The only residual effect of the stroke that caused any real problem was my poor equilibrium. A week after I came home, I was reaching up to straighten a picture while standing on the kitchen stepstool. The room began to whirl around; I lost my balance and fell, completely smashing a table lamp but not breaking anything else, including any body parts. The doctor suggested I use a walker for a while—and stay off stepstools.

I had promised to appear in the Westbrook Follies, our annual community amateur talent show to be held in late February. I was playing the role of Adelaide in the concert presentation of *Guys and Dolls*. Rehearsals for the event were scheduled immediately following my return from the hospital, so I was using the walker for most of the rehearsals. When I sang, "You promise me this, you promise me that, you promise me everything under the sun," stomping from one side of the stage to the other with my walker, the rest of the cast laughed so hard they said, "Keep the walker!" However, I had graduated to a cane by the time of the performance.

For a year, I would suffer an attack of atrial fibrillation about every ninety days, until doctors found the correct combination of drugs to treat the condition. I was beginning to think I was affected by the phases of the moon! On two separate occasions, I received the cardio-conversion treatment, an interesting procedure in which the heart is stopped by electric shock and then re-started, which usually returns the heart to sinus rhythm. You've probably seen those shows on television where the handsome doctor yells, "Clear!" and then applies the paddles to the patient's heart, delivering a severe shock.

I was wheeled into the treatment room, rails were set up around the gurney, and then the nurse began stuffing pillows around my body. I asked why. She replied, "So you won't accidentally bump the sides during the procedure." Hmm.

I began to envision all sorts of horrible scenes. When she placed two large electrode pads on my back and chest and then tilted my head back, chin high, I asked, "Aren't you going to put a stick between my teeth?" But the procedure worked well and kept my heart in rhythm for several months.

Finally, I was able to determine most of the circumstances that would trigger the a-fib. Now, I know what to avoid: no stress (good luck with that one), no caffeine, no heavy lifting (no problem!), and no ice cold drinks (good-bye frozen margaritas!)

However, I still have a-fib attacks now and then, usually after something stressful, such as a fight with my homeowner's association. Because I'm so familiar with my body's reaction, I simply drive myself to the hospital emergency room, tell them I need an injection of Cardizem, and within a few hours I'm fine. This way, my car is in the parking lot and I can simply drive myself home.

My next-door neighbor chastised me for driving myself to the hospital. I said, "But I take the less-traveled roads and I drive slowly, never more than thirty miles per hour."

"Yeah," he said, "and you piss off every other driver on the road."

Okay, so I'm independent—and stubborn!

# CHAPTER 30

---
·•❈•·
---

# LIL' ORPHAN ANNIE

Honor thy Father and thy Mother, that
thy days may be long upon the land
which the Lord thy God giveth thee.
—The Holy Bible (Exod. 20:12)

William Elwood Blevins
(January 11, 1916-April 2, 2006)

About six weeks after my brother, Bill, returned to Indiana following my stroke, he called me to say that Daddy had been admitted to the hospital with congestive heart failure and that I should come home as soon as possible. Daddy had lost a kidney to cancer in 1993, and recently doctors had taken him off diuretics because his one remaining kidney was functioning at only 38 percent effectiveness. Apparently, diuretic drugs can cause kidney problems.

Unfortunately, the withholding of the diuretics caused Daddy's body to fill with fluid and his system was unable to cope with the excess. My brother could give the exact diagnosis; he used words such as "left mitral valve regurgitation" and "pulmonary edema."

Daddy was hospitalized for several weeks while doctors attempted to reverse the negative effects. However, the efforts at damage control were not successful and the doctors concluded there was nothing more to be done. Daddy was released to home care on Thursday, March 30. I was there to help Mom, but the home nurse provided by the hospital to assess his condition said Daddy needed hospice care, which could not begin until the following Monday.

On Friday, my niece, Kristi, and her husband, Nick, came down from Chicago for the weekend, and we had a poignant family reunion with Mom and Dad, their children and grandchildren. After dinner, Daddy called my brother and me into the living room and looked us in the eyes, as he had done when we were born. "I want you to promise you will take care of your mother."

We hastened to assure him we would look after Mom. Then he said, "And I want you two to stop fighting."

"Oh, Daddy," I joked, "Bill and I don't fight—we just have differences of opinion."

Unfortunately, pain from the congestive heart failure increased to such a point that, on Saturday evening, Daddy said, "I need to go back to the hospital." The ambulance came and neighbors gathered outside, somehow knowing that the end was near. All the family followed the ambulance to the hospital.

Daddy was placed on a respirator and given sedatives so he would feel no pain. However, my brother knew that Daddy did not want to be kept alive by any artificial means, so Bill, with aching heart, gave the attending physicians the official order to remove life support. With every one of us touching him, we said our good-byes, and I sang "Amazing Grace," so that the last thing Daddy felt and heard was an affirmation of his family's love and his enduring faith in God.

## Edna Marie Smith Blevins
### (May 21, 1920-January 30, 2008)

After Daddy died, the life seemed to go out of Mom, as well. After all, she had been married to this man for almost sixty-eight years. I coaxed her into coming with me to Arizona for a few months, and I believe she did find some relief from the agony of widowhood. She enjoyed my friends and attended a volunteer reception with me at

Sun Sounds of Arizona, the radio reading service for the blind and print-disabled. I have volunteered there as a reader since shortly after Michael died. We were both surprised when the recipient of the Golden Microphone award for volunteer of the year was announced—*me!* At that reception, I also received a plaque for Program of the Year, awarded by the International Association of Audio Information Services, for my reading of *Christ the Lord: Out of Egypt.* I was so glad that my mother was there to see me receive these honors.

Despite having a good time with me, Mom said she had to return to Indiana and attempt to live her life as a widow. My father's brother, Uncle Charles, would visit her from time to time, and my brother Bill tried to look after her, as best he could.

Mom's eyesight was worsening, so she could no longer drive. Fortunately, her younger sister, my Aunt Elma, lived nearby and was able to drive her to the doctor and to the grocery store. I would call Mom twice a week, and visit her every two or three months. My brother and I bought her a hearing aid so she could hear the television, and she had cataract surgery so she could see what was on the screen. I contracted with the local hospital to have a special telephone put in her home that required Mom to check in with the hospital morning and evening. If she failed to call in, they would contact a neighbor.

By Christmas, 2007, Mom could no longer walk. She also had congestive heart failure, caused by a diseased heart and lungs that failed to get blood to her extremities, and her body was, literally, dying from the feet upward. Again, my brother Bill made the sad call to tell me the bad news, and on my birthday, January 8, 2008, I flew to Indiana on what was—as it had been sixty-eight years earlier—the coldest day of the year. Mom's problem was in the right side of her heart, which Bill says causes "the most painful, inhumane, and drawn-out death." The doctors said there was nothing that could be done for her, so Mom was sent to the St. Anthony Care Center in Lafayette on January 20, 2008. (My brother always called the place "Holy Tony's.") She was given the best of care, and I was with her every morning and evening. Her friends and other family members would visit every afternoon.

One evening, Mom began to show agitation, a clear sign that she was in pain. I went to the nurses' station to see if she could be given some pain medication. The nurse told me that Mom's pain medication was not due to be given for another two hours.

I smiled at the nurse. "Did you ever see the movie, *Terms of Endearment*? There is a scene in which Debra Winger, a cancer patient, is in pain, so her mother, played by Shirley MacLaine, pounds on the nurse's desk and screams, 'My daughter needs pain medication—*now!*'"

"Oh, yes, I saw that movie—it was really good."

"Okay." I smiled and then leaned over the nurse's desk, put my fist on the counter, and said loudly and forcefully, "My mother needs pain medication—*now!*" She got it.

On January 29, Lafayette had the worst snow and ice storm in history. When I left the nursing home that night, I couldn't get my car door open; it had frozen shut. Luckily, I was able to flag down my brother as he was pulling out of the parking lot and he opened the door for me. The town lost electricity that night, but the home had a generator for emergency lights. They wheeled Mom's bed down to the nurses' station, and she passed away at three-thirty in the morning of January 30, 2008.

Both Mom and Dad were interred in the Montgomery Cemetery at Oakland City, near our hometown in southern Indiana. The weather was cooperative when Daddy died April 2, 2006, and there was a spring-like day for his funeral. But the weatherman was definitely not cooperative when Mom died January 30, 2008. A tornado-like winter storm swept through southern Indiana the day before Mom's burial, and the cemetery ground was so hard I pitied the gravediggers.

Daddy had been a member of the Freemasons for nearly fifty years, and was a former worshipful master of his lodge. All throughout his life, even at the last, he was constantly refreshing his memory of the Masonic rituals. He knew them so well he was always asked to prompt the participants when they would forget their words during the meetings. To honor him, the Masons provided an impressive ceremony at his funeral, burying him wearing his white leather Masonic apron. Daddy's brother, my uncle Charles, also a Mason, participated in the ceremony. My high school quartet sang "Amazing Grace" and "Beyond the Sunset," and my brother, Bill, gave an extremely moving and emotional eulogy.

At the time of her death, Mom was a member of the Eastern Star—a women's group whose husbands, fathers, sons, or brothers are Masons. She was just three months shy of being eligible for her fifty-year pin. The Eastern Star also gave a special ceremony for Mom's funeral and placed a fifty-year ribbon in her casket. Again, my high school quartet sang and I gave the eulogy, some of which follows:

> When Mom died early Wednesday morning, Lafayette had a terrible winter storm and electrical outage, and Fort Branch had a tornado ripping through town. I believe that the poet, Dylan Thomas, might have said, "Mom did not go gently into that dark night."
>
> Mom and Dad instilled in their two children many values, but especially these two: "Get an education," and "Work hard in life."
>
> Mom always told me that Daddy held us in the palm of his hand when we were born, pointed a finger at our newborn baby selves, and commanded, *"You* are going to get an education." Both Bill and I certainly loved school, and Mom and Dad sacrificed a lot so that we could earn those degrees: BA, BS, MS, MBA, DVM, PhD, yada, yada, blah, blah, blah.
>
> During our growing up years, I remember seeing a crocheted antimacassar (a large doily used to protect chair backs or table tops) that I believe was crocheted by my Grandma Dorsam and which reflects the way our parents lived:
>
> *Life is mostly froth and bubble; two things stand like stone:*
> *Kindness in another's trouble, courage in your own.*

Bud and Edna Blevins were wonderful parents. They didn't intend to raise a "schizo"; they thought they had raised a normal girl who would bring them love, honor—and grandchildren. Two out of three ain't bad.

The decade of loss was not finished, however. In December 2010, my stepdaughter, Shari, called to say that her cancer had returned. After a month of hospitalization, my darling Shari left us—her brother Scott, her beloved John, her Aunt Rose, and me—on February 11, 2011.

# CHAPTER 31

·•◈•·

# SING, SING, SING, SING

You're the flower of my heart, Sweet Adeline.
—Richard Gerard and Harry Armstrong, 1903

By 1995 I had been singing for five years with a large, championship chorus in Arizona whose members were very talented but not very warm or welcoming. For example, at one rehearsal I facilitated a values clarification exercise to ascertain the closely held beliefs of the group, as well as to reveal to each of us individual members how our own beliefs and values might differ from those of the group. Most people in the chorus valued youthfulness, a winning attitude, and "fitting in with the chorus." I looked at my values list; I valued diversity and empathy. I believed that everyone was valuable to the group, no matter what they could contribute. Most others in the chorus apparently disagreed.

The director would not allow riser chairs—those are special chairs affixed to the risers for members who had difficulty standing. Nor did she allow anyone who was not thin and svelte to stand in the front row. Other championship choruses I had joined or counseled had very different closely held values. Gem City Chorus, in Dayton, Ohio, had several heavy ladies in the front row, but those gals could really dance! San Diego Chorus had special chairs on the risers for the older or infirm members, but those women could really sing!

227

Therefore, when a small chorus that met closer to my home asked me to audition to be their director, I thought, Why not? I've directed a small chorus before, in Lafayette, Indiana, and although it can be a challenge, I enjoy the closeness and camaraderie of a smaller group. There were thirteen members when I started directing the Cactus Country Chorus, and within four years we had grown to seventy members and won the midsize chorus award at regional competition. They were truly a diverse group of women—young and not-so-young, slender and not-so-slender, talented and not-so-talented—but they were like a big family that loved each other—even the irrepressible Dolores.

Dolores was a postal worker, and we all know how we must be careful of them! I approached her window at the Sun City Post Office one day and showed her the documentation I was sending to Sweet Adelines headquarters, together with my application to be accepted to the international faculty of the organization. There were videotapes, syllabi, documentation of my experience, and letters of recommendation. I asked her advice on the best method of safely mailing those materials. She looked all through the stack and exclaimed, "What the heck *is* this!?"

After I explained, she was intrigued and asked me more about our chorus, what we sang, where we rehearsed and performed. I invited her to attend one of our rehearsals, just to listen to the chorus. Much to my surprise, she showed up the next week. The welcoming committee greeted her and, as is the normal procedure, took her to a back room where she was voice tested to determine which of the four barbershop voice parts best matched her vocal range.

Later, after Dolores joined the chorus and was one of our best contributing members, she told me she almost walked out the first night. "When those women grabbed me, took me to the back room and made me sing, 'Happy Birthday,' I was ready to wrestle 'em to the ground and hightail it out o' there." (Dolores was from Kentucky.)

Early in 1997, Judy X., a former member of the chorus, called me with a proposition. Her country-western combo had been a performer in the New Year's Day parade festival in London, England, the previous year, and she wanted to participate again. However, the parade organizers did not allow the same group to perform in two consecutive years. So, Judy asked me to apply for the Cactus Country Chorus to participate in the 1997/98 London parade festival, and her combo would perform as part of our group.

The chorus applied, and won a spot in the London parade festival, but the country-western combo opted out. Most of the groups who performed in the New Year's Day parade in London were high school and college marching bands. Our chorus did not march, of course, so we performed in the pre-parade festivities, singing in concerts in Westminster—the inner section of London, home of the Queen's palace. We also performed for the lord mayors of the major cities in Great Britain and gave a London concert for the general population.

We made costumes that reflected our Arizona connection: silver-fringed black boots, black riding skirts, white shirts with silver vests lined in red paisley and trimmed in black fringe, silver concho-trimmed bolo string ties, red paisley bandanas, and silver cowboy hats. After we sang for the lord mayors, who were splendidly robed in velvet with massive silver chains of office, one buxom lady approached me and cooed in her aristocratic British accent, "Your costume is ever so much lovelier than mine!"

The next year the chorus was again invited by the London parade festival group to sing—this time at the 1999 Easter parade festival in Maastricht, Netherlands. The directors of each chorus or band were invited on an all-expense-paid trip to visit the performance venue in Maastricht a few months prior to the chorus trip.

When I returned to Phoenix from Amsterdam, my bags did not return with me. The airline searched but couldn't locate them. About a week later, someone from Phoenix Sky Harbor Airport called me to say that my bags had been found in a dumpster at the airport. Apparently, a baggage handler had rifled my bags, stolen some jewelry and, more importantly, the book of trip instructions containing the London festival bank account number for our chorus trip deposits. I made a hasty phone call to London and was assured that the bank account was for deposits only—no one except the festival company could withdraw the money.

A few weeks later, the Phoenix police called me and reported they had apprehended a burglar in the middle of a hotel theft, and at his apartment they had found my jewelry and the account notebook that contained my name and address. I was told to report to the police precinct to recover my possessions. The detective at the precinct asked me to pose with my possessions while they took a photograph for the files. I stood against the wall, as requested, smiled triumphantly, and presented the notebook and my jewelry like Vanna White presenting the vowels on *Wheel of Fortune.* The detective shook his head in disbelief. "We've never had anyone pose like that before." (Obviously, he'd never had a Sweet Adeline before!)

As soon as Cactus Country Chorus arrived in Amsterdam the week before Easter 1999, we were whisked away on a tour of some of its well-known attractions: the queen's palace, the bustling city square, and the infamous red light district. One of our members, a former nun, looked at the narrow streets with scantily clad women sitting in picture windows, and grumbled, "This is a tourist attraction? To think we could have been seeing some of Amsterdam's famous churches instead." The tour was followed by a magnificent Indonesian *rijsttafel* (rice table) dinner at a floating restaurant. Indonesian food is popular in the Netherlands, probably because the Dutch colonized the East Indies for centuries before Indonesia became independent in 1945.

We were then bused to Maastricht where we visited the caverns beneath the city, the cobble-stoned and restored old part of the city that had been bombed during World War II, as well as the historic churches and city hall buildings. Two days a week there was an open market in the town square that sold everything from fine hand-made laces and tooled leather bags to slabs of freshly butchered sides of beef. Another intriguing aspect of Maastricht was its unique blend of modern and ancient technology. I saw the latest in automatic street-sweeping machines, which were accompanied by workers sweeping the sidewalks, wielding handcrafted brooms made of twigs.

We performed on the holiday weekend in front of the city hall while the Maastricht Easter parade marched past the reviewing stand, where the chorus stood while singing. It rained so much during the event that when I took a bow after our first number, the water that had collected on the rim of my cowboy hat cascaded, Niagara-like, down the front of my costume.

The highlight of our trip was a visit to the American Veterans Memorial Cemetery, between Maastricht, Netherlands, and Achen, Germany. The cemetery land was a gift to the United States by the grateful Netherlanders. We could see row upon row of crosses, denoting the final resting place of thousands of American soldiers who lost their lives during the liberation of the Dutch people from the Nazis in World War II. A monumental map depicted the liberation campaign trail, and a nearby chapel provided a place for visitors to pray or simply contemplate the solemnity of the place. Our Cactus Country Chorus stood on the steps of the chapel and sang, "The Star Spangled Banner" and "Amazing Grace." There was not a dry eye in the place.

The chorus was scheduled to perform a concert later in the week at the Maastricht Performing Arts Center, a magnificent new facility that was the showplace of this bustling, modern *Nederlander* community. Prior to that, on one of the group's sightseeing stops, I'd been chatting with our tour bus driver and asked him to teach me a phrase in the Dutch language to use when addressing the audience—something that would express our delight in being there and performing for them.

After considering my request for a moment, he said, "Well, there is a phrase we often use when greeting friends. It's a sort of poem that means 'How are you doing?'"

"That sounds great! Teach me."

"Okay. It goes like this: *Is alles kits achter der rits?*"

I repeated the phrase to him until he assured me I was pronouncing the greeting perfectly. When the evening of our big performance came, I was ready.

We sang and danced through the first number in our musical spoof, "LaWanda Darlene, the Rodeo Queen," the story of a girl of the Golden West who longs to become a star on the Broadway stage. We were dressed appropriately—in cowboy hats, silver vests, and black boots, every item in our costumes dripping with silver fringe and sequins. After our chorus sang the opening song, I went to the microphone.

"Good evening, ladies and gentlemen. We are so happy to be here, performing for you. I wanted to be able to greet you in your native language, and I persuaded our tour bus driver to teach me a phrase of greeting. So, here goes: '*Guten aben, mein damen und herren. Is alles kits achter der rits?*'"

The audience erupted, as if thousands of sharp pins had jabbed their seats simultaneously! They applauded madly, they roared with laughter, they slapped their knees, and when the laughter began to die down, it would break out again in waves throughout the audience. I was so proud!

We gave a terrific performance, and when the concert was over and we were down in front of the stage, visiting with audience members, a tall man pushed and elbowed his way through the crowd. When he finally reached me, he asked, "Did your bus driver really teach you to say that?"

"Yes, he did."

"Well, I'm the manager of the bus company. Do you know what you said?"

"Uh—I hope I pronounced it correctly. I think it means something like 'How are you doing?'"

"Actually, it means, literally, 'Is everything okay behind your zipper?'"

I was stunned momentarily. "Well—at least the audience enjoyed it. Please don't fire the bus driver!"

When Michael died on November 1, 1999, I was on the management team (the board of directors) of Region 21, Sweet Adelines. The region includes West Texas, New Mexico, Arizona, and Southern California. I also had been appointed the previous year to the international faculty of Sweet Adelines and was teaching in St. Louis when my husband had that fatal heart attack. In addition, I was due to lead a weekend retreat in Vancouver, Canada, later in November, despite the fact that I had broken my ankle in Atlanta, Georgia, at the Sweet Adelines International competition a few weeks before Michael died.

But being the stalwart (okay, stubborn!) Capricorn that I am, I refused to let anything slow me down; I flew (and limped) to Vancouver the last week in November to do my thing. I sparkled, I laughed, I told my humorous stories, and I was accepted with love and attention. However, when I presented Learning Style Inventory and Analysis—for which I always used my four husbands as illustrations—I broke down and cried when discussing the converger, my husband Michael. The audience was typical of Sweet Adelines throughout the world. They were warm, loving, caring, and made me feel as though they shared every ounce of my pain.

One source of both love and pain came about when I was nominated to run for a position on the international board of Sweet Adelines, which was headquartered in Tulsa, Oklahoma. Although I was beginning to become known to members around the globe, I was running against some women who, in my opinion, made serving on the international board their life's work—not unlike the members of the US Congress.

I was not elected for the three-year term, but I *was* appointed to serve a one-year term on the international board. I thought, "Now, I can show them what I can do!" I literally (well, figuratively) rolled up my sleeves and set to work. I accepted every task that I was assigned, and I volunteered to lead the group—board members and permanent headquarters staff—in several strategic planning sessions. After all, I had taught business leaders of several countries to lead their corporations in planning strategically for success. I hit them with all barrels: mission, vision, values, goals, action plans, and implementation targets. I was a planning dynamo!

About midway through my term of office, the board prepared the slate of nominees for the following year's election. I assumed I would be on the slate because of my work on the board of directors, and the fact that, by now, I had been teaching the organization's membership in almost every one of the international regions.

However, when the slate was announced, my name was not included. I was crushed. I went back to my hotel room and sobbed as though my heart were breaking, which it was. I couldn't understand why this had happened. Hadn't I done everything that was asked of me, and hadn't I done a good job? I begged one of the members of the nominating committee to tell me why I was not chosen. She told me the committee was sworn to secrecy, but she could see how brokenhearted I was, so she gave me this morsel, "The committee felt that you would try to change the board."

Well, yes! That's what strategic planning is all about! If things are not going well, the planners must obviously change things or the organization will sink—just like the metaphorical ship and its deserting rats. And things definitely were not going well for Sweet Adelines; the life blood of the membership was hemorrhaging. Once again, my old bugaboo, academic excellence, reared its ugly head and I was hoisted on my own petard—my knowledge and talents.

Although I would no longer be on the international board, I was still a much sought after international faculty member. I was chosen to teach at the International Education Symposium in New Zealand and Australia in the summer (their winter) of 2000. The people of New Zealand were so warm and friendly. They took me on a tour of Auckland, the Americas Cup basin, and the central part of the country, where I saw sheep grazing on the lawn of some of the national monuments.

One of my tasks in the symposium was to direct a chorus of Kiwis, the affectionate term for New Zealanders, in a delightfully comic song written and arranged by Arizona's own Nancy Bergman: "I've Been Waiting for Your Phone Call for Eighteen Years." When the Kiwis sang that song, it sounded like, "Oive beeeen whyting foah yewuh phaon cawl foah eyeteen yeeeers."

I said to the group, "I think we need to work on vowels."

When I returned home to Arizona, I was faced with a chorus that was split by conflicting loyalties. Some members wanted to work and become bigger and better. Others were the girls who "just wanted to have fun." Although I had taken the Cactus Country Chorus to winning performances and exciting concerts and tours in Europe, another woman who had directed the chorus twenty years previously and then resigned to raise her family had decided she wanted to be the director again. Once more, rather than stay and fight through the conflict, I fled.

My good friend, Judy B., who had sung with me in The Right Arrangement and Just One More Time quartets in Indiana, now lived in California. She suggested I join the San Diego Chorus with her. I told the director, Kim H., that I could not meet the attendance requirements, but I would do everything I could for the chorus. She told me, "You will do more in one rehearsal a month than most members do in four." So, from 2000 until 2006, I commuted to San Diego from Phoenix once or twice a month. Kim named me the lead section leader, and in October 2001, the San Diego Chorus won the first place championship in the Sweet Adelines International competition in Portland, Oregon. (Whoopee!)

When one is part of a worldwide organization such as Sweet Adelines, one is never truly alone. We members often say, "I can always tell if a woman is a Sweet Adeline—she smiles at everything and everybody."

And, she's not afraid to ask people in another country, "Is everything okay behind your zipper?"

# CHAPTER 32

———•◦✸◦•———

# THANKS FOR THE MEMORY

It is therefore necessary that memorable things
should be committed to writing, and not
wholly committed to slippery memory.
—Sir Edward Coke, 1660

E ven at my age, I'm still a member of Sweet Adelines International
and still singing with my comedy quartet, Lilac Crazy. As we
say to our audiences, "We chose that name, not because we are
crazy about the color lilac, but because—we *lie* like crazy!"

It's not easy to describe the thrill, the hair-raising emotion, and
the visceral experience of singing four-part harmony, *a cappella* (i.e.,
unaccompanied), barbershop style, and singing it correctly. Some have
described it as "ringing chords," resulting from the fifth note that sounds
when all four voices sing in perfect precision of vowels and frequencies.
This creates a harmonic—the fifth note—that causes a ringing effect.
When it happens, those of us who are hooked on barbershop would do
just about anything to make it happen again. This experience happens
most frequently when one sings in a quartet.

Once, several years ago, a lady on the entertainment committee for
a group that was hiring my quartet asked me, "How many are in your
quartet?" It's difficult to keep a straight face in answering that question.
As I recall, I replied, "Oh, the usual number."

I have been singing in barbershop quartets since I joined Sweet Adelines in 1972. My garage wall is covered, floor to ceiling, with pictures of all my barbershop choruses and quartets. I have been a member of a quartet that placed last in contest, and another one that placed first. I've been in some quartets for only a few weeks, and others for several years. I have sung with quartet members who lived in the same town and others who lived thousands of miles away. Some quartets were friends and some were not. While it's fun to sing with people who are friends, it is difficult to self-coach the quartet and to offer feedback to them without hurting the feelings of those you love. On the other hand, it's not fun to sing with people who are not friends, even when they sing like angels.

The barbershop quartet I have sung with more years than any other is my current quartet, Lilac Crazy. While we may not be the best in terms of barbershop contest criteria, we are the best at providing entertainment and joy, both for the members of the quartet and for the audiences. And we ring those chords, too!

We got together in 2000, after Claudia (bass), Kay (tenor), and Sherm (baritone) were singing with another lead in the Cactus Country Chorus. They had a different quartet name, All That Glitters, and they were not all that successful. (I suppose one could say, "It was not gold.") Sherm's name is actually Connie, but none of us thought she seems like a Connie and neither does she, so she became Sherm, a shortening of her last name. When their lead dropped out, the three of them asked me, the director of their chorus, to substitute until they found a suitable replacement. They never found a replacement; they stopped looking.

It soon became apparent that our forte was comedy, not serious traditional barbershop. We generated many possible names for the new foursome, including Four-on-the-Floor. We were rolling on the floor in hysterical laughter when someone suggested that one. But when Claudia proposed Lilac Crazy, we all said, "That's it!" For our theme song, we chose the song with the longest title ever written: "How Could You Believe Me When I Said I Loved You When You Know I've Been a Liar All My Life." (Written by Burton Lane, composer, and Alan Jay Lerner, lyricist, for the film *Royal Wedding*, © 1951 MGM Studio)

We bought lilac-colored wigs and purple boas to go with our costumes, and we learned songs that we knew would entertain our audiences: "Somewhere Overweight People" (a parody sung to the familiar song, "Over the Rainbow"), "Mister Sandman" (updated with lines about Richard Gere and Queen Latifah), and "Renaissance Woman" (a song bemoaning the fact that we women of a certain age and size are living in a Diet Coke world full of young, skinny girls.)

To enhance our comedic performances, I would write parodies to familiar songs, which we sang to the delight of our listeners. One that audiences loved and we enjoyed singing was introduced as a dedication to my second husband (see Chapter 18):

> I'll be seeing you in all the old familiar places,
> Gambling halls and greyhound races all day through.
> In that rude café, the bar where bimbos play
> And wrestle in mud galore,
> The honky-tonk, the porno store.
> I'll be seeing you in every gloomy rainy day,
> In gutters where you always lay
> By garbage cans in alleyways.
> I'll find you when I walk the dog
> And when the doggie's through,
> I'll be looking at his mmm—but,
> I'll be seeing—you!

The quartet was fairly successful, and after we formed, we would go on a retreat every other year—a trip in which we planned to have fun, work on our music, and bond as a unit. Our first retreat, in 2003, was a cruise on the Royal Caribbean cruise liner to the Mexican Riviera. Not only did we enjoy visiting the various ports, but also we had a serendipitous entertainment opportunity in a Puerto Vallarta bar—and we *were* sober. In Cabo San Lucas, we took a boat across the bay to a bar called the Office, where we enjoyed *mucho* margaritas and got henna tattoos on various parts of our bodies, then rolled into another boat to take us back to the dock. (And did we bond!)

In 2005, the quartet went to Hawaii to spend a week in my time-share condo. While we were waiting in Honolulu for our plane flight to the Big Island, we were singing (of course) while waiting in line. A lady came up to us and asked if we would be willing to sing at the elementary school on the Big Island where she taught. We agreed and made the arrangements.

On the agreed-upon date, we showed up at the school and were given a tour of the facility, which had a Montessori curriculum. The student body was filled with youngsters of all ages and nationalities who were learning the three Rs with methods unknown to *my* elementary teachers. We saw children on the floor playing with a Rubik's cube-type device with which they were learning mathematics. Other children were singing songs—and learning—in Japanese.

We were led to an open-air lanai—a large, empty, covered area about half the size of my house and open on two sides. Students began bringing their own chairs out to the meeting area and setting them up in rows, the first-graders in front with their tiny little chairs, followed by the other students, row-by-row and class-by-class, until the area was filled, teachers sitting and standing at the back.

Fortunately, we had brought our hand puppet, Kitten, with us and we entertained the children with our puppet routine and some of our funniest songs. We called the puppet Kitten because she always said, "I've seen everything, been everywhere, and done it all—the whole kit 'n' kaboodle!" That puppet became so real to us that at one performance, I actually held the microphone in front of the puppet's mouth instead of Claudia, who was the voice of Kitten.

The day after our performance we received a call from the school's principal, saying that we had left something at the school. Puzzled, we agreed to return that day and retrieve it, whatever it was. When we walked into the school, we were asked to wait in the principal's office. After about five minutes, several little children marched into the office carrying huge, fragrant flower leis. We had to bend over while the little tykes put them around our necks and gave us big hugs. They were so short they actually hugged our knees. The students had also written stories and thank you notes to give us as mementos of our visit. It was a thrill for us, and a memory we will cherish, always.

239

In the summer of 2006, we planned to have our retreat in a mountain cabin in Montana that belonged to Claudia's sister, a legislator for the state. Even though I had had my stroke in January, I had recovered sufficiently to make the trip. I was not looking forward to experiencing nature while living in a non-air-conditioned cabin accessible only by boat. But I was anticipating our performance in Helena, where we entertained a large group of business leaders and government officials. I must confess my favorite part of the trip was singing in Helena's famous watering hole—a bar in town where we were fawned over by semi-drunken but handsome young men. (Montana has a lot of those!)

A few years ago we were invited by the San Diego Chorus of Sweet Adelines to entertain at their annual show, doing our Andrews Sisters package, complete with army uniforms (sequin-trimmed, of course), 1940s hairdos, and truckin'-down-the-avenue choreography. We drove over to San Diego on a Friday afternoon, performed that night, did a little sightseeing on Saturday, and performed again Saturday night.

We decided to drive back to Arizona on Saturday night so that a couple of our members could get some rest before heading to work on Monday. I'm fine with driving at night while the others doze, but I do have to stop for frequent bladder breaks. As you may know, between California and Gila Bend, Arizona, on Interstate 8, there are very few towns and no restaurants open in the middle of the night. I pulled in to one of the desert rest stops—not much more than a big outhouse. All the lights were turned off, but I boldly led the way into the rest stop, turned on the lights, and was greeted by thousands of cockroaches scurrying for cover. (What is it with me and cockroaches!?!) We all used the facilities, gingerly holding our clothing off the floor and away from the sides of the stalls, breathed sighs of relief (no pun intended), and hurried back to the car.

When we were just a few miles west of Gila Bend, I noticed an itchy feeling on my thigh. I absent-mindedly scratched the itch and felt something hard. Overcome by horror, I realized that a cockroach from the rest stop had made its way up my leg inside my blue jeans! I clamped my hand on the insect, squeezed hard enough to crush it, and held my hand there, driving one-handed until I reached Gila Bend and could pull off the road into the parking lot of the truck stop.

I jumped out of the car and shook my leg to drop the cockroach out of my blue jeans. Well, it must be true that cockroaches will be here long after the earth is destroyed, because the big fellow fell out of my jeans and then raced off to terrorize Gila Bend! The girls in the quartet were not at all sympathetic to my plight, and they laughed so hard I thought they would wake up the town. They still make fun of me and my losing battle with the cockroach.

In August 2006, the quartet had a rather confrontational meeting at which time Sherm ranted at me—I didn't quite catch all that she said—and Claudia finally concluded the discussion, "I don't want to sing with you anymore." Maybe they thought I was too old and wasn't going to be able to come back after my stroke. Or, perhaps they resented the fact that I was doing everything in the quartet: arranging the music, making learning tapes on the four-track recorder I had purchased for that purpose, teaching the music, keeping track of our money, paying our bills, creating our business cards and performance cue cards on my computer, lugging the sound equipment to every rehearsal, sewing our costumes, and much, much more. Why did I do all that? Because it needed to be done and no one else volunteered! But I suppose they thought of it as controlling behavior. *Hmmm.*

After a couple of years, when they had sung with one lead who didn't like to perform comedy and another one who would rather go back East to visit family, they asked me to sing with them again. I had been extremely angry with them for dumping me and frankly was pleased that they hadn't had all that much success without me, but I thought to myself, *On the one hand, you could hold a grudge; on the other hand, you could sing again.* Grudge? Sing? No contest—singing wins every time!

In 2010, Lynda M. replaced Kay as tenor, when Kay decided to hang up her lilac wig and retire. During January 2011, the new foursome had an opportunity to join a Carnival cruise to the Caribbean, on which Sherm's grandson, Johnny Cooper, was a featured performer. We visited Jamaica, Grand Cayman Islands, and Cozumel, Mexico, and we did get a few opportunities to sing, informally, on the ship. But the high point of the trip was an impromptu concert at Margaritaville, the famous bar on Grand Cayman Island that pays tribute to the singer, Jimmy Buffett.

We also entertained *sober* people by singing one of our favorite gospel songs, "One Size Fits All," in the oldest church on the island.

Today, I try hard not to exhibit any controlling behavior and just go along with the group's choices, unless there is something that just cries to be changed or fixed—a joke, a chord, or a song. Ironically, Claudia is now the one who has taken charge of everything in the quartet: the marketing, the money, the program, the song choices, and most everything else. It helps that our new tenor, Lynda, was a baritone previously and reads music, so she helps Sherm. I still make the learning CDs, singing each of their parts. I don't know how much longer we will be able to perform, but recently we did win the senior citizens talent show at the Montecito Retirement Village. What a thrill to be handed a gigantic check—just like the Publisher's Clearing House—for five hundred dollars!

Although three of us have lost our husbands, widowhood hasn't slowed down Sherm. I call her our "serial dater." She told me I should write a book entitled, "How to Be Arm Candy After Seventy."

I replied, "Yeah—and be prepared for a lot of pain."

How long can I, an over-seventy senior citizen, continue to sing and entertain audiences? When I was a teacher, we had an inside joke: Question: How long do I have to keep repeating myself before you learn this? Answer: As long as it takes. So, to answer my own question, I'll keep singing as long as it takes to keep entertaining an audience, ringing those chords, and making memories to last the rest of my life, however long that is.

# CHAPTER 33

---•❋•---

# LIVE ALONE AND LIKE IT

*If you don't learn to be alone,*
*you will only know how to be lonely.*
—Sherry Turkle, author of *Alone Together*

After Michael died, I was bereft and very depressed. My doctor tried different ways to deal with my tears and first prescribed the usual treatment for such cases—antidepressant medication. I filled the prescription and took the first dose. When I woke up a few hours later, I declared that I would *not* live the rest of my life asleep.

My doctor next prescribed a psychotherapist. It seemed my insurance coverage would pay for the first six sessions without referral. I looked over the roster of psychiatrists affiliated with the clinic and simply picked the first one on the list—Dr. Anderson.

I had no idea what to expect, and was surprised to find there was no couch in his office, just two comfortable armchairs. During our first session, he elicited the usual demographic information and encouraged me to talk about my late husband and his death. I think I cried most of the hour.

During the second session, something he said triggered a response. He mentioned the Albert Brooks movie about dying and being doomed to repeat life's mistakes before getting on the train to a higher level of existence.

Suddenly the solution dawned: I have been paid considerable sums of money helping large corporations do strategic turnarounds when they're faced with hostile competition, reduced profits, dissatisfied/disgruntled employees, and uncertain or unfriendly futures. Why couldn't I use the same techniques to do a turnaround for myself?

The next session I came armed with a strategic plan for my life, complete with mission and values statements, goals, action plans, and target dates for completion. Dr. Anderson looked at my plan and then at me. "I don't think you need any more sessions."

One of the action plans I wrote for myself was to volunteer at KBAQ, the local public radio station that broadcasts classical music twenty-four hours a day. I had often heard on their broadcasts that they welcomed volunteers to help answer phones and stuff envelopes during fund drives.

I answered the call to man (or woman) the phones for the spring fund drive. While there, I met John, the station's development officer, as well as Sterling Beeaff, the early morning DJ. When Sterling and I were introduced, I blurted out, "Oh! I just love waking up with you every morning!"

He was very forgiving: "I get that a lot."

John and I chatted about my being a member of Sweet Adelines and my love of singing and performing. He recommended that I audition to be a reader for Sun Sounds of Arizona, a radio reading service for the visually handicapped and print-disabled. The studio was located in the same building and broadcast on a subcarrier of the public radio band. Sun Sounds was a member of the International Association of Audio Information Services (IAAIS). They had over two hundred volunteers reading newspapers, magazines, and books to thousands of print-disabled people in Arizona, broadcasting 24/7 from the studios in Tempe, Flagstaff, Tucson, and Yuma.

"Oh, my, I could never do that. I'd be terrified to audition."

"I'll call the program manager and set up an audition for today." John called Lettie, and then told me they expected me in the studio in half an hour.

I met with Lettie, who dealt with me swiftly and matter-of-factly. She explained the audition process to me, set up a recording booth, and instructed me to read from each of several pages, which included representations of the many types of publications that were read and broadcast to their audiences. These included a long list of words to recite, words that were obviously difficult to pronounce, like "ideologically." There were also excerpts from newspapers such as *The Arizona Republic, USA Today,* and *The Christian Science Monitor,* as well as magazines including *The Economist, Newsweek,* and special interest publications such as *TV Guide.* Also, I was given grocery ads and comics, which I had to describe as well as read.

After the audition, Lettie told me that someone would listen to the audition recording, determine what type of publication I would be best suited to read, and then match that with any openings they might have. She said, "For a while, you'll probably be a substitute for other readers when they are sick or on vacation."

In other words, "Don't call us, we'll call you."

I headed home, saying to myself, "Well, at least I tried."

When I arrived home about an hour later, there was a message on my answering machine from Lettie. "We want you to read the weekly *Christian Science Monitor* international news. Can you start Tuesday?"

That was 2002, and I still read the *Christian Science Monitor* international news every Tuesday, and I have added a program called *Reminiscing*—stories of the good old days taken from the *Reminisce* and *Good Old Days* magazines. I am amused by the fact that the "good old days" now includes the 1960s! From time to time, I will read and broadcast books, both fiction and non-fiction, for the program, *A Good Book.*

In 2006 I was awarded The Golden Microphone, an award given by Sun Sounds of Arizona to the volunteer of the year. Also, that year, my reading of the book, *Christ the Lord: Out of Egypt,* was awarded first prize in the narrative reading category by the IAAIS. In 2011, I received another honor; the radio play I had written, *Voices from the Front,* received first place at the IAAIS annual conference.

When the price of gasoline rose to nearly four dollars per gallon, I decided that the thirty-five miles one-way to the studios in Tempe was too costly. I then learned how to record programs on my computer at home and transmit them, via a process called file transfer protocol, to the studio. I drive to the studio every other month to touch base with the program manager, pick up new copies of magazines, and trade gossip with the staff.

At a recent reception at Sun Sounds studio to which listeners, as well as media, were invited, I was chatting and laughing with some of the staff when I heard my name being called excitedly, "Mary Ellen! Mary Ellen!" It was an elderly woman on the arm of a younger lady. It seems she was a regular listener who recognized my voice from having heard me on the radio. There is something special about doing what you love to do and knowing that you are also helping bring some measure of joy into the lives of others. I believe the best way to relieve your own burden of pain is to help relieve the pain for someone else.

Here are a few things I have enjoyed since being alone:

Reading: I can read in bed without bothering someone else who will tell me, "Aren't you ready to turn off that light yet? Some of us have to get up early, you know."

Silence: You can soak it up, uninterrupted by television, irrelevant conversation, or arguments about whose turn it is to take out the garbage.

Music: I can listen to any type of music I like, and not hear "Do we have to listen to A Cappella Gold quartet singing "Bald-Headed Men" one more time?"

Crying: You don't have to be embarrassed because you cry at schmaltzy movies, episodes of *Ghost Whisperer*, or Hallmark greeting card commercials.

Singing: I love to sing along with the contestants on *American Idol*, with the *West Side Story* movie, and—even though my cat objects—with the soprano in *Aida*. A passerby in another auto once caught me in the act of conducting Beethoven's Fifth Symphony, which was playing on KBAQ classical radio. A California policeman started laughing when he saw me singing and playing air guitar to "Johnny Be Good" while listening to the CD of Buddy Holly's life. Unfortunately, I was driving through Riverside at the time. (Oops!)

Housecleaning: I no longer pick up dirty glasses left on end tables, underwear and socks left on the bedroom floor, or myself after falling into the toilet bowl because the seat was left open. Oh! That's right—there's no man in the house!

Petting: Uh—petting my cat, that is. I always swore I would not be one of those old ladies with a houseful of cats. However, this one (Cookie) looked at me as though she knew me when I visited a local animal shelter. I said I'd take her home on trial. When I let her out of the cat carrier, she walked around the house, examined every nook and cranny, then jumped on my bed, started to purr, and made herself at home—in my house and in my heart.

Having a living being around the house, whether it's a spouse, a pet, or a tropical plant, is important to one's soul. However, the pet is the easiest to care for, by far. An added benefit of having a pet is often better health. I was suffering an atrial fibrillation attack one evening, moaning and groaning, trying to decide whether I should go to the hospital. Cookie jumped into my lap and curled up, and after about twenty minutes of my stroking her, my heart went back to sinus rhythm.

It was difficult to go out to dinner by myself after I was widowed, probably because I had enjoyed dinners out with my husband more than I had enjoyed dinners at home. (What, me, cook?!) However, I have discovered that being alone while dining means you will have a chance to connect with other people—those at nearby tables or even the waitress who is happy to have someone smile and joke with her, rather than complain. On the other hand, I must admit that recently, while dining alone at Tlaquepaque in Sedona, Arizona, the waitress did look behind me to see if my dinner partner was hiding somewhere. By the way, no one else at the restaurant was dining alone.

One of my friends, Dolores, called me in May 2010 to describe a research project she'd heard about that I might enjoy. It was called the Longevity Study and was conducted by the Sun Health Research Institute at the nearby Banner Boswell Hospital. I called the number she gave me and made an appointment to be interviewed as a research subject by one of their volunteers.

At the end of the data-gathering interview, after the volunteer had learned about my background teaching behavioral science, she said, "I think you belong on *this* side of the desk."

My training as a research volunteer followed shortly afterward. Because Banner Boswell sponsored the study, I was required first to attend a training class for hospital volunteers, even though I would not be working with hospital patients (for which they should be thankful). One of the issues emphasized by my trainer at SHRI was the importance of keeping the subjects on task during the interviews. "Sometimes, the older people go off on tangents and start telling side stories. You have to bring them back to focus on the questions you're asking."

What I've found is that I *love* hearing the older people's stories, they enjoy sharing with me, and before we know it, I'm swapping stories with them. Consequently, I have asked the scheduler to give me an extra half-hour at every interview.

I can't help but remember the song, "Lots of Things That You Can Do Alone," as Pearl Bailey sang it, listing the many activities one can do alone, including napping, nipping, crooning, laughing, and simply "going to pot."

However, the song ends with this reminder:

> It takes two to tango, two to tango,
> Two to really get the feeling of romance,
> Let's do the tango, do the tango,
> Do the dance of love.

I have been dancing the tango for more than seventy years, and my knees are beginning to complain, not to mention other parts of my body. Although it took a few years, I have discovered that, even in widowhood, there are many activities that I can do alone and that I enjoy. Better yet, I've helped a lot of other people in the process.

# CHAPTER 34

⸱•❁•⸱

# THE SONG HAS ENDED

I'm right where I'm supposed to be,
thanks to where I've been.
—Jennifer Lopez, Singer/Actress

As I said in my Note to Reader, this memoir is more of a how-not-to book rather than a how-to book—specifically, how not to program your children to be dysfunctional adults who will make disastrous choices. However, I must acknowledge that the cultural environment surrounding growing youngsters today is such that it would be a miracle if children managed to grow up to be functioning adults and not "schizos."

For inspiration on child rearing, I look no further than my niece, Melissa, whose children display healthy curiosity and love of learning, value and respect life of all types, and embrace diversity in people and friends. Of course, their mother closely guards their environments, especially in schools; they attend charter schools where class sizes are smaller and students are given more attention and guidance.

This is also a how-to book—how to live alone and lead a healthy, happy, and useful life as a single woman, either through choice or widowhood.

Since my stroke in 2006, I have tried to keep to a fairly regular daily schedule, making sure I'm doing some activity in which I interact with others every day. That way, if I am inexplicably absent, it will be noticed, and therefore my body will not be lying undiscovered for days while I rot away (like my college statistics professor, Dr. Winer). Monday is my quartet rehearsal with Lilac Crazy. Tuesday I broadcast my programs on Sun Sounds Radio for the blind and print-disabled. Wednesday is grocery shopping—it's senior citizens discount day, you know. Thursday I get my hair done, and Friday I volunteer at the Sun Health Research Institute (SHRI), interviewing subjects for their longevity study. My neighbor will notice and investigate if I don't put the trashcan out by the curb on weekends.

Although I always have a regular hairdresser appointment on Thursday, one Wednesday last year I experienced another atrial fibrillation attack that continued unabated for almost two days. Reluctantly, I called 911, as well as my sister-in-law, Rose. As I was being hauled away in the ambulance, I yelled to Rose, "Call Cathy, my hairdresser! Tell her I won't be coming in Thursday morning!" Rose either forgot or couldn't find the hairdresser's number, because she did not call.

When I didn't show up for my hair appointment, Cathy called Melba, another friend: "Melba, Mary Ellen didn't show up this morning for her hair appointment, and she *never* misses her appointment. Can you go over to her house and see if something is wrong? Maybe she had another stroke!" Melba hurried to my house and looked through all the windows to see if she could see my body lying comatose inside. There were a few anxious moments until the facts became known. (And I learned that Rose was not reliable in such situations.)

Volunteering has added a special dimension to my single life. Doing things for others keeps the focus off one's own aloneness. My sister-in-law, Rose, lost her husband in the same year that I lost Michael, her brother. She was not able to find satisfaction in volunteering, however. Both Michael and Rose had the same attitude: "If I'm not paid, I'm not going to do it." I happen to feel that a hug and a smile from someone I've helped is worth more than any salary.

One of the female subjects in the Sun Health Research Institute's longevity study was asked if there was anything else she would recommend to others who were embarking on retirement. She remarked, "Focus on the inner journey." By that, I believe she was saying that so much of our lives are focused on the *outer* journey—which person we'll marry, what career we will pursue, and how much wealth we can accumulate. Rather, we should focus on the *inner* journey—what sparks or motivates us, and our relationship with our inner self and our spiritual guide.

Of course, when I asked one of the eighty-eight-year-old male subjects in the longevity study if there was a question we should ask in the survey that we had not, he responded, almost with pride, "You didn't ask me about my sex life!" (Men! As Celeste Holm's character said in *High Society*, "The little dears.")

The results of the SHRI longevity study are not finalized, but they seem to be echoing the ingredients of "A Recipe for a Healthy Brain," published in the *Banner Alzheimer Institute Newsletter, 2012:*

> One daily dose of thirty minutes of exercise
> One daily dose of a heart-healthy diet
> One daily dose of mental activity
> Three weekly doses of social activity
> One daily dose of positive thinking
> One daily dose of seven to eight hours of sleep
> Mix together on a routine basis and enjoy a longer, happier life.
>
> (Used by permission)

Am I living up to that recipe? I'm okay on the first one, *if* I can count as exercise my several minutes of attempting to get out of my recliner. I certainly have a heart-healthy diet—isn't chocolate good for your heart? I am doing well on mental activity, social activity, and positive thinking. I'm *positive* that trying to learn all the words, music, and choreography for my quartet performances must be good for me. Sleep? I'll sleep when I'm dead.

When I perform with Lilac Crazy, I tell a story that Mae West once told. She is a performer I have admired for years for her wit and her unabashed sexuality—even in her seventies! When people would ask how many husbands she'd had, she would respond in that special petulant, sex-infused pout of hers, "I've had eight husbands . . . four of them were mine!"

Recently, after a performance by my quartet, a man in the audience came up to me and said, "I can see why you had all those divorces."

My response? "Yeah, but think of all the fun they had while it lasted!"

So, what about all those divorces? After giving it some thought, I believe this is the value I've embraced:

When you are in a relationship that becomes transparent and you realize that the bonds that bound you at the beginning are no longer present, that the tie that binds is one of discontent and discord rather than a ribbon of contentment and companionship, then I say: Cut the cord! I have seen too many couples hanging on when there is nothing concrete left but a desire to avoid losing community property. Being alone and comfortable in one's skin is far superior to being thus bound.

Here's a frightening thought—it comes from a volume of daily teachings from *The Secret*, by Rhonda Byrne: "We attract to ourselves what we hold inside. Every circumstance, every person, and every situation is a reflection of what you hold inside you, and what you hold inside you is always under your control." This means to me that when I hold fear inside me, I will be afraid: afraid to be alone, to dine alone, to take a trip alone. When I hold a grudge inside me—against my parents, my fellow quartet members, or an uncaring world—I'm attracting more grudges to myself. When I am annoyed with the action of another person, someone else will be annoyed with me. When I—well, you get the picture. The secret is to realize that each of us has the power to control what is inside us, to change it, and therefore change the circumstances of our lives.

Like most people born and value programmed in the 1940s, I was bombarded throughout my young life with conflicting messages that resulted in confusing goals and actions. In adulthood, those messages, somewhat Garbo-like, became "I want to be alone." Yet my actions seemed to reveal the pursuit of an apparently opposing goal, "I want to be loved." Is it possible to be loved and still be left alone? I wanted a husband to love me but not to suffocate me. I will forever regret the fact that when Michael would grab my hand to lead me across the street, I shook his hand away, because I did not want to be led (i.e., controlled.) I saw controlling behavior in what he probably meant as loving behavior.

I wanted to be the director of a large chorus or the lead singer in a quartet, and I wanted them to listen to what I thought, felt, reasoned, or imagined. I was so hurt when I realized they didn't care what I thought, felt, reasoned, or imagined. What I failed to understand at the time was that they also wanted to be left alone to do it their way.

Perhaps this inner conflict is the result of being an "in-betweener" or "schizo," as Dr. Morris Massey describes my generation. Or is it possible that all human beings are plagued by such conflicts? I am reminded of the push-me-pull-me animal immortalized by Dr. Doolittle. Many times I have felt as though I'd been pushed into situations in which I found myself floundering and wishing there was someone to pull me out. Why did I think I had to *marry* those guys?

When we are old (well—older*)* and wiser perhaps, and we actually are alone—widowed or otherwise—we find that we are not really alone but are surrounded by the ghosts and memories of all whom we have loved, hated, feared, or adored and all the things we have been and have done. As Sigmund Freud said, "We are what we are because we have been what we have been."

Echoing that thought is a saying by Saint Augustine of Hippo, who lived more than sixteen centuries ago: "If we live good lives, the times are also good. As we are, such are the times." I suppose that means when the times in my life were bad, I was living a less than stellar life. What does that say about today's world? There must be a lot of people living bad lives!

My brother recently found my great-grandfather Smith's high school autograph book among my late mother's possessions. Written in beautiful, flowing Spenserian script was this message from one of his teachers:

> Not years, but actions, tell how long we live,
> so in all things, dare to do right, dare to be true,
> for you have a work no other can do.
> Do it bravely, so kindly, so well,
> that angels will hasten the story to tell.
>
> July 9, 1888, Lou Owen

Neil Armstrong, one of America's astronauts and cultural icons, said, "I believe every human has a finite number of heartbeats. I don't intend to waste any of mine."

As this memoir has illustrated, I have lived with many men and in many places. I have tried to be true to my parents and my early value programmers, but most of all I have been true to myself and to my own notions of right and wrong.

In a way, you could say that I have lived many lives. I say "thank you" to the universe for that opportunity, because *all* of those lives—thank you, God—were mine.

# EPILOGUE

## OH, BURY ME OUT ON THE LONE PRAIRIE

# A EULOGY

———————•❂•———————

**M**ary Ellen Blevins Trowbridge Brannen Batterton Stepanich was born on one of the coldest nights of the year in Fort Branch, Indiana, on January 8, 1940. She died in one of the hottest climates in the country in Peoria, Arizona on [to be filled in later]. As the poem, "The Dash," suggests, she filled those in-between years with as much life and gusto as she could manage.

Her parents, William "Bud" Blevins and Edna Marie Smith Blevins, preceded her in death. They tried to teach her everything they knew and what they thought she ought to know, but couldn't teach her to keep her mouth shut, do what she was told, or listen to (but not necessarily respect) the opinion of others.

William Robert "Billy Bob" Trowbridge, Carlton Hunt Brannen, George Beverley Batterton, and Rudolph Michael Stepanich, all of whom taught her valuable lessons, also preceded her in death. Billy Bob taught her to be self-reliant—he was gone so much with the navy and really didn't care what she did, anyway. Hunt taught her to beware of artists—they paint a pretty picture but what you see is never what it appears to be. George taught her to avoid any man from Texas with a girl's middle name and who was a private pilot—they can be mean. Michael taught her that love is possible, even later in life, but it rarely lasts long enough—so savor every minute. (And drink a lot of champagne!)

Her stepdaughter, Shari Michael, who was like a daughter to her, also preceded her in death. Shari Ann Stepanich legally changed her last name to Michael, her father's middle name, because Stepanich was such a mouthful and so often misspelled and mispronounced by others.

257

Shari taught Mary Ellen how to help her students remember the correct pronunciation and spelling of the name: "Think of a bug scurrying across the sidewalk: you *step*, an' *ich*!" She would then mime scraping the bug off her shoe. Shari and Mary Ellen enjoyed many girls' nights or weeks out, even though Shari would have to fib to her mother about where she was going and with whom. (A husband's ex-wife can be so difficult!)

Mary Ellen is survived by her brother, Dr. William (Karin Koorman) Blevins; nieces Kristina (Nick) Butler and Melissa (Logan) Wilcoxson; great niece and nephew Sarah and Noah Wilcoxson; stepson Scott Stepanich; daughter-in-law Jennifer and step-grandson Carter Stepanich.

By many accounts, Mary Ellen was a success. She earned three college degrees—BS, MS, and PhD—but as her father once remarked, "We all know what BS stands for, right? Well, MS is just 'more of the same,' and PhD simply means 'piled higher and deeper.'"

Being a child of the 1940s, Mary Ellen learned early that it is men who rule the world, and who establish the rules for the lesser beings— children, animals, and women, in that order. Therefore, if a man said, "Move," she moved, even if it meant leaving a job and/or a home that she had come to love. Perhaps that explains her peripatetic career: business school teacher, corporate tax clerk, research assistant, public school teacher, private secretary, civil servant, finance assistant, law school registrar, and college professor (with tenure, she would stress.)

Of course, a career that was so varied also took her to many exciting—and some not so exciting—locations: Chicago, Illinois; Terre Haute and Clinton, Indiana; Virginia Beach and Norfolk, Virginia; San Francisco, Anaheim, and Fullerton, California; West Lafayette, Indiana; and finally Phoenix and Peoria, Arizona. In between those places were occasional brief, and often delightful, visits to Germany, France, Switzerland, Austria, Italy, Spain, the Netherlands, Belgium, England, Scotland, Wales, New Zealand, Australia, Canada, Mexico, Jamaica, Grand Caymans, and *(sigh)* Hawaii.

But Mary Ellen was more than jobs she had done, men she had married—and divorced—or places she had lived or visited. She was a woman who loved life and loved to make other people laugh. She was a born entertainer whose star was never allowed to ascend as high as she would have wished. Nevertheless, she did manage to reach the hearts and minds of a few people: the students she taught (who often said, "Dr. Stepanich taught us how to *do* something!"), the audiences she entertained ("I laughed so hard I wet my pants!"), and even some members of her family ("You're not a great aunt, you're an *awesome* aunt!)

Mary Ellen was a former Girl Scout, so she always tried to follow the Scout motto, "Be Prepared." She made all the arrangements for her final interment before she was seventy years of age. In selecting the urn for her cremation, she did allow a bit of vanity to influence her choice. She told the funeral parlor manager, "I want a black box for the ashes, because as everyone knows, black makes you look slimmer."

Despite the fact that her generation has been dubbed "schizo" and the value programming by parents and teachers attempted to make her a dutiful and obedient young lady (without success, we might add), Mary Ellen did achieve her life-long goal. She wanted to be left alone—not necessarily to be alone as in "by herself," but to be alone as in "in control of herself" (with a little help from Poise pads, of course.)

Although there may be no people to mourn her passing, may the trees and the breeze and the wind from the seas breathe a sigh and a fond farewell to this Hoosier schizo.

*Footnote*: Her ashes will be interred at the National Memorial Cemetery in Cave Creek, Arizona, in the same "post office box" as her Air Force veteran husband, Rudolph Michael Stepanich. However, she would prefer to have songs at the ceremony that reflect her life-long love of the US Navy: "Anchors Aweigh," "The Navy Hymn," and "Yo Ho Ho and a Bottle of Rum."

CPSIA information can be obtained at www.ICGtesting.com
Printed in the USA
BVOW030453250613

324202BV00002B/2/P